Hands-On Functional Programming with C++

An effective guide to writing accelerated functional code using C++17 and C++20

Alexandru Bolboaca

BIRMINGHAM - MUMBAI

Hands-On Functional Programming with C++

Commissioning Editor: Richa Tripathi
Acquisition Editor: Shriram Shekhar
Content Development Editor: Manjusha Mantri
Senior Editor: Afshaan Khan
Technical Editor: Riddesh Dawne
Copy Editor: Safis Editing
Project Coordinator: Prajakta Naik
Proofreader: Safis Editing
Indexer: Rekha Nair
Production Designer: Nilesh Mohite

First published: June 2019

Production reference: 1270619

Published by Packt Publishing Ltd.
Livery Place
35 Livery Street
Birmingham
B3 2PB, UK.

ISBN 978-1-78980-733-2

www.packtpub.com

To all the people in my life who pushed me forward – Luc Rogge, Corey Haines, JB Rainsberger, Samir Talwar, Thomas Sundberg, Johan Martinsson, and Peter "CodeCop" Kofler, to name a few.

To my brother, Adi, for being a conversation partner on difficult topics. To my mother, Raluca, for her support throughout my formative years.

To David Hussman, for sowing the seeds of inspiration that continued even after his premature passing. RIP dude—I miss you, but you keep inspiring me.

And finally, to my best friend, mentor, wife, and CEO/entrepreneur, Maria, for her continuous support and patience, and for building our story together, with more to come!

- Alex Bolboaca

Packt.com

Subscribe to our online digital library for full access to over 7,000 books and videos, as well as industry leading tools to help you plan your personal development and advance your career. For more information, please visit our website.

Why subscribe?

- Spend less time learning and more time coding with practical eBooks and Videos from over 4,000 industry professionals

- Improve your learning with Skill Plans built especially for you

- Get a free eBook or video every month

- Fully searchable for easy access to vital information

- Copy and paste, print, and bookmark content

Did you know that Packt offers eBook versions of every book published, with PDF and ePub files available? You can upgrade to the eBook version at www.packt.com and as a print book customer, you are entitled to a discount on the eBook copy. Get in touch with us at customercare@packtpub.com for more details.

At www.packt.com, you can also read a collection of free technical articles, sign up for a range of free newsletters, and receive exclusive discounts and offers on Packt books and eBooks.

Contributors

About the author

With 20 years' experience in the software development industry, **Alexandru Bolboaca** has gone from being a junior C++ programmer to a technical lead and software architect, before becoming a technical coach and trainer. He has extensive experience in helping customers to improve the way they work, as well as their code and approach to testing. He is also the author of *Usable Software Design*, and the co-author of *Coderetreat*.

The team at Packt Publishing were a great help in writing this book. I've learned a lot in the process. Thank you for your patience and support. I hope I was easy to work with.

About the reviewers

Trevor Hickey is a software engineer at Uber. He holds a bachelor's degree in computer science from Edinboro University of Pennsylvania. He has experience in literature peer review and specializes in computational pasigraphy. His research interests include pragmatics and relevance theory.

Will Brennan is a C++/Python software engineer based in London, with experience of working on high-performance image processing and machine learning applications.

Ryan Riley has been involved in the futures and derivatives industry for almost 20 years. He received a bachelor's degree and a master's degree from DePaul University in applied statistics. Doing his course work in math meant that he had to teach himself how to program, thereby forcing him to read more technical books on programming than he would otherwise have done. Ryan has worked with numerous AI libraries in various languages, and is currently using the Caffe2 C++ library to develop and implement futures and derivatives trading strategies at PNT Financial.

Andreas Oehlke is a professional full-stack software engineer. He holds a bachelor's degree in computer science and loves to experiment with software and hardware. His trademark has always been his enthusiasm and affinity for electronics and computers. His hobbies include game development, building embedded systems, sports, and making music. He currently works full time as a senior software engineer for a German financial institution. He has also worked as a consultant and game developer in San Francisco, CA. He is also the author of the book, *Learning LibGDX Game Development*.

Packt is searching for authors like you

If you're interested in becoming an author for Packt, please visit `authors.packtpub.com` and apply today. We have worked with thousands of developers and tech professionals, just like you, to help them share their insight with the global tech community. You can make a general application, apply for a specific hot topic that we are recruiting an author for, or submit your own idea.

Table of Contents

Preface

Welcome to a hands-on tour of functional programming in C++! This book is about an old idea, that is, functional programming, and a classic programming language, that is, C++, finally uniting forces.

Functional programming has been around since the 1950s; however, due to its mathematical underpinnings, it has been of limited interest to mainstream software development for many years. With the advent of multicore CPUs and big data leading to the need for parallelization, and with programming language designers becoming more interested in immutability and lambdas, functional programming concepts have been gradually introduced in all major programming languages, including C#, Java, PHP, JavaScript, Python, and Ruby. C++ has never been far from functional programming, with features such as function pointers, functors, and the algorithms from STL allowing many programmers to take advantage of certain constructs. However, starting with C++ 11, we see the introduction of lambdas, and of higher-order functions such as all_of, any_of, and none_of. In C++ 17, we see more progress, with the introduction of map (implemented as transform). Additionally, the features coming in C++ 20 are very exciting; for example, the ranges library, which allows composable, lightweight, and lazily evaluated transformations, is a great addition to the standard.

This brings us to what you will learn from this book. Whether you are a seasoned programmer or a C++ beginner, you will learn about functional programming concepts, how to use them in C++, and why they are useful for managing and improving existing code bases. Every idea will be showcased with clear code samples and verified with unit tests; we highly encourage you to take these code samples and play around with them yourself.

Special effort has been put into ensuring that every idea is presented in a clear manner, and that a flow of understanding is followed; in other words, we've been looking at optimizing your learning experience. In order to do that, we have decided to exaggerate the use of certain constructs. For example, the sample code uses a lot of lambdas since we wanted to show how they can be used. We believe that the best way to learn functional programming is to fully dive into the world of lambdas and operations on lambdas. We expect the reader to separate this approach from a production approach; in fact, I advise you to experiment with these concepts on your own, then on small parts of production code, and only then use those that are promising to their full extent. To support this goal, we have documented multiple ways of using operations on functions so that you will possess enough tools to use in various contexts.

It's important to note that we made a calculated decision to present the C++ 17 standard in most of the book. We don't use external libraries (other than the unit testing library), and we stick to the standard features of the language and of **Standard Template Library** (STL). The focus is on functional programming concepts and on how to implement them using a minimalistic approach. The only exception is the last section of the book that looks at the future of C++ and STL. We did this because we believe that it's more important for you to understand the concepts and be ready to apply them with minimal tooling than to provide a multitude of implementation options. This has left out the ranges library for most of the book, the Boost library support for functional programming, and, most likely, other useful libraries that can extend or simplify the code. I will leave it to the reader to try them out for themselves and let us know how they worked.

Who this book is for

This book is for programmers who already know C++ (including the language syntax, STL containers, and elements of templates) and who want to add more tools to their toolkit. You don't need to know anything about functional programming to read the book; we took care to explain every idea in a clear and practical manner.

You do, however, need to be curious about the set of tools coming from the world of functional programming. A hefty dose of experimentation will help you to make the most of this book, so I encourage you to play around with the code and to let us know what you find.

What this book covers

Chapter 1, *An Introduction to Functional Programming*, introduces you to the fundamental ideas of functional programming.

Chapter 2, *Understanding Pure Functions*, teaches you the fundamental building blocks of functional programming, functions that focus on immutability, and how to write them in C++.

Chapter 3, *Deep Dive into Lambdas*, focuses on lambdas and how to write them in C++.

Chapter 4, *The Idea of Functional Composition*, looks at how to compose functions with a higher order operation.

Chapter 5, *Partial Application and Currying*, teaches you how to use two fundamental operations on functions—partial application and currying in C++.

Chapter 6, *Thinking in Functions – from Data in to Data out*, introduces you to another way of organizing your code, enabling function-centric design.

Chapter 7, *Removing Duplication with Functional Operations*, is an overview of the **Don't Repeat Yourself (DRY)** principle, the types of code duplication and code similarities, and how to write more DRY code using functional operations such as composition, partial application, and currying.

Chapter 8, *Improving Cohesion Using Classes*, demonstrates how functions can evolve into classes and how classes can be turned into functions.

Chapter 9, *Test-Driven Development for Functional Programming*, looks at how to use **Test-Driven Development (TDD)** with functional programming and at how immutability and pure functions simplify tests.

Chapter 10, *Performance Optimization*, dives into specific methods of how to optimize the performance of function-centric design, including memoization, tail recursion optimization, and parallel execution.

Chapter 11, *Property-Based Testing*, looks at how functional programming enables a new paradigm of writing automated tests that enhances example-based testing with data generation.

Chapter 12, *Refactoring to and through Pure Functions*, explains how any existing code can be refactored to pure functions and then back into classes with minimal risk. It also looks at classic design patterns and a few functional design patterns.

Chapter 13, *Immutability and Architecture – Event Sourcing*, explains that immutability can move at the data storage level, looks at how to use event sourcing, and discusses its advantages and disadvantages.

Chapter 14, *Lazy Evaluation Using the Ranges Library*, dives into the awesome ranges library and demonstrates how to use it in C++ 17 and C++ 20.

Chapter 15, *STL Support and Proposals*, looks at STL functional features in the C++ 17 standard and at a few interesting additions to C++ 20.

Chapter 16, *Standard Language Support and Proposals*, closes the book with an overview of the fundamental building blocks of functional programming and the various options for using them in the C++ 17 standard.

To get the most out of this book

This book assumes a good knowledge of the C++ syntax and of basic STL containers. However, it does not assume any knowledge of functional programming, functional constructs, category theory, or math. We've gone to great lengths to ensure that each concept is explained clearly and from a practical, programmer-centric perspective.

We strongly encourage you to play around with the code after reading the chapters or try to replicate the code from the samples after finishing a chapter. Even better, pick a coding kata (for example, from http://codingdojo.org/kata/) problem and try to solve it using the techniques from this book. You will learn much more by combining reading with toying with code than by simply reading the theory on its own.

Most of the content in this book requires you to think differently about the code structure and, sometimes, this will be contrary to what you are used to. However, we see functional programming as another tool in your toolkit; it doesn't contradict what you already know, instead, it just provides you with additional instruments to use with your production code. When and how you use them is your decision.

To run the code samples from the book, you will need g++ and the make command. Alternatively, you can run the samples using any compiler that supports C++ 17, but you will need to manually run each file. All the code samples compile and automatically run with make or make [specific example], and provide the output on the console with a few caveats that follow.

The memory optimization samples from Chapter 10, *Performance Optimization*, need to run with make allMemoryLogs or a specific target, require a keyboard press after each target run, and will create log files in the out/ folder, showing the evolution of allocated memory for the process. This will only work on Linux systems.

The reactive programming sample from Chapter 10, *Performance Optimization* and requires user input. Just input numbers and the program will compute in a reactive way whether they are prime or not. The program should receive inputs even while computing. The code samples from Chapter 16, *Standard Language Support and Proposals*, require a compiler that supports C++20; at this point, g++-8 is used. You will need to install g++-8 separately.

Download the example code files

You can download the example code files for this book from your account at www.packt.com. If you purchased this book elsewhere, you can visit www.packt.com/support and register to have the files emailed directly to you.

You can download the code files by following these steps:

1. Log in or register at www.packt.com.
2. Select the **SUPPORT** tab.
3. Click on **Code Downloads & Errata**.
4. Enter the name of the book in the **Search** box and follow the onscreen instructions.

Once the file is downloaded, please make sure that you unzip or extract the folder using the latest version of:

- WinRAR/7-Zip for Windows
- Zipeg/iZip/UnRarX for Mac
- 7-Zip/PeaZip for Linux

The code bundle for the book is also hosted on GitHub at https://github.com/PacktPublishing/Hands-On-Functional-Programming-with-Cpp. In case there's an update to the code, it will be updated on the existing GitHub repository.

We also have other code bundles from our rich catalog of books and videos available at https://github.com/PacktPublishing/. Check them out!

Code in Action

Visit the following link to see the code being executed:

http://bit.ly/2ZPw0KH

Conventions used

There are a number of text conventions used throughout this book.

CodeInText: Indicates code words in text, database table names, folder names, filenames, file extensions, pathnames, dummy URLs, user input, and Twitter handles. Here is an example: "In STL, it's implemented with the find_if function. Let's see it in action."

A block of code is set as follows:

```
class Number{
    public:
        static int zero(){ return 0; }
        static int increment(const int value){ return value + 1; }
}
```

When we wish to draw your attention to a particular part of a code block, the relevant lines or items are set in bold:

```
First call: 1,367 ns < 16,281 ns
Second call: 58,045 ns < 890,056 ns
Third call: 16,167 ns > 939 ns
Fourth call: 1,334 ns > 798 ns
```

 Warnings or important notes appear like this.

 Tips and tricks appear like this.

Get in touch

Feedback from our readers is always welcome.

General feedback: If you have questions about any aspect of this book, mention the book title in the subject of your message and email us at customercare@packtpub.com.

Errata: Although we have taken every care to ensure the accuracy of our content, mistakes do happen. If you have found a mistake in this book, we would be grateful if you would report this to us. Please visit www.packt.com/submit-errata, selecting your book, clicking on the Errata Submission Form link, and entering the details.

Piracy: If you come across any illegal copies of our works in any form on the Internet, we would be grateful if you would provide us with the location address or website name. Please contact us at copyright@packt.com with a link to the material.

If you are interested in becoming an author: If there is a topic that you have expertise in and you are interested in either writing or contributing to a book, please visit authors.packtpub.com.

Reviews

Please leave a review. Once you have read and used this book, why not leave a review on the site that you purchased it from? Potential readers can then see and use your unbiased opinion to make purchase decisions, we at Packt can understand what you think about our products, and our authors can see your feedback on their book. Thank you!

For more information about Packt, please visit packt.com.

Section 1: Functional Building Blocks in C++

In this section, we will learn about the basic building blocks of functional programming and how to use them in C++. First, we will look at what functional programming is and how it is different from and similar to **object-oriented programming** (OOP). Then, we will dive into the fundamental idea of immutability and learn how to write pure functions in C++—that is, functions that don't change state. We will then learn how to use lambdas and how to write pure functions using them.

Once we master those building blocks, we can move on to operations with functions. In functional programming, functions are data, so we can pass them around and make operations with them. We will learn about partial application and currying, two fundamental and closely-related operations. We will also see how to compose functions. These operations will take us from simple functions to very complex ones with just a few lines of plumbing code.

The following chapters will be covered in this section:

- Chapter 1, *An Introduction to Functional Programming*
- Chapter 2, *Understanding Pure Functions*
- Chapter 3, *Deep Dive into Lambdas*
- Chapter 4, *The Idea of Functional Composition*
- Chapter 5, *Partial Application and Currying*

An Introduction to Functional Programming

1

Why is functional programming useful? Functional programming constructs have popped up in all major programming languages in the past decade. Programmers have enjoyed their benefits—simplified loops, more expressive code, and simple parallelization. But there's more to it—decoupling from time, enabling opportunities to remove duplication, composability, and a simpler design. Higher adoption of functional programming (including the large-scale adoption of Scala in the financial sector) means more opportunities for you once you know and understand it. While we will take a deep dive into functional programming in this book to help you learn, remember that functional programming is another tool to add to your toolbox—one that you can choose to use when the problem and the context fits.

The following topics will be covered in this chapter:

- An introduction to functional programming and an examination of how you've already been using functional constructs
- Structured loops versus functional loops
- Immutability
- **Object-oriented programming (OOP)** versus functional design
- Composability and removing duplication

Technical requirements

The code works with g++ 7.3.0 and C++ 17; it includes a `makefile` for your convenience. You can find it in the GitHub repository (`https://github.com/PacktPublishing/Hands-On-Functional-Programming-with-Cpp`) in the `Chapter01` directory.

An introduction to functional programming

My first experience with functional programming was at university. I was a 20-year-old geek who was interested in Sci-Fi, reading, and programming; programming was the highlight of my academic life. Everything to do with C++, Java, MATLAB, and a few other programming languages that we used was fun for me. Unfortunately, I can't say the same thing about the disciplines around electrical engineering, circuits, or compiler theory. I just wanted to write code!

Based on my interests, functional programming should have been a very fun course for me. Our teacher was very passionate. We had to write code. But something went wrong—I didn't click with what the teacher was telling us. Why were lists so interesting? Why was the syntax so backward and full of parentheses? Why would I use these things when it was much simpler to write the same code in C++? I ended up trying to translate all the programming constructs I knew from BASIC and C++ into Lisp and OCaml. It completely missed the point of functional programming, but I passed the course and forgot about it for many years.

I imagine that many of you can relate to this story, and I have a possible reason for this. I now believe that my teacher, despite being extremely passionate, used the wrong approach. Today, I understand that functional programming has a certain elegance at its core, due to its strong relationship with mathematics. But that elegance requires a sense of insightful observation that I didn't have when I was 20, that is, a sense that I was lucky to build on after years of various experiences. It's obvious to me now that learning functional programming shouldn't be related to the ability of the reader to see this elegance.

So, what approach could we use instead? Thinking about the past me, that is, the geek who just wanted to write code, there's only one way to go—look at the common problems in code and explore how functional programming reduces or removes them entirely. Additionally, start from the beginning; you've already seen functional programming, you've already used some of the concepts and constructs, and you might have even found them very useful. Let's examine why.

Functional programming constructs are everywhere

Around 10 years after I finished the university functional programming course, I had a casual chat with my friend, Felix. As any two geeks, we would rarely see each other, but we had, for years, an ongoing conversation on instant messaging discussing all kinds of nerdy topics and, of course, programming.

Somehow, the topic of functional programming came up. Felix pointed out that one of my favorite and most enjoyable programming languages, LOGO, was, in fact, a functional programming language.

 LOGO is an educational programming language whose main characteristic is utilization of so-called **turtle graphics**.

It was obvious in retrospect; here is how to write a function that draws a square in the KTurtle version of LOGO:

```
learn square {
    repeat 4 {forward 50 turnright 90}
}
```

The result is shown in the following screenshot:

Can you see how we're passing two lines of code to the repeat function? That's functional programming! A fundamental tenet of functional programming is that code is just another type of data, which can be packed in a function and passed around to other functions. I used this construct in LOGO hundreds of times without making the connection.

This realization made me think: could there be other functional programming constructs that I've used without knowing? As it turns out, yes, there were. In fact, as a C++ programmer, you've most likely used them as well; let's take a look at a few examples:

```
int add(const int base, const int exponent){
    return pow(base, exponent);
}
```

This function is a typical example of recommended C++ code. I first learned about the benefits of adding `const` everywhere from the amazing books of Bertrand Meyer: *Effective C++*, *More Effective C++*, and *Effective STL*. There are multiple reasons this construct works well. First, it protects the data members and parameters that shouldn't change. Second, it allows a programmer to reason more easily about what happens in the function by removing possible side effects. Third, it allows the compiler to optimize the function.

As it turns out, this is also an example of immutability in action. As we'll discover in the following chapters, functional programming places immutability at the core of the programs, moving all side effects to the edges of the program. We already know the basic construct of functional programming; to say that we use functional programming just means to use it much more extensively!

Here's another example from STL:

```
std::vector aCollection{5, 4, 3, 2, 1};
sort (aCollection.begin(), aCollection.end());
```

The STL algorithms have great power; this power comes from polymorphism. I'm using this term in a more fundamental sense than in OOP—it merely means that it doesn't matter what the collection contains, because the algorithm will still work fine as long as a comparison is implemented. I have to admit that when I first understood it, I was impressed by the smart, effective solution.

There's a variant of the `sort` function that allows the sorting of elements even when the comparison is not implemented, or when it doesn't work as we'd like; for example, when we are given a `Name` structure, as follows:

```
using namespace std;

// Parts of code omitted for clarity
struct Name{
    string firstName;
    string lastName;
};
```

If we'd like to sort a `vector<Name>` container by first name, we just need a `compare` function:

```
bool compareByFirstName(const Name& first, const Name& second){
    return first.firstName < second.firstName;
}
```

Additionally, we need to pass it to the `sort` function, as shown in the following code:

```
int main(){
    vector<Name> names = {Name("John", "Smith"), Name("Alex",
    "Bolboaca")};

    sort(names.begin(), names.end(), compareByFirstName);
}
// The names vector now contains "Alex Bolboaca", "John Smith"
```

This makes a kind of *higher-order function*. A high-level function is a function that uses other functions as parameters in order to allow higher levels of polymorphism. Congratulations—you've just used a second functional programming construct!

I will go as far as to state that STL is a good example of functional programming in action. Once you learn more about functional programming constructs, you'll realize that they are used everywhere in STL. Some of them, such as function pointers or functors, have been in the C++ language for a very long time. In fact, STL has stood the test of time, so why not use similar paradigms in our code as well?

There's no better example to support this statement other than the functional loops present in STL.

Structured loops versus functional loops

It's hardly a surprise that one of the first things that we learn as programmers is how to write a loop. One of my first loops in C++ was printing the numbers from 1 to 10:

```
for(int i = 0; i< 10; ++i){
    cout << i << endl;
}
```

As a curious programmer, I took this syntax for granted, went over its peculiarities and complications, and just used it. Looking back, I realize that there are a few unusual things about this construct. First, why start with 0? I've been told it's a convention, due to historical reasons. Then, the `for` loop has three statements—an initialization, a condition, and an increment. This sounds slightly too complicated for what we're trying to achieve. Finally, the end condition forced me into more off-by-one errors than I'd like to admit.

At this point, you will realize that STL allows you to use iterators when looping over collections:

```
for (list<int>::iterator it = aList.begin(); it != aList.end(); ++it)
    cout << *it << endl;
```

This is definitely better than the `for` loop using a cursor. It avoids off-by-one errors and there are no 0 convention shenanigans. There's still a lot of ceremony around the operation, however. Even worse is that the loop tends to grow as the complexity of the program grows.

There's an easy way to show this symptom. Let's take a look back at the first problems that I've solved using loops.

Let's consider a vector of integers and compute their sum; the naive implementation will be as follows:

```
int sumWithUsualLoop(const vector<int>& numbers){
    int sum = 0;
    for(auto iterator = numbers.begin(); iterator < numbers.end();
    ++iterator){
        sum += *iterator;
    }
    return sum;
}
```

If only production code was so simple! Instead, the moment we implement this code, we'll get a new requirement. We now need to sum only the even numbers from the vector. Hmm, that's easy enough, right? Let's take a look at the following code:

```
int sumOfEvenNumbersWithUsualLoop(const vector<int>& numbers){
    int sum = 0;
    for(auto iterator = numbers.begin(); iterator<numbers.end();
    ++iterator){
        int number = *iterator;
        if (number % 2 == 0) sum+= number;
    }
    return sum;
}
```

If you thought this is the end, it's not. We now require three sums for the same vector—one of the even numbers, one of the odd numbers, and one of the total. Let's now add some more code, as follows:

```
struct Sums{
    Sums(): evenSum(0), oddSum(0), total(0){}
    int evenSum;
```

```
        int oddSum;
        int total;
};

const Sums sums(const vector<int>& numbers){
    Sums theTotals;
    for(auto iterator = numbers.begin(); iterator<numbers.end();
    ++iterator){
        int number = *iterator;
        if(number % 2 == 0) theTotals.evenSum += number;
        if(number %2 != 0) theTotals.oddSum += number;
        theTotals.total += number;
    }
    return theTotals;
}
```

Our loop, which initially started relatively simple, has become more and more complex. When I first started professional programming, we used to blame users and clients who couldn't make up their minds about the perfect feature and give us the final, frozen requirements. That's rarely possible in reality, however; our customers learn new things every day from the interaction of users with the programs we write. It's up to us to make this code clear, and it's possible with functional loops.

Years later, I learned Groovy. A Java virtual machine-based programming language, Groovy focuses on making the job of programmers easier by helping them to write less code and avoid common errors. Here's how you could write the previous code in Groovy:

```
def isEven(value){return value %2 == 0}
def isOdd(value){return value %2 == 1}
def sums(numbers){
    return [
        evenSum: numbers.filter(isEven).sum(),
        oddSum: numbers.filter(isOdd).sum(),
        total: numbers.sum()
    ]
}
```

Let's compare the two for a moment. There's no loop. The code is extremely clear. There's no way to make off-by-one errors. There's no counter, so, therefore, there is no *starting from* 0 weirdness. Additionally, there's no scaffolding around it—I just write what I want to achieve, and a trained reader can easily understand it.

While the C++ version is more verbose, it allows us to achieve the same goals:

```cpp
const Sums sumsWithFunctionalLoops(const vector<int>& numbers){
    Sums theTotals;
    vector<int> evenNumbers;
    copy_if(numbers.begin(), numbers.end(),
    back_inserter(evenNumbers), isEven);
    theTotals.evenSum = accumulate(evenNumbers.begin(),
    evenNumbers.end(), 0);

    vector<int> oddNumbers;
    copy_if(numbers.begin(), numbers.end(), back_inserter(oddNumbers),
    isOdd);
    theTotals.oddSum= accumulate(oddNumbers.begin(), oddNumbers.end(),
    0);

    theTotals.total = accumulate(numbers.begin(), numbers.end(), 0);

    return theTotals;
}
```

There's still a lot of ceremony though, and too much code similarity. So, let's get rid of it, as follows:

```cpp
template<class UnaryPredicate>
const vector<int> filter(const vector<int>& input, UnaryPredicate
filterFunction){
    vector<int> filtered;
    copy_if(input.begin(), input.end(), back_inserter(filtered),
    filterFunction);
    return filtered;
}

const int sum(const vector<int>& input){
    return accumulate(input.begin(), input.end(), 0);
}

const Sums sumsWithFunctionalLoopsSimplified(const vector<int>& numbers){
    Sums theTotals(
        sum(filter(numbers, isEven)),
        sum(filter(numbers, isOdd)),
        sum(numbers)
    );
    return theTotals;
}
```

We've just replaced a complex `for` loop with a number of simpler, more readable, and composable functions.

So, is this code better? Well, that depends on your definition of *better*. I like to think of any implementation in terms of advantages and disadvantages. The advantages of functional loops are simplicity, readability, reduced code duplication, and composability. Are there any disadvantages? Well, our initial `for` loop only requires one pass through the vector, while our current implementation requires three passes. This can be a burden for very large collections, or when response time and memory usage are very important. This is definitely worth discussing, and we will examine it in more detail in `Chapter 10`, *Performance Optimization,* which is focused solely on performance optimization for functional programming. For now, I recommend that you focus on understanding the new tool of functional programming.

In order to do that, we need to revisit immutability.

Immutability

We've already understood that a certain level of immutability is preferred in C++; the common example is as follows:

```
class ...{
    int add(const int& first, const int& second) const{
        return first + second;
    }
}
```

The `const` keyword clearly communicates a few important constraints on the code, such as the following:

- The function does not change any of its arguments before returning.
- The function does not change any data member of the class it belongs to.

Let's now imagine an alternate version of `add`, as follows

```
int uglyAdd(int& first, int& second){
    first = first + second;
    aMember = 40;
    return first;
}
```

I called this `uglyAdd` for a reason—I don't tolerate code like this when I'm programming! This function violates the principle of minimal surprise and does too many things. Reading the function code reveals nothing about its intent. Imagine the surprise of the caller, if not careful, then, just by calling an `add` function, two things changed—one in the parameters passed, and the second in the class where the function is located.

While this is an extreme example, it contributes to an argument for immutability. Immutable functions are boring; they receive data, change nothing in the received data, change nothing in the class containing them, and return a value. When it comes to maintaining code over long periods of time, however, boring is good.

Immutability is the core property of functions in functional programming. Of course, there's at least one part of your program that cannot be immutable—**input/output (I/O)**. We will accept I/O for what it is, and we will focus on increasing the immutability of our code as much as possible.

Now, you are probably wondering whether you have to completely rethink the way you write programs. Should you forget all that you learned about OOP? Well, not really, and let's see why.

OOP versus functional design styles

An important part of my job is to work with programmers and help them to improve the way they write code. To do so, I try my best to come up with simple explanations for complex ideas. I have one such explanation for software design. Software design is, for me, the way we structure the code such that we optimize it for business purposes.

I like this definition because it's plain and short. But one thing bugged me after I started experimenting with functional constructs; that is, functional programming leads to code such as the following:

```
const Sums sumsWithFunctionalLoopsSimplified(const vector<int>& numbers){
    Sums theTotals(
        sum(filter(numbers, isEven)),
        sum(filter(numbers, isOdd)),
        sum(numbers)
    );
    return theTotals;
}
```

Writing similar code in OOP style would most likely mean creating classes and using inheritance. So, which style is better? Additionally, if software design is about code structure, is there an equivalence between the two styles?

First, let's take a look at what the two design styles really promote. What is OOP? For many years, I believed all the books that listed the following three properties of object-oriented languages:

- Encapsulation
- Inheritance
- Polymorphism

Alan Kay, the thinker behind OOP, does not really agree with this list. For him, OOP is about communication between many small objects. As a biology major, he saw an opportunity to organize programs like the body organizes cells, and to allow objects to communicate much like cells do. He places more importance on objects over classes, and on communication over the commonly listed OOP properties. I would best summarize his position as follows: the dynamic relations in the system are more important than its static properties.

This changes a lot about the OOP paradigm. So, should classes match the real world? Not really. They should be optimized for the representation of the real world. Should we focus on having clear, well-thought out class hierarchies? No, since those are less important than the communication between objects. What is the smallest object that we can think of? Well, either a combination of data, or a function.

In a recent answer on Quora (https://www.quora.com/Isnt-getting-rid-of-the-evil-state-like-Haskells-approach-something-every-programmer-should-follow/answer/Alan-Kay-11), Alan Kay stated an interesting idea when answering a question on functional programming. Functional programming came from mathematics and from an effort to model the real world in order to enable artificial intelligence. This effort hit the following problem—*Alex is in Bucharest* and *Alex is in London* can both be true, but at different points in time. The solution to this modeling issue is immutability; that is, time becomes a parameter to functions, or a data member in the data structures. In any program, we can model data changes as time-bound versions of the data. Nothing stops us from modeling the data as small objects, and the changes as functions. Additionally, as we will see later, we can easily turn functions into objects and vice versa.

So, to summarize, there's no real tension between OOP as Alan Kay meant it and functional programming. We can use them together and interchangeably, as long as we focus on increasing the immutability of our code, and on small objects that communicate with one another. We'll discover, in the following chapters, how easy it is to replace a class with functions and vice versa.

But there are many ways to use OOP that are different from Alan Kay's vision. I've seen a lot of C++ code with my clients, and I've seen it all—big functions, huge classes, and deep inheritance hierarchies. Most of the time, the reason I'm called is because the design is too hard to change and because adding new features slows down to a crawl. Inheritance is a very strong relationship and overusing it leads to strong coupling, and, therefore, to code that's difficult to change. Long methods and long classes are harder to understand and harder to change. Of course, there are situations when inheritance and long classes make sense, but, in general, going for small objects with loose coupling enables changeability.

But classes can be reused, can't they? Can we do that with functions? Let's visit this topic next.

Composability and removing duplication

We have already seen an example of where we had a fair amount of duplication:

```
const Sums sumsWithFunctionalLoops(const vector<int>& numbers){
    Sums theTotals;
    vector<int> evenNumbers;
    copy_if(numbers.begin(), numbers.end(), back_inserter(evenNumbers),
    isEven);
    theTotals.evenSum = accumulate(evenNumbers.begin(),
    evenNumbers.end(), 0);

    vector<int> oddNumbers;
    copy_if(numbers.begin(), numbers.end(), back_inserter(oddNumbers),
    isOdd);
    theTotals.oddSum= accumulate(oddNumbers.begin(), oddNumbers.end(),
    0);

    theTotals.total = accumulate(numbers.begin(), numbers.end(), 0);

    return theTotals;
}
```

We managed to reduce it using functions, as shown in the following code:

```
template<class UnaryPredicate>
const vector<int> filter(const vector<int>& input, UnaryPredicate
filterFunction){
    vector<int> filtered;
    copy_if(input.begin(), input.end(), back_inserter(filtered),
    filterFunction);
    return filtered;
}
```

```
const int sum(const vector<int>& input){
    return accumulate(input.begin(), input.end(), 0);
}

const Sums sumsWithFunctionalLoopsSimplified(const vector<int>& numbers){
    Sums theTotals(
        sum(filter(numbers, isEven)),
        sum(filter(numbers, isOdd)),
        sum(numbers)
    );

    return theTotals;
}
```

It's interesting to see how the functions are composed in various ways; we have
sum(filter()) called twice, and sum() called once. Moreover, filter can be used with
multiple predicates. Additionally, with a bit of work, we can make both filter and sum
polymorphic functions:

```
template<class CollectionType, class UnaryPredicate>
const CollectionType filter(const CollectionType& input, UnaryPredicate
filterFunction){
    CollectionType filtered;
    copy_if(input.begin(), input.end(), back_inserter(filtered),
    filterFunction);
    return filtered;
}
template<typename T, template<class> class CollectionType>
const T sum(const CollectionType<T>& input, const T& init = 0){
    return accumulate(input.begin(), input.end(), init);
}
```

It's now easy to call filter and sum with arguments of type other than vector<int>. The
implementation is not perfect, but it illustrates the point that I'm trying to make, that is,
small, immutable functions can easy become polymorphic and composable. This works
especially well when we can pass functions to other functions.

Summary

We've already covered a lot of interesting topics! You've just realized that you know the basics of functional programming. You can write immutable functions in C++ with the help of the `const` keyword. You've already used high-level functions from STL. Additionally, you don't have to forget anything about OOP, but, instead, just see it from a different perspective. Finally, we discovered how small immutable functions can be composed to offer complex functionality, and how they can become polymorphic with the help of C++ templates.

It's now time to take an in-depth look at the building blocks of functional programming and learn how to use them in C++. This includes pure functions, lambdas, and operations with functions such as functional composition, currying, or partial functional application.

Questions

1. What is an immutable function?
2. How do you write an immutable function?
3. How do immutable functions support code simplicity?
4. How do immutable functions support simple design?
5. What is a high-level function?
6. What example of high-level function can you give from STL?
7. What are the advantages of functional loops over structured loops? What are the potential disadvantages?
8. What is OOP from the perspective of Alan Kay? How does it relate to functional programming?

Understanding Pure Functions

2

Pure functions are the core building blocks of functional programming. They are immutable functions, which allow them to be simple and predictable. Writing pure functions in C++ is easy, but there are a few things that you'll need to be aware of. Since functions in C++ are mutable by default, we need to learn the syntax that tells the compiler how to prevent mutations. We'll also explore how to separate mutable code from immutable code.

The following topics will be covered in this chapter:

- Understanding what a pure function is
- Writing pure functions in C++ and functions that return multiple arguments using tuples
- Ensuring immutability in C++ pure functions
- Understanding why I/O is mutable and needs to be separated from pure functions

Technical requirements

You will need a C++ compiler that supports C++ 17. I'm using GCC version 7.3.0. Code samples are on GitHub (`https://github.com/PacktPublishing/Hands-On-Functional-Programming-with-Cpp`) in the `Chapter02` folder and have a `makefile` file for your convenience.

What is a pure function?

Let's take a moment to think about a simple everyday experience. When you turn the light switch, one of two things happen:

- If the light is on, it turns off
- If the light is off, it turns on

The behavior of a light switch is highly predictable. It's so predictable that, when the light doesn't turn on, you immediately think that something is wrong—that is, with the light bulb, the fuses, or the switch itself.

Here are some of the things that you don't expect to happen when you turn the switch on or off:

- Your fridge doesn't go off
- Your neighbor's lights don't turn on
- Your bathroom sink water doesn't turn on
- Your mobile phone doesn't reset

Why would all these things happen when you turn the light switch on? That would be highly chaotic; we wouldn't want chaos in our lives, right?

Yet, programmers often experience such behaviors in code. Calling a function often results in changes to the state of the program; when this happens, we say that a function has **side effects**.

Functional programming tries to reduce the chaos caused by a state change through the extended use of pure functions. Pure functions are functions that have two constraints:

- They always return the same output values for the same argument values.
- They don't have side effects.

Let's explore how we would write the code for the light switch. We'll assume that the bulb is an external entity that we can call; think of it as the output from **input/output (I/O)** for our program. The natural code for a structured/object-oriented programmer would look something like this:

```
void switchLight(LightBulb bulb){
    if(switchIsOn) bulb.turnOff();
    else bulb.turnOn();
}
```

There are two things happening with this function. Firstly, it uses an input that's not part of the list of parameters, that is, switchIsOn. Secondly, it directly produces side effects on the bulb.

So, what does a pure function look like? Well, in the first instance, all of its parameters are visible:

```
void switchLight(boolean switchIsOn, LightBulb bulb){      if(switchIsOn)
    bulb.turnOff();
    else bulb.turnOn();
}
```

Second, we need to get rid of the side effect. How can we do that? Let's separate the computation of the next state from the action of turning the light bulb on or off:

```
LightBulbSignal signalForBulb(boolean switchIsOn){
    if(switchIsOn) return LightBulbSignal.TurnOff;
    else return LightBulbSignal.TurnOn;
}
// use the output like this:
sendSignalToLightBulb(signalForBulb(switchIsOn))
```

The function is now pure, and we'll discuss this in more detail later; however, for now, let's simplify it as follows:

```
LightBulbSignal signalForBulb(boolean switchIsOn){
    return switchIsOn ? LightBulbSignal.TurnOff :
    LightBulbSignal.TurnOn;
}
// use the output like this:
sendSignalToLightBulb(signalForBulb(switchIsOn))
```

Let's make things even clearer (I'll assume the function is part of a class):

```
static LightBulbSignal signalForBulb(const boolean switchIsOn){
    return switchIsOn ? LightBulbSignal.TurnOff :
    LightBulbSignal.TurnOn;
}
// use the output like this:
sendSignalToLightBulb(signalForBulb(switchIsOn))
```

This function is terribly uninteresting: it's very predictable, it's easy to read, and it doesn't have side effects. This sounds exactly like a well-designed light switch. Moreover, it sounds exactly like what we want when we maintain a huge number of lines of code for tens of years.

We now understand what a pure function is and why it's useful. We also demonstrated an example of separating pure functions from side effects (usually I/O). It's an interesting concept, but where can it take us? Can we really build complex programs using such simple constructs? We'll discuss how to compose pure functions in the following chapters. For now, let's focus on understanding how to write pure functions in C++.

Pure functions in C++

You've already seen, in the preceding example, the basic syntax that we need to use for pure functions in C++. You just need to remember the following four ideas:

- Pure functions don't have side effects; if they are part of a class, they can be `static` or `const`.
- Pure functions don't change their parameters, so every parameter has to be of the `const`, `const&`, or `const* const` type.
- Pure functions always return values. Technically, we can return a value through an output parameter, but it's usually simpler to just return a value. This means that pure functions usually don't have a void return type.
- None of the preceding points guarantee the lack of side effects or immutability, but they take us close. For example, data members can be marked as mutable and the `const` methods could change them.

We'll explore, in the following sections, how to write pure functions both as free functions and as class methods. When we go through the examples, remember that we are exploring the syntax for now, focusing on how to use the compiler to get as close as possible to pure functions.

Pure functions without arguments

Let's start simple. Can we use pure functions without arguments? Certainly. One example is when we need a default value. Let's consider the following example:

```
int zero(){return 0;}
```

This is a standalone function. Let's understand how to write a pure function inside a class as well:

```
class Number{
    public:
        static int zero(){ return 0; }
}
```

Now, `static` tells us that the function doesn't change any non-static data member. However, this doesn't prevent the code from changing the value of a `static` data member:

```
class Number{
    private:
        static int accessCount;
    public:
        static int zero(){++accessCount; return 0;}
        static int getCount() { return accessCount; }
};
int Number::accessCount = 0;
int main(){
Number::zero();
cout << Number::getCount() << endl; // will print 1
}
```

Fortunately, we'll see that we can solve most mutable state problems with well-placed `const` keywords. The following case is no exception:

```
static const int accessCount;
```

Now that we have gained some understanding of how to write pure functions without arguments, it's time to add more arguments.

Pure functions with one or more arguments

Let's start with one pure class method with one parameter, as shown in the following code:

```
class Number{
    public:
        static int zero(){ return 0; }
        static int increment(const int value){ return value + 1; }
}
```

How about two parameters? Sure, let's consider the following code:

```
class Number{
    public:
        static int zero(){ return 0; }
        static int increment(const int value){ return value + 1; }
        static int add(const int first, const int second){ return first
        + second; }
};
```

We can do the same with reference types, as follows:

```
class Number{
    public:
        static int zero(){ return 0; }
        static int increment(const int& value){ return value + 1; }
        static int add(const int& first, const int& second){ return
        first + second; }
};
```

Additionally, we can do the same with pointer types, albeit with a bit more syntactic sugar:

```
class Number{
    public:
        static int incrementValueFromPointer(const int* const value )
        {return *value + 1;}
};
```

Congratulations—you now know how to write pure functions in C++!

Well, kind of; unfortunately, immutability is a bit more complex to implement in C++ than what we've seen so far. We need to look at various situations in more depth.

Pure functions and immutability

The 1995 movie, *Apollo 13*, is one of my favorite thrillers. It involves space, a real story, and multiple engineering problems. Between many memorable scenes, there's one in particular that can teach us a lot about programming. While the team of astronauts is preparing a complex procedure, the commander, played by Tom Hanks notices, that his colleague placed a sticker on one of the command switches saying *Don't flip this*. The commander asks his colleague why he did that, and his answer is something along the lines of *My head wasn't clear, and I was afraid I would flip this and send you to space. So, I wrote this to remind myself not to make this mistake.*

If this technique works for astronauts, it should work for programmers. Fortunately, we have the compiler to tell us when we do something wrong. However, we need to tell the compiler what we want it to check.

After all, we can write pure functions without any `const` or `static`. Function purity is not a matter of syntax, but a concept. Having the right stickers in place can prevent us from making mistakes. We'll see, however, that the compiler can only go so far.

Let's take a look at another way to implement the increment function that we discussed previously:

```
class Number{
    public:
        int increment(int value){ return ++value; }
};
int main(){
    Number number;
    int output = number.increment(Number::zero());
    cout << output << endl;
}
```

This is not a pure function. Can you see why? The answer is on the following line:

```
int increment(int value){ return ++value; }
```

`++value` not only increments `value`, but it also changes the input parameter. While it's not a problem in this case (the `value` parameter is passed by value, so only its copy is modified), it's still a side effect. This shows how easy it is to write side effects in C++, or in any language that doesn't enforce immutability by default. Fortunately, the compiler can help us, as long as we tell it exactly what we want.

Recall the previous implementation as follows:

```
static int increment(const int value){ return value + 1; }
```

If you try to write `++value` or `value++` in the body of this function, the compiler will immediately tell you that you're trying to change a `const` input parameter. That's very nice of the compiler, isn't it?

What about the parameters passed by reference though?

Immutability and passing by reference

The problem could have been worse. Imagine the following function:

```
static int increment(int& value){ return ++value; }
```

We're avoiding a pass by value, which involves a few more bytes of memory. But what happens with the value? Let's take a look at the following code:

```
int value = Number::zero(); //value is 0
    cout << Number::increment(value) << endl;
    cout << value << endl; // value is now 1
```

The `value` parameter started at `0`, but when we called the function, it was incremented, so now its `value` is `1`. That's like every time you turn on the light, your refrigerator door opens. Fortunately, if we just add a small `const` keyword, we will see the following:

```
static int increment(const int& value) {return value + 1; }
```

Then, the compiler is once again nice enough to tell us that we can't use `++value` or `value++` in its body.

That's cool, but what about pointer arguments?

Immutability and pointers

When using pointers as input parameters, preventing unwanted changes becomes more complex. Let's see what happens when we try calling this function:

```
static int increment(int* pValue)
```

The following things could change:

- The value pointed by `pValue` could change.
- The pointer could change its address.

The value pointed by `pValue` can change in similar conditions, as we discovered previously. For example, consider the following code:

```
static int increment(int* pValue){ return ++*pValue; }
```

This will change the pointed value as well as return it. To make it impossible to change, we need to use a well-placed `const` keyword:

```
static int increment(int* const pValue){ return *pValue + 1; }
```

The changes to the pointer address are trickier than you'd expect. Let's take a look at an example that will behave in an unexpected way:

```
class Number {
    static int* increment(int* pValue){ return ++pValue; }
}

int main(){
    int* pValue = new int(10);
    cout << "Address: " << pValue << endl;
    cout << "Increment pointer address:" <<
    Number::incrementPointerAddressImpure(pValue) << endl;
    cout << "Address after increment: " << pValue << endl;
    delete pValue;
}
```

Running this on my laptop gives the following result:

```
Address: 0x55cd35098e80
Increment pointer address:0x55cd35098e80
Address after increment: 0x55cd35098e80
Increment pointer value:10
```

The address doesn't change, even though we're incrementing it in the function by using `++pValue`. The same also happens with `pValue++`, but why is this the case?

Well, the pointer address is a value, and it's passed by value, so any change within the function body only applies to the function scope. To make the address change, you need to pass the address by reference, as follows:

```
static int* increment(int*& pValue){ return ++pValue; }
```

This tells us that, fortunately, it's not easy to write functions that change a pointer address. I still feel safer telling the compiler to enforce this rule for me:

```
static int* increment(int* const& pValue){ return ++pValue; }
```

Of course, this doesn't block you from changing the value pointed to:

```
static int* incrementPointerAddressAndValue(int* const& pValue){
    (*pValue)++;
    return pValue + 1;
}
```

To enforce immutability for both the value and the address, you need to use even more `const` keywords, as shown in the following code:

```
static const int* incrementPointerAddressAndValuePure(const int*
    const& pValue){
        (*pValue)++;//Compilation error
        return pValue + 1;
}
```

This covers all types of class functions. However, C++ allows us to write functions outside classes. So, does `static` still work in this situation? (Spoiler alert: not quite as you would expect).

Immutability and non-class functions

All the examples so far assume that the functions are part of a class. C++ allows us to write functions that are not part of any class. For example, we could write the following code:

```
int zero(){ return 0; }
int increment(int& value){ return ++value; }
const int* incrementPointerAddressAndValuePure(const int* const& pValue){
    return pValue + 1;
}
```

You may have noticed that we're not using `static` anymore. You can use `static`, but you need to be aware that it has a completely different meaning to the functions in a class. `static` applied to a standalone function means that *you can't use it from a different translation unit*; so, if you write the function in a CPP file, it will just be available in that file and it will be ignored by the linker.

We've covered all types of class and non-class functions. But what about functions that have output parameters? As it turns out, they need a bit of work.

Immutability and output parameters

Sometimes, we want a function to change the data that we pass in. There are many examples in **Standard Template Library (STL)**, and the easiest one to provide as an example is `sort`:

```
vector<int> values = {324, 454, 12, 45, 54564, 32};
    sort(values.begin(), values.end());
```

However, this doesn't fit the idea of pure functions; a pure equivalent of `sort` would be as follows:

```
vector<int> sortedValues = pureSort(values);
```

 I can hear you thinking, *but the STL implementation works in place for optimization reasons, so are pure functions less optimized?* Well, as it turns out, pure functional programming languages, such as Haskell or Lisp, also optimize such operations; a `pureSort` implementation would just move the pointers around and only allocate more memory when one of the pointed values is changed. These are, however, two different contexts; C++ has to support multiple programming paradigms, while Haskell or Lisp optimize for immutability and functional style. We will discuss optimization further in `Chapter 10`, *Performance Optimization*. For now, let's examine how to make these types of functions pure.

We've discovered how to deal with one output parameter. But how can we write pure functions that will have multiple output parameters? Let's consider the following example:

```
void incrementAll(int& first, int& second){
    ++first;
    ++second;
}
```

A simple solution to this problem would be to replace the two arguments with `vector<int>`. But what happens if the parameters have different types? Then, we could use a struct. But what if this is the only time we need it? Fortunately, STL offers a solution to this problem, that is, through tuples:

```
const tuple<int, int> incrementAllPure(const int& first, const int&
    second){
        return make_tuple(first + 1, second + 1);
}
int main(){
    auto results = incrementAllPure(1, 2);
    // Can also use a simplified version
    // auto [first, second] = incrementAllPure(1, 2);
    cout << "Incremented pure: " << get<0>(results) << endl;
    cout << "Incremented pure: " << get<1>(results) << endl;
}
```

Tuples have a number of advantages, as follows:

- They can be used with multiple values.
- The values can have different data types.
- They are easy to build—just one function call.
- They don't require an additional data type.

From my experience, tuples are a great solution when you are trying to render a function that has multiple output parameters pure, or a return value and an output parameter. However, I often try to refactor them toward named *struct*s or data classes after I figure out how to design them. Nonetheless, using tuples is a very useful technique; just use them sparingly.

By now, we have used a lot of `static` functions. But aren't they bad practice? Well, that depends on a number of things; we'll discuss this in more detail next.

Aren't static functions bad practice?

By now, you may be wondering whether pure functions are good since they contradict with the rules of **object-oriented programming (OOP)** or clean code, that is, to avoid `static`. However, until now, we've only written `static` functions. So, are they good or bad?

There are two arguments against using `static` functions.

The first argument against `static` functions is that they hide the global state. Since `static` functions can only access `static` values, those values become global state. Global state is bad because it's hard to understand who changes it, and it's also hard to debug when its value is unexpected.

But remember the rules for pure functions—a pure function should return the same output values for the same input values. Therefore, a function is pure if, and only if, it does not depend on global state. Even when the program has a state, all the necessary values are sent to the pure functions as input parameters. Unfortunately, we cannot easily enforce this using the compiler; it has to be the practice of the programmer to avoid using any kind of global variable and to turn it into a parameter instead.

There's an edge case for this situation, specifically when using global constants. While constants are an immutable state, it's important to consider their evolution as well. For instance, consider the following code:

```
static const string CURRENCY="EUR";
```

Here, you should know that there will come a time when the constant will become a variable, and then you'll have to change a bunch of code to implement the new requirement. My advice is that it's usually better to pass in the constants as well.

The second argument against `static` functions is that they shouldn't be part of a class. We will discuss this argument in more detail in the following chapters; suffice to say that, for now, classes should group cohesive functions, and, sometimes, the pure functions should fit together neatly in a class. There's also an alternative to grouping cohesive pure functions in a class—just use a namespace.

Fortunately, we don't necessarily have to use `static` functions in classes.

Alternatives to static functions

We discovered in the previous section how to write pure functions in a Number class by using `static` functions:

```
class Number{
    public:
        static int zero(){ return 0; }
        static int increment(const int& value){ return value + 1; }
        static int add(const int& first, const int& second){ return
        first + second; }
};
```

However, there's another alternative; C++ allows us to avoid `static`, but keep the functions immutable:

```
class Number{
    public:
        int zero() const{ return 0; }
        int increment(const int& value) const{ return value + 1; }
        int add(const int& first, const int& second) const{ return
        first + second; }
};
```

The `const` keyword after each function signature just tells us that the function can access data members of the Number class, but can never change them.

If we change this code slightly, we can ask an interesting question about immutability in the context of a class. If we initialize the number with a value and always add to the initial value, we obtain the following code:

```
class Number{
    private:
        int initialValue;

    public:
        Number(int initialValue) : initialValue(initialValue){}
        int initial() const{ return initialValue; }
        int addToInitial(const int& first) const{ return first +
        initialValue; }
};

int main(){
    Number number(10);
    cout << number.addToInitial(20) << endl;
}
```

Here is an interesting question: is the `addToInitial` function pure? Let's check the criteria as follows:

- Does it have side effects? No, it doesn't.
- Does it return the same output value for the same input value? This is a tricky question because the function has a hidden parameter, that is, the `Number` class or its initial value. However, nobody can change `initialValue` from outside the `Number` class. In other words, the `Number` class is immutable. Therefore, the function will return the same output value for the same `Number` instance and the same parameter.
- Does it change the values of its parameters? Well, it only receives one parameter, and it doesn't change it.

The result is that the function is, in fact, pure. We will discover in the following chapter that it is also a *partially applied function*.

We previously mentioned that everything can be pure inside a program, except I/O. So, what do we do with the code that does I/O?

Pure functions and I/O

Take a look at the following and consider whether the function is pure:

```
void printResults(){
    int* pValue = new int(10);
    cout << "Address: " << pValue << endl;
    cout << "Increment pointer address and value pure:" <<
    incrementPointerAddressAndValuePure(pValue) << endl;
    cout << "Address after increment: " << pValue << endl;
    cout << "Value after increment: " << *pValue << endl;
    delete pValue;
}
```

Well, let's see—it doesn't have arguments, so no value is changed. But something is off when compared to our previous example, that is, it doesn't return values. Instead, it calls a few functions, of which at least one is pure.

So, does it have side effects? Well, yes; one on almost every line of code:

```
cout << ....
```

This line of code writes a line of string on the console, which is a side effect! cout is based on a mutable state, so it's not a pure function. Moreover, due to its external dependency, cout may fail, leading to exceptions.

We need I/O in our programs though, so what can we do? Well, that's easy—simply separate the mutable from the immutable parts. Separate the side effects from the non-side effects and reduce the impure functions as much as possible.

So, how can we make this happen here? Well, there's a pure function waiting to get out of this impure function. The key is to start from the problem; so, let's separate cout as follows:

```
string formatResults(){
    stringstream output;
    int* pValue = new int(500);
    output << "Address: " << pValue << endl;
    output << "Increment pointer address and value pure:" <<
    incrementPointerAddressAndValuePure(pValue) << endl;
    output << "Address after increment: " << pValue << endl;
    output << "Value after increment: " << *pValue << endl;
    delete pValue;
    return output.str();
}

void printSomething(const string& text){
```

```
        cout << text;
    }

    printSomething(formatResults());
```

We have moved the side effects due to `cout` into another function, and have made the intent for the initial function clearer—which is that it's formatting something rather than printing. It seems as though we cleanly separated the pure function from the impure one.

But did we? Let's check `formatResults` again. It doesn't have side effects, as it did before. We are using `stringstream`, which might not be pure, and are allocating memory, but all these things are local to the function.

 Is memory allocation a side effect? Can a function that allocates memory be pure? After all, memory allocation may fail. However, it's virtually impossible to avoid some kind of memory allocation in functions. We will accept, therefore, that a pure function may fail if there's some kind of memory failure.

So, what about its output? Does it change? Well, it has no input parameters, but its output can change depending on the memory address allocated by the `new` operator. So, it's not yet a pure function. How do we make it pure? That's easy—let's pass in a parameter, `pValue`:

```
string formatResultsPure(const int* pValue){
    stringstream output;
    output << "Address: " << pValue << endl;
    output << "Increment pointer address and value pure:" <<
    incrementPointerAddressAndValuePure(pValue) << endl;
    output << "Address after increment: " << pValue << endl;
    output << "Value after increment: " << *pValue << endl;
    return output.str();
}

int main(){
    int* pValue = new int(500);
    printSomething(formatResultsPure(pValue));
    delete pValue;
}
```

Here, we isolated ourselves from the side effects and mutable state. The code no longer depends on I/O or the `new` operator. Our function is pure, which brings additional benefits—it only does one thing, it's easier to understand what it does, it's predictable, and we can test it pretty easily.

As for our function with side effects, consider the following code:

```cpp
void printSomething(const string& text){
    cout << text;
}
```

I think that we can all agree that it's easy to understand what it does, and we can safely ignore it as long as all our other functions are pure.

In conclusion, to obtain code that's more predictable, we should separate pure from impure functions, and push the impure functions to the boundaries of the system as much as possible. There may be situations when this change is expensive, and it's perfectly fine to have impure functions in your code. Just make sure you know which are which.

Summary

In this chapter, we explored how to write pure functions in C++. Since there are a few tricks that you need to remember, here's a list of the recommended syntax:

- Class functions for pass by value:
    - `static int increment(const int value)`
    - `int increment(const int value) const`

- Class functions for pass by reference:
    - `static int increment(const int& value)`
    - `int increment(const int&value) const`

- Class functions for pass pointer by value:
    - `static const int* increment(const int* const value)`
    - `const int* increment(const int* const value) const`

- Class functions for pass pointer by reference:
    - `static const int* increment(const int* const& value)`
    - `const int* increment(const int* const& value) const`

- A standalone function for pass by value: `int increment(const int value)`

- A standalone function for pass by reference: `int increment(const int& value)`
- A standalone function for pass pointer by value: `const int* increment(const int* value)`
- A standalone function for pass pointer by reference: `const int* increment(const int* const& value)`

We've also discovered that, while the compiler is helpful to reduce side effects, it doesn't always tell us when a function is pure or not. We always need to remember the criteria to use when writing a pure function, as follows:

- It always returns the same output values for the same input values.
- It has no side effects.
- It does not change the values of the input parameters.

Finally, we saw how to separate side effects, usually related to I/O, from our pure functions. It's pretty easy, and it usually requires passing in values and extracting functions.

It's now time to move forward. We can do much more with functions when we treat them as first class citizens of our designs. To do that, we need to learn what lambdas are and how they are useful. We'll do this in the next chapter.

Questions

1. What is a pure function?
2. How is immutability related to pure functions?
3. How can you tell the compiler to prevent changes to a variable that's passed by value?
4. How can you tell the compiler to prevent changes to a variable that's passed by reference?
5. How can you tell the compiler to prevent changes to a pointer address that's passed by reference?
6. How can you tell the compiler to prevent changes to the value that's pointed by a pointer?

3
Deep Dive into Lambdas

Congratulations! You've just mastered the power of pure functions! It's now time to move on to the next level—pure functions on steroids, or the legendary lambdas. They've been around for longer than objects, they have a mathematical theory around them (if you like that sort of thing), and they're very powerful, as we'll discover in this chapter and the next.

The following topics will be covered in this chapter:

- Understanding the concept and history of lambdas
- How to write lambdas in C++
- How pure functions compare to lambdas
- How to use lambdas with classes

Technical requirements

You will need a C++ compiler that supports C++ 17. The code can be found in the GitHub repository (https://github.com/PacktPublishing/Hands-On-Functional-Programming-with-Cpp) in the Chapter03 folder. A makefile file is provided to make it easier for you to compile and run the code.

What is a lambda?

The year was 1936. A 33-year old mathematician, Alonzo Church, published his research on the foundations of mathematics. In doing so, he created the so-called **lambda calculus**, which was a model for the recently created field of computation. In collaboration with Alan Turing, he would then go on to prove that the lambda calculus is equivalent to a Turing machine. The relevance of this discovery is fundamental to programming—it means that we can write any program for a modern computer by using lambdas and by taking advantage of lambda calculus. That explains why it's called **lambda**—mathematicians have long preferred single Greek letters for every notation. But what exactly is it?

If you ignore all the mathematical notations, a lambda is just a **pure function** that can be applied to variables or values. Let's take a look at an example. We will learn how to write lambdas in C++, but, for now, I will use the Groovy syntax since it's the simplest syntax that I know:

```
def add = {first, second -> first + second}
add(1,2) //returns 3
```

add is a lambda. As you can see, it's a function that has two parameters and returns their sum. Since Groovy has optional types, I don't have to specify the type of the argument. Additionally, I don't need to use a return statement to return the sum; it will automatically return the value of the last statement. In C++, we can't skip types or the return statements, as we'll discover in the next section.

For now, let's take a look at another property of a lambda, that is, the ability to capture values from the context:

```
def first = 5
def addToFirst = {second -> first + second}
addToFirst(10) // returns 5 + 10 = 15
```

In this example, first is not a parameter to the function, but a variable defined in the context. The lambda *captures* the value of the variable and uses it inside its body. We can use this property of lambdas to simplify the code or to gradually refactor toward immutability.

We'll explore how to use lambdas in future chapters; for now, let's demonstrate how to write them in C++, how to ensure they are immutable, and how to capture values from the context.

Lambdas in C++

We explored how to write lambdas in Groovy. So, can we use their power in C++? Well, since C++ 11, a specific syntax was introduced. Let's take a look at how our add lambda would look in C++:

```
int main(){
    auto add = [](int first, int second){ return first + second;};
    cout << add(1,2) << endl; // writes 3
}
```

Let's unpack the syntax as follows:

- Our lambda starts with []. This block specifies the variables we capture from the context, and we'll see how to use it in a moment. Since we don't capture anything, the block is empty.
- Next, we have the parameter list, (int first, int second), as in any other C++ function.
- Finally, we write the body of the lambda, using a return statement: { return first + second; }.

The syntax has a bit more ceremony than in Groovy, but it feels like C++ and that's a good thing; uniformity helps us to remember things.

Alternatively, we can use the arrow syntax, as shown in the following code:

```
auto add = [](int first, int second) -> int { return first +
    second;};
```

The arrow syntax is a staple of lambdas since Alonzo Church used the notation in his lambda calculus. In addition to this, C++ requires the return type specification before the lambda body, which may provide clarity in situations where type casts are involved.

Due to its history, the arrow syntax is present, in one way or another, in all functional programming languages. It's rarely useful in C++; however, it's useful to know if you want to get used to functional programming in general.

It's now time to explore how to capture variables from the context. As we mentioned previously, it's all in the [] block.

Capturing variables

So, what if we wanted to capture the variable? In Groovy, we just used the variable inside the lambda scope. This won't work in C++, because we need to specify what variables we are capturing and how we are capturing them. So, if we just use the `first` variable inside our `add` lambda, we will get a compilation error as follows:

```
int main(){
    int first = 5;
    auto addToFirst = [](int second){ return first + second;};
    // error: variable 'first' cannot be implicitly captured
    cout << add(10) << endl;
}
```

In order to capture variables in C++, we need to use a capture specifier inside the `[]` block. There are multiple ways of doing this, depending on what you want. The most intuitive way is to write the name of the variable we're capturing directly. In our case, since we are trying to capture the first variable, we just need to add `[first]` before the lambda parameters:

```
int main(){
    int first = 5;
    auto addToFirst = [first](int second){ return first + second;};
    cout << addToFirst(10) << endl; // writes 15
}
```

As we will see, this means that the `first` variable is captured by a value. Since C++ gives a lot of control to programmers, we expect it to provide specific syntax for capturing variables by reference. Now, let's explore the capture syntax in more details.

Capturing variables by value and by reference

We know that the specifier for capturing a variable by value is just writing the name of the variable, that is, `[first]`. This means that the variable is copied, so we're wasting a few bytes of memory. The solution is to capture the variable by reference. The syntax for the capture specifier is very intuitive—we can just use the name of the variable as a `[&first]` reference:

```
int main(){
    int first = 5;
    auto addToFirstByReference = [&first](int second){ return first +
        second;};
    cout << addToFirstByReference(10) << endl; // writes 15
}
```

I know what you're thinking: can the lambda now modify the value of the `first` variable since it's passed by reference? Spoiler alert—yes, it can. We'll revisit immutability, pure functions, and lambdas in the next section. For now, there's more syntax to learn. For example, if we want to capture multiple variables from the context, do we have to write them all in the capture specifier? As it turns out, there are shortcuts to help you avoid this.

Capturing multiple values

So, what if we want to capture multiple values? Let's explore what our lambda would look like if we added five captured values:

```
int second = 6;
int third = 7;
int fourth = 8;
int fifth = 9;

auto addTheFive = [&first, &second, &third, &fourth, &fifth]()
{return first + second + third + fourth + fifth;};
cout << addTheFive() << endl; // writes 35
```

Our current syntax is a bit redundant, isn't it? We could use a default capture specifier instead. Fortunately, the language designers thought the same way; notice the `[&]` syntax before the lambda parameters:

```
auto addTheFiveWithDefaultReferenceCapture = [&](){return first +
second + third + fourth + fifth;};
cout << addTheFiveWithDefaultReferenceCapture() << endl; // writes 35
```

The `[&]` syntax is telling the compiler to capture all the specified variables from the context by reference. This is the *default capture by reference* specifier.

If we want to copy their values instead, we need to use the *default capture by value* specifier, which you'll have to remember because this is the only place where it's used like this. Notice the `[=]` syntax before the lambda parameters:

```
auto addTheFiveWithDefaultValueCapture = [=](){return first +
second + third + fourth + fifth;};
cout << addTheFiveWithDefaultValueCapture() << endl; // writes 35
```

The `[=]` syntax tells the compiler that all the variables will be captured by copying their values. At least, this is the default. If, for some reason, you'd like all variables except `first` to be passed by value, then you just combine the default with a variable specifier:

```
auto addTheFiveWithDefaultValueCaptureForAllButFirst = [=, &first](){return
first + second + third + fourth + fifth;};
cout << addTheFiveWithDefaultValueCaptureForAllButFirst() << endl; //
writes 35
```

We know now how to capture variables by value and by reference, and how to use default specifiers. This leaves us with one important type of variable—pointers.

Capturing pointer values

Pointers are just simple values. If we want to capture a pointer variable by value, we could just write its name, as shown in the following code:

```
int* pFirst = new int(5);
auto addToThePointerValue = [pFirst](int second){return *pFirst +
    second;};
cout << addToThePointerValue(10) << endl; // writes 15
delete pFirst;
```

If we want to capture the pointer variable by reference, the capture syntax is the same as for capturing any other type of variable:

```
auto addToThePointerValue = [&pFirst](int second){return *pFirst +
    second;};
```

The default specifiers work exactly as you'd expect; that is, `[=]` captures pointer variables by value:

```
auto addToThePointerValue = [=](int second){return *pFirst + second;};
```

In comparison, `[&]` captures pointer variables by reference, as shown in the following code:

```
auto addToThePointerValue = [&](int second){return *pFirst +
    second;};
```

We'll explore what effects capturing variables by reference can have on immutability. But first, since there are multiple ways of capturing variables for a lambda, we need to check which one we prefer and when to use each of them.

What capture should we use?

We've seen a few options for capturing values, as follows:

- Name the variable to capture it by value; for example, `[aVariable]`
- Name the variable and precede it with the reference specifier to capture it by reference; for example, `[&aVariable]`
- Use the default value specifier to capture all the used variables by value; the syntax is `[=]`
- Use the default reference specifier to capture all the used variables by reference; the syntax is `[&]`

In practice, I find that using the default value specifier is the best version for most situations. This is probably influenced by my preference for very small lambdas that don't mutate their captured values. I believe that simplicity is very important; when you have multiple options, it's very easy to make the syntax more complex than necessary. Think through each context and use the simplest syntax that works; my advice is to start from `[=]` and to only change it if required.

We've explored how to write lambdas in C++. What we haven't mentioned is how they are implemented. The current standard implements lambdas as a C++ object with an unknown type, created on the stack. Like any C++ object, it has a class behind it, with a constructor, a destructor, and the captured variables stored as data members. We can pass a lambda to a `function<>` object, in which case the `function<>` object will store a copy of the lambda. Moreover, *lambdas use lazy evaluation*, unlike `function<>` objects.

Lambdas appear to be an easier way to write pure functions; so, what's the relationship between lambdas and pure functions?

Lambdas and pure functions

We learned in `Chapter 2`, *Understanding Pure Functions*, that pure functions have three characteristics:

- They always return the same values for the same argument values
- They don't have side effects
- They don't change the values of their parameters

We also discovered that we need to pay attention to immutability when writing pure functions. This is easy, as long as we remember where to place the `const` keyword.

So, how do lambdas deal with immutability? Do we have to do anything special or do they just work?

Lambda immutability and pass by value arguments

Let's start with a very simple lambda, as follows:

```
auto increment = [](int value) {
    return ++value;
};
```

Here, we're passing the argument by value, so we don't expect any change in the value after calling the lambda:

```
int valueToIncrement = 41;
cout << increment(valueToIncrement) << endl;// prints 42
cout << valueToIncrement << endl;// prints 41
```

Since we copy the value, we're probably using a few extra bytes of memory and an additional assignment. We can add a const keyword to make things clearer:

```
auto incrementImmutable = [](const int value) {
    return value + 1;
};
```

Due to the const specifier, the compiler will give an error if the lambda tries to change value.

But we're still passing the argument by value; how about passing by reference?

Lambda immutability and pass by reference arguments

Let's explore the effect on the input parameter when we call this lambda:

```
auto increment = [](int& value) {
    return ++value;
};
```

As it turns out, it's relatively close to what you'd expect:

```
int valueToIncrement = 41;
cout << increment(valueToIncrement) << endl;// prints 42
cout << valueToIncrement << endl;// prints 42
```

Here, the lambda changes the value of the argument. That's not good enough, so let's make it immutable, as shown in the following code:

```
auto incrementImmutable = [](const int& value){
    return value + 1;
};
```

Once again, the compiler will help us with an error message if the lambda tries to change value.

Well, that's better; but what about pointers?

Lambda immutability and pointer arguments

Just like we saw in Chapter 2, *Understanding Pure Functions*, there are two questions regarding pointer arguments, as follows:

- Can the lambda change the pointer address?
- Can the lambda change the pointed value?

Once again, if we pass in the pointer by value, there's no change in the address:

```
auto incrementAddress = [](int* value) {
    return ++value;
};

int main(){
    int* pValue = new int(41);
    cout << "Address before:" << pValue << endl;
    cout << "Address returned by increment address:" <<
    incrementAddress(pValue) << endl;
    cout << "Address after increment address:" << pValue << endl;
}

Output:
Address before:0x55835628ae70
Address returned by increment address:0x55835628ae74
Address after increment address:0x55835628ae70
```

Passing the pointer by reference changes that though:

```
auto incrementAddressByReference = [](int*& value) {
    return ++value;
};

void printResultsForIncrementAddressByReference(){
    int* pValue = new int(41);
    int* initialPointer = pValue;
    cout << "Address before:" << pValue << endl;
    cout << "Address returned by increment address:" <<
    incrementAddressByReference(pValue) << endl;
    cout << "Address after increment address:" << pValue << endl;
    delete initialPointer;
}
```

```
Output:
Address before:0x55d0930a2e70
Address returned by increment address:0x55d0930a2e74
Address after increment address:0x55d0930a2e74
```

So, once again, we need to use a well-placed `const` keyword to protect ourselves from this change:

```
auto incrementAddressByReferenceImmutable = [](int* const& value) {
    return value + 1;
};
```

```
Output:
Address before:0x557160931e80
Address returned by increment address:0x557160931e84
Address after increment address:0x557160931e80
```

Let's also make the value immutable. As expected, we need another `const` keyword:

```
auto incrementPointedValueImmutable = [](const int* const& value) {
    return *value + 1;
};
```

While this works, I suggest that you favor a simpler way to pass the `[](const int& value)` value—that is, just dereference the pointer and pass an actual value to the lambda, which will make the parameter syntax easier to understand and more reusable.

So, no surprises! We can use the same syntax we use for pure functions to ensure immutability.

But can lambdas call mutable functions, such as I/O, for example?

Lambdas and I/O

What better way to test lambdas and I/O than the `Hello, world` program:

```
auto hello = [](){cout << "Hello, world!" << endl;};

int main(){
    hello();
}
```

Obviously, lambdas aren't protected from calling mutable functions. This is no surprise, given that we learned the same thing about pure functions. This means that, similar to pure functions, programmers need to pay extra attention to separate I/O, which is fundamentally mutable, from the rest of the code, which can be immutable.

Since we're trying to get the compiler to help us with enforcing immutability, can we do that for captured values?

Lambda immutability and capturing values

We've discovered that lambdas can capture variables from the context, both by value and by reference. So, does this mean we can mutate their value? Let's check it out, as follows:

```
int value = 1;
auto increment = [=](){return ++value;};
```

This code immediately gives you a compilation error—*cannot assign to a variable captured by copy*. This is an improvement from passing parameters by value; that is, there is no need to use the `const` keyword—it just works as expected.

Immutability for values captured by reference

So, what about values captured by reference? Well, we can just use the default reference specifier, `[&]`, and check the value of the variable before and after the call to our `increment` lambda:

```
void captureByReference(){
    int value = 1;
    auto increment = [&](){return ++value;};

    cout << "Value before: " << value << endl;
    cout << "Result of increment:" << increment() << endl;
    cout << "Value after: " << value << endl;
```

```
}
```

```
Output:
Value before: 1
Result of increment:2
Value after: 2
```

As expected, the `value` changes. So, how do we protect against this mutation?

Unfortunately, there's no easy way to do this. C++ assumes that if you capture variables by reference, you want to modify them. While it's possible, it requires a bit more syntactic sugar. Specifically, we need to capture its cast to a `const` type, instead of the variable:

```
#include <utility>
using namespace std;
...

    int value = 1;
    auto increment = [&immutableValue = as_const(value)](){return
        immutableValue + 1;};
```

```
Output:
Value before: 1
Result of increment:2
Value after: 1
```

Given the choice, I prefer using simpler syntax. So, I'd rather use the capture by value syntax unless I really need to optimize performance.

We've explored how to make lambdas immutable when capturing value types. But can we ensure immutability when capturing pointer types?

Immutability for pointers captured by value

Things get interesting when we use pointers. If we capture them by value, we can't modify the address:

```
    int* pValue = new int(1);
    auto incrementAddress = [=](){return ++pValue;}; // compilation
    error
```

However, we can still modify the pointed value, as shown in the following code:

```
int* pValue = new int(1);
auto increment= [=](){return ++(*pValue);};
```

```
Output:
Value before: 1
Result of increment:2
Value after: 2
```

Constraining immutability requires a variable of the `const int*` type:

```
const int* pValue = new int(1);
auto increment= [=](){return ++(*pValue);}; // compilation error
```

However, there's a much easier solution—that is, just capture the value of the pointer instead:

```
int* pValue = new int(1);
int value = *pValue;
auto increment = [=](){return ++value;}; // compilation error
```

Immutability for pointers captured by reference

Capturing pointers by reference allows you to change the memory address as well:

```
auto increment = [&](){return ++pValue;};
```

We could use the same trick as before to enforce the constant nature of the memory address:

```
auto increment = [&pImmutable = as_const(pValue)](){return pImmutable
    + 1;};
```

However, this is getting quite complicated. The only reason to do this is due to the following:

- We want to avoid copying 64 bits at most
- The compiler doesn't optimize it for us

It's simpler to stick to the values that are passed by value instead, that is, unless you want to do pointer arithmetic in your lambda.

You now know how lambdas work with immutability. But, in our C++ code, we're used to classes. So, what is the relationship between lambdas and classes? Can we use them together?

Lambdas and classes

So far, we have learned how to write lambdas in C++. All the examples use lambda expressions outside classes, either as variables or as part of the `main()` function. However, most of our C++ code lives in classes. This begs the question—how can we use lambdas in classes?

To explore this question, we need an example of a simple class. Let's use a class that represents basic imaginary numbers:

```
class ImaginaryNumber{
    private:
        int real;
        int imaginary;

    public:
        ImaginaryNumber() : real(0), imaginary(0){};
        ImaginaryNumber(int real, int imaginary) : real(real),
        imaginary(imaginary){};
};
```

We want to use our new-found lambda superpowers to write a simple `toString` function, as shown in the following code:

```
string toString(){
    return to_string(real) + " + " + to_string(imaginary) + "i";
}
```

So, what options do we have?

Well, lambdas are simple variables so they can be a data member. Alternatively, they can be `static` variables. Perhaps we can even convert class functions to lambdas. Let's explore these ideas next.

Lambdas as data members

Let's first try to write it as a member variable, as follows:

```cpp
class ImaginaryNumber{
...
    public:
        auto toStringLambda = [](){
            return to_string(real) + " + " + to_string(imaginary) +
                "i";
        };
...
}
```

Unfortunately, this results in a compilation error. We need to specify the type of the lambda variable if we want to have it as a non-static data member. To make this work, let's wrap our lambda into a `function` type, as follows:

```cpp
include <functional>
...
    public:
        function<string()> toStringLambda = [](){
            return to_string(real) + " + " + to_string(imaginary) +
                "i";
        };
```

The function type has a special syntax, allowing us to define lambda types. The `function<string()>` notation means the function returns a `string` value and receives no parameters.

However, this still doesn't work. We receive another error because we haven't captured the variables that we're using. We can use any of the captures that we've learned about so far. Alternatively, we can capture `this` instead:

```cpp
function<string()> toStringLambda = [this](){
    return to_string(real) + " + " + to_string(imaginary) +
        "i";
};
```

This is, therefore, how we can write a lambda as part of a class while capturing the data members of the class. Capturing `this` is a useful shortcut when refactoring existing code. However, I would avoid it in more permanent situations. It's best to capture the required variables directly rather than the whole pointer.

Lambdas as static variables

We could also define our lambda as a `static` variable. We can't capture the values any more, so we need to pass in a parameter, but we can still access the `real` and `imaginary` private data members:

```
        static function<string(const ImaginaryNumber&)>
            toStringLambdaStatic;
...
// after class declaration ends
function<string(const ImaginaryNumber&)>
ImaginaryNumber::toStringLambdaStatic = [](const ImaginaryNumber& number){
    return to_string(number.real) + " + " + to_string(number.imaginary)
        + "i";
};

// Call it
cout << ImaginaryNumber::toStringLambdaStatic(Imaginary(1,1)) << endl;
// prints 1+1i
```

Converting a static function to a lambda

Sometimes, we need to convert a `static` function to a lambda variable. This is very easy in C++, as shown in the following code:

```
static string toStringStatic(const ImaginaryNumber& number){
    return to_string(number.real) + " + " + to_string(number.imaginary)
        + "i";
  }
string toStringUsingLambda(){
    auto toStringLambdaLocal = ImaginaryNumber::toStringStatic;
    return toStringLambdaLocal(*this);
}
```

We can simply assign a function from a class to a variable, as you can see in this line from the preceding code:

```
    auto toStringLambdaLocal = ImaginaryNumber::toStringStatic;
```

We can then use the variable in the same way that we would use the function. As we'll discover, this is a very powerful concept because it allows us to compose functions even when they are defined inside a class.

Lambdas and coupling

We have many options when it comes to interaction between lambdas and classes. They can become both overwhelming and they can make design decisions more difficult.

While it's good to know the options since they help when going through difficult refactorings, I've found, through practice, that it's best to follow one simple principle when it comes to lambdas; that is, to choose the option that reduces the coupling area between your lambda and the rest of the code.

For example, we've seen that we can write our lambda as a `static` variable in a class:

```
function<string(const ImaginaryNumber&)>
ImaginaryNumber::toStringLambdaStatic = [](const ImaginaryNumber& number){
    return to_string(number.real) + " + " + to_string(number.imaginary)
        + "i";
};
```

This lambda has a coupling area as large as the `ImaginaryNumber` class. However, it only needs two values: the real and the imaginary part. We could easily rewrite it as a pure function, as follows:

```
auto toImaginaryString = [](auto real, auto imaginary){
    return to_string(real) + " + " + to_string(imaginary) + "i";
};
```

If, for some reason, you decide to change the representation of the imaginary number by adding members or methods, removing members or methods, splitting it into multiple classes, or changing data member types, this lambda will not need to be changed. Of course, it takes two parameters instead of one, but the parameter type no longer matters, as long as `to_string` works for them. In other words, this is a polymorphic function that leaves your options for representing the data structure open.

But we'll discuss more about how to use lambdas for design in the following chapters.

Summary

You've just obtained lambda superpowers! Not only can you write simple lambdas in C++, but you also know the following:

- How to capture variables from the context
- How to specify the default capture type—by reference or by value
- How to write immutable lambdas even when capturing values
- How to use lambdas in classes

We've also touched on the design principle of low coupling and how lambdas can help with this. We'll keep mentioning this principle in the following chapters.

Would you believe me if I told you that lambdas are even more powerful than what we've seen so far? Well, we'll discover that we can grow from simple to complex lambdas through functional composition.

Questions

1. What is the simplest lambda you can write?
2. How can you write a lambda that concatenates two string values passed as parameters?
3. What happens if one of the values is a variable that's captured by value?
4. What happens if one of the values is a variable that's captured by reference?
5. What happens if one of the values is a pointer that's captured by value?
6. What happens if one of the values is a pointer that's captured by reference?
7. What happens if both values are captured by value using the default capture specifier?
8. What happens if both values are captured by reference using the default capture specifier?
9. How can you write the same lambda as a data member in a class that has the two string values as data members?
10. How can you write the same lambda as a `static` variable in the same class?

4
The Idea of Functional Composition

We've seen in the past chapters how to write pure functions and lambdas. These are the basic building blocks of functional programming. It's time to take them to the next level.

In this chapter, we will learn how to obtain more functions from existing functions, thus building complex behavior from the simple examples that we've looked at so far.

The following topics will be covered in this chapter:

- Composing functions in C++
- A basic decomposition strategy for functions with multiple arguments
- Removing duplication (or code similarity) using functional composition

Technical requirements

You will need a compiler that supports C++ 17. I used GCC 7.3.0.

The code is on GitHub at `https://github.com/PacktPublishing/Hands-On-Functional-Programming-with-Cpp`, in the `Chapter04` folder. It includes and uses `doctest`, which is a single-header open source unit testing library. You can find it in its GitHub repository here: `https://github.com/onqtam/doctest`.

What is functional composition?

Pure functions and lambdas are the basic blocks of functional programming. But all the examples we've looked at so far use very simple functions. We obviously deal with much more complex problems in our industry. However, as we've seen, we still want our basic blocks to be very simple, since we want to understand and maintain them easily. So, how can we create complex programs from the simple lambdas and pure functions we've seen so far? Functional programming has a simple answer—let's create more complex functions by combining the simple functions we have. The fundamental way to create complex functions in functional programming is functional composition.

Functional composition

At its core, functional composition is very simple. We'll use a basic example to illustrate it. We will start with our `increment` function. Also, from now on, I will use test cases to show how the code works. I'm using `doctest`, a single-header open source unit testing library (`https://github.com/onqtam/doctest`).

Let's look at our `increment` function with a test case:

```
auto increment = [](const int value) { return value + 1; };

TEST_CASE("Increments value"){
    CHECK_EQ(2, increment(1));
}
```

Let's also say that, for some reason, we need to increment the value twice. Since we're thinking in functions, we want to reuse our function. We could, therefore, call it twice:

```
TEST_CASE("Increments twice"){
    CHECK_EQ(3, increment(increment(1)));
}
```

This works fine if we only need a double increment in a single place. If we need it in multiple places in our code, we will need a function. It's easy enough to extract a function that performs a double increment:

```
auto incrementTwiceLambda = [](int value){return
increment(increment(value));};

TEST_CASE("Increments result of addition with lambda"){
    CHECK_EQ(3, incrementTwiceLambda(1));
}
```

If we look at `incrementTwiceLambda`, we can see that it is formed by `increment` called on the result of `increment`.

Let's let it rest for now, and move on to another case. We now want to compute the square of a number, still using functions. It's easy to write, once again:

```
auto square = [](int value){ return value * value; };

TEST_CASE("Squares the number"){
    CHECK_EQ(4, square(2));
}
```

Our next requirement is to compute the incremented square of a value. Once again, we could extract a lambda that combines `increment` and `square` as we need them:

```
auto incrementSquareLambda = [](int value) { return
increment(square(value));};

TEST_CASE("Increments the squared number"){
    CHECK_EQ(5, incrementSquareLambda(2));
}
```

That's very nice. However, we have a hidden similarity in the code. Let's look at the `incrementTwiceLambda` and `incrementSquareLambda` functions:

```
auto incrementTwiceLambda = [](int value){ return
increment(increment(value)); };
auto incrementSquareLambda = [](int value) { return
increment(square(value)); };
```

They both have the same pattern—we created a function, C, by having a function, *f*, call on the result of another function, *g*, applied to the value passed to our function, C. This is a kind of code similarity that we can expect to see a lot when we use small, pure functions. It would be nice to have a name and maybe even a way to implement it without writing so much boilerplate code.

It turns out, it does have a name—this is functional composition. In general terms, for any *f* or *g* function with single arguments, we can obtain a function, C, as follows:

$C = f \circ g$ meaning that for every value of *x*, $C(x) = f(g(x))$.

The ○ symbol is the mathematical operator for functional composition.

As you can see, what we're actually trying to do is to obtain functions from other functions by having operations on the functions themselves! It's a type of calculus that uses lambdas instead of numbers, and defines operations on lambdas. Lambda calculus is an apt name, don't you think?

This is the concept of functional composition. The next question is—can we eliminate the boilerplate code?

Implementing functional composition in C++

It would be nice to have an operator that allows us to perform functional composition. Indeed, other programming languages provide one; for example, in Groovy, we can use the << operator as follows:

```
def incrementTwiceLambda = increment << increment
def incrementSquareLambda = increment << square
```

Unfortunately, C++ doesn't (yet) have a standard operator for functional composition. However, C++ is a powerful language, so it should be possible to write our own function that performs functional composition, at least for limited cases.

First, let's clearly define the problem. We would like to have a compose function that receives two lambdas, f and g, and returns a new lambda that calls value -> f(g(value)). The simplest implementation in C++ would look like the following code:

```
auto compose(auto f, auto g){
    return [f, g](auto x){ return f(g(x)); };
}

TEST_CASE("Increments twice with composed lambda"){
    auto incrementTwice = compose(increment, increment);
    CHECK_EQ(3, incrementTwice(1));
}
```

Unfortunately, this code doesn't compile because C++ doesn't allow parameters with auto types. One way would be to specify the function type:

```
function<int(int)> compose(function<int(int)> f,  function<int(int)> g){
    return [f, g](auto x){ return f(g(x)); };
}

TEST_CASE("Increments twice with composed lambda"){
```

```
    auto incrementTwice = compose(increment, increment);
    CHECK_EQ(3, incrementTwice(1));
}
```

This works fine and passes the tests. But now our `compose` function depends on the function type. That's not very useful, since we will have to reimplement `compose` for every type of function that we need. It's less boilerplate than before, but still far from ideal.

But this is exactly the type of problem resolved by C++ templates. Maybe they can help:

```
template <class F, class G>
auto compose(F f, G g){
    return [=](auto value){return f(g(value));};
}

TEST_CASE("Increments twice with composed lambda"){
    auto incrementTwice = compose(increment, increment);
    CHECK_EQ(3, incrementTwice(1));
}

TEST_CASE("Increments square with composed lambda"){
    auto incrementSquare = compose(increment, square);
    CHECK_EQ(5, incrementSquare(2));
}
```

Indeed, this code works! So, we now know that, although there is no operator for functional composition in C++, we can implement it with an elegant function.

Please note how compose returns a lambda, which uses lazy evaluation. Therefore, our functional composition function also uses lazy evaluation. This is an advantage, since the composed lambda will only be initialized when we use it.

Functional composition is not commutative

It's important to realize that functional composition is not commutative. Indeed, it's easy to see why when we speak—*the increment square of a value* is different from *squaring the increment of a value*. However, we need to be careful in code because the two differ just by the order of the parameters for the compose function:

```
auto incrementSquare = compose(increment, square);
auto squareIncrement = compose(square, increment);
```

We've seen what functional composition is, how to implement it in C++, and how to use it for simple cases. I bet you're eager to try it now for more complex programs. We'll get there, but first let's look at more complex situations. What about functions with multiple parameters?

Complex functional composition

Our compose function has a problem—it only works with lambdas that receive one argument. So, what do we do if we want to compose functions with multiple arguments?

Let's take the following example—given two lambdas, `multiply` and `increment`:

```
auto increment = [](const int value) { return value + 1; };
auto multiply = [](const int first, const int second){ return first *
second; };
```

Can we obtain a lambda that increments the result of the multiplication?

Unfortunately, we cannot use our `compose` function since it assumes that both functions have one parameter:

```
template <class F, class G>
auto compose(F f, G g){
    return [=](auto value){return f(g(value));};
}
```

So, what are our options?

Implementing more compose functions

We could implement a variant of the `compose` function that takes a function, `f`, which takes one argument, and another function, `g`, which takes two arguments:

```
template <class F1, class G2>
auto compose12(F1 f, G2 g){
    return [=](auto first, auto second){ return f(g(first, second)); };
}

TEST_CASE("Increment result of multiplication"){
    CHECK_EQ(5, compose12(increment, multiply)(2, 2));
}
```

This solution is simple enough. However, if we need to obtain a function that multiplies the incremented values of its arguments, we need yet another compose variant:

```
template <class F2, class G1>
auto compose21(F2 f, G1 g){
    return [=](auto first, auto second){ return f(g(first), g(second)); };
}

TEST_CASE("Multiplies two incremented values"){
    CHECK_EQ(4, compose21(multiply, increment)(1, 1));
}
```

What if we only want to increment one of the arguments? There are a lot of possible combinations, and while we can cover them with multiple variants of compose, it's worth visiting other options as well.

Decomposing functions with multiple arguments

Instead of implementing more variations of compose, we could look into the multiply function itself:

```
auto multiply = [](const int first, const int second){ return first *
    second; };
```

There's a trick we can use to decompose it into two lambdas, each taking one argument. The key idea is that a lambda is just a value, so it can be returned by a function. We've already seen this in action in our compose function; it creates and returns a new lambda:

```
template <class F, class G>
auto compose(F f, G g){
    return [=](auto value){return f(g(value));};
}
```

We can, therefore, decompose a function with two arguments by returning a new lambda with a single argument that captures the first argument from the context:

```
auto multiplyDecomposed = [](const int first) {
    return [=](const int second){ return first * second; };
};

TEST_CASE("Adds using single parameter functions"){
    CHECK_EQ(4, multiplyDecomposed(2)(2));
}
```

Let's unpack this code, because it's quite complex:

- `multiplyDecomposed` takes one argument, `first`, and it returns a lambda.
- The returned lambda captures `first` from the context.
- It then receives one parameter, `second`.
- It returns the result of the addition of `first` and `second`.

It turns out that any function with two arguments can be decomposed like this. We can, therefore, write a generic implementation using templates. We just need to use the same trick—specify the function type as a template type, and proceed with using it in our decomposition:

```
template<class F>
auto decomposeToOneParameter(F f){
    return [=](auto first){
        return [=](auto second){
            return f(first, second);
        };
    };
}

TEST_CASE("Multiplies using single parameter functions"){
    CHECK_EQ(4, decomposeToOneParameter(multiply)(2)(2));
}
```

This method is promising; it might simplify our implementation of functional composition. Let's see if it works.

Incrementing the result of multiplication

Let's move forward toward our goal. Can we use `compose` to obtain a function that increments the result of the multiplication? It's easy now, since `add` is decomposed into lambdas that receive one argument. We would expect to just compose `multiplyDecomposed` with `increment`:

```
TEST_CASE("Increment result of multiplication"){
    int first = 2;
    int second = 2;
    auto incrementResultOfMultiplication = compose(increment,
        multiplyDecomposed);
    CHECK_EQ(5, incrementResultOfMultiplication(first)(second));
}
```

However, this doesn't compile. Our compose function assumes that the result of `multiplyDecomposed(first)` can be passed to increment. But `multiplyDecompose(first)` returns a lambda, and `increment` takes an integer.

We need, therefore, to compose `increment` with `multipyDecomposed(first)`:

```
TEST_CASE("Increment result of multiplication"){
    int first = 2;
    int second = 2;
    auto incrementResultOfMultiplication = compose(increment,
        multiplyDecomposed(first));
    CHECK_EQ(5, incrementResultOfMultiplication(second));
}
```

This works, but we have not yet achieved our goal. We didn't obtain a function that takes the two values in; instead, the first value is passed to `multiplyDecomposed` when composing it with the `increment` function.

Fortunately, this is the perfect place to use a lambda, as shown in the following code:

```
TEST_CASE("Increment result of multiplication final"){
    auto incrementResultOfMultiplication = [](int first, int second) {
        return compose(increment, multiplyDecomposed(first))(second);
    };

    CHECK_EQ(5, incrementResultOfMultiplication(2, 2));
}
```

This definitely works, and we've achieved our goal! The `incrementResultOfMultiplication` lambda takes two parameters and returns the increment of the multiplication. It would be nicer, though, if we didn't have to rewrite `multiply`. Fortunately, we have our `decomposeToOneParameter` function to help us:

```
TEST_CASE("Increment result of multiplication"){
    auto incrementResultOfMultiplication = [](int first, int second) {
        return compose(increment, decomposeToOneParameter(multiply)
            (first)) (second);
    };
    int result = incrementResultOfMultiplication(2, 2);
    CHECK_EQ(5, result);
}
```

It's time to look at the reversed composition—what if we wanted to multiply the increments of both our arguments?

Multiplying increments

We would like to obtain a function that multiplies the increments of our arguments, by using our `compose` function. The simplest code, which doesn't use `compose`, is the following:

```
TEST_CASE("Multiply incremented values no compose"){
    auto multiplyIncrementedValues = [](int first, int second){
        return multiply(increment(first), increment(second));
    };
    int result = multiplyIncrementedValues(2, 2);
    CHECK_EQ(9, result);
}
```

As we've seen, we need to decompose the `multiply` lambda first if we want to use our version of compose:

```
TEST_CASE("Multiply incremented values decompose"){
    auto multiplyIncrementedValues = [](int first, int second){
        return multiplyDecomposed(increment(first))(increment(second));
    };
    int result = multiplyIncrementedValues(2, 2);
    CHECK_EQ(9, result);
}
```

Now we can see the call to `multiplyDecomposed(increment(first))`, which is the composition between `multiplyDecomposed` and `increment`. We can replace it with our `compose` function, as shown in the following code:

```
TEST_CASE("Multiply incremented values compose simple"){
    auto multiplyIncrementedValues = [](int first, int second){
        return compose(multiplyDecomposed, increment)(first)
            (increment(second));
    };

    int result = multiplyIncrementedValues(2, 2);
    CHECK_EQ(9, result);
}
```

Again, it would be nice if we didn't have to rewrite our `multiply` function. But remember that we implemented a useful function that can decompose any function with two parameters into two functions with a parameter. We don't have to rewrite `multiply`; we just have to call our decomposition utility on it:

```
TEST_CASE("Multiply incremented values decompose first"){
    auto multiplyIncrementedValues = [](int first, int second){
        return compose(
```

```
                  decomposeToOneParameter(multiply),
                  increment
              )(first)(increment(second));
      };
      int result = multiplyIncrementedValues(2, 2);
      CHECK_EQ(9, result);
  }
```

We've achieved our goal!

Reflections on the composition and decomposition of functions

Let's take a moment to look at the results and at our working method. Here's the good news—we made good progress with learning how to think in functions. Our previous examples work just by operating on functions as first-class citizens of our code, which is exactly the mindset we need if we want to design applications using the functional paradigm. The decomposition and recomposition of functions is incredibly powerful; master it and you will be able to implement very complex behavior with very little code.

As for the resulting code, it has an interesting property—we can generalize it to reuse on many combinations of functions.

But we're not done yet! We can use these functions to remove certain types of duplication from our code. Let's see how.

Using functional composition to remove duplication

So far, we've seen how we can write functions that compose lambdas in various ways. But code tends to repeat itself, so we would like to make this method more general. We can indeed take this even further; let's look at a few examples.

Generalizing incrementResultOfMultiplication

Let's take another look at our `incrementResultOfMultiplication` lambda:

```
auto incrementResultOfMultiplication = [](int first, int second) {
    return compose(increment, decomposeToOneParameter(multiply)
```

```
            (first))(second);
    };
```

There's something interesting about it—it's not specific to `increment` and `multiply`. Since lambdas are just values, we can pass them as parameters and obtain a general `composeWithTwoParameters` function:

```
template <class F, class G>
auto composeWithTwoParameters(F f, G g){
    return [=](auto first, auto second) {
        return compose(
                f,
                decomposeToOneParameter(g)(first)
                )(second);
    };
};

TEST_CASE("Increment result of multiplication"){
    auto incrementResultOfMultiplication =
    composeWithTwoParameters(increment, multiply);
    int result = incrementResultOfMultiplication(2, 2);
    CHECK_EQ(5, result);
}
```

This function allows us to *compose any other two functions,* f *and* g, *where* g *takes two parameters and* f *only one parameter.*

Let's do some more of this. Let's generalize `multiplyIncrementedValues`.

Generalizing multiplyIncrementedValues

Similarly, we can easily generalize our `multiplyIncrementedValues` lambda, as shown in the following code:

```
auto multiplyIncrementedValues = [](int first, int second){
    return compose(
            decomposeToOneParameter(multiply),
            increment
            )(first)(increment(second));
};
```

In the same manner, we need to pass the `multiply` and `increment` lambdas as parameters:

```
template<class F, class G>
auto composeWithFunctionCallAllParameters(F f, G g){
    return [=](auto first, auto second){
        return compose(
                decomposeToOneParameter(f),
                g
                )(first)(g(second));
    };
};

TEST_CASE("Multiply incremented values generalized"){
    auto multiplyIncrementedValues =
    composeWithFunctionCallAllParameters(multiply, increment);
    int result = multiplyIncrementedValues(2, 2);
    CHECK_EQ(9, result);
}
```

We can use this new function to create a function, C, which implements `g(f(first),` `f(second))`, no matter what `g` and `f` are.

Our work here is done for now.

Summary

If you thought that pure functions and lambdas are powerful, you will now realize how much you can do by composing them! In this chapter, you learned what functional composition is and how to compose functions in C++.

We also worked on something much more important. In this chapter, we really started to think in functions. Here are some things we learned:

- A lambda is just a value, so we can have functions that return lambdas, or lambdas that return lambdas.
- Also, we can have functions that receive one or more lambdas and return a new lambda.
- Any function with multiple arguments can be decomposed into multiple lambdas with single arguments and captured values.
- Operations with functions are quite complex. If you feel your head spinning, that's OK—we've been playing with very powerful and abstract concepts.

- It's very difficult to instantly come up with a solution when it comes to various ways of composing functions. The best way is to go step by step, have a clear goal and a clear mind, and use the techniques described in this chapter to improve.
- Functional composition can help remove some types of duplication; for example, when you have multiple compositions between different functions with similar signatures.
- However, there is a cost to implementing the compose family of functions as we did in this chapter—a higher level of abstraction. It's quite difficult to understand how the functions that perform operations on lambdas work; indeed, trust me that I also have trouble understanding the results. Still, they are quite easy to use once you understand their goal.

After all this effort, let's take a moment to consider the result. Imagine that any two functions you already have in your code base, or in libraries that you use, could be composed just with a function call and expressed as variables. Moreover, these calls can stack; the functions you obtain can be composed even more. Functional composition is extremely powerful; with very simple lambdas and a few operations with functions, we can very quickly implement complex behavior.

We've seen how to compose two functions. There's yet another operation on functions we need to learn—obtaining new functions by playing around with arguments.

Questions

1. What is functional composition?
2. Functional composition has a property that is usually associated with mathematical operations. What is it?
3. How can you turn an `add` function with two parameters into two functions with one parameter?
4. How can you write a C++ function that comprises two single argument functions?
5. What are the advantages of functional composition?
6. What are the potential disadvantages of implementing operations on functions?

Partial Application and Currying

5

We've already gone far in our quest to understand functional programming! We learned about pure functions and lambdas and dived into lambda calculus with the help of functional composition. We now know how to create functions from other functions.

There's still one more thing to learn about the basis of lambda calculus. Besides functional composition, we can also create functions from other functions through two operations—currying and partial application. This will complete our discussion on functional building blocks and allow you to move forward towards designing with functions.

The following topics will be covered in this chapter:

- What is partial application?
- How to use partial application in C++
- What is currying?
- How to curry functions in C++
- The relationship between currying and partial application
- How to combine currying with functional composition

Technical requirements

You will need a compiler that supports C++ 17. I used GCC 7.3.0.

The code is on GitHub at `https://github.com/PacktPublishing/Hands-On-Functional-Programming-with-Cpp` in the `Chapter05` folder. It includes and uses `doctest`, which is a single header open source unit testing library. You can find it on its GitHub repository here: `https://github.com/onqtam/doctest`.

Partial application and currying

If you think about lambdas and what operations we could do on them to obtain other lambdas, two things spring to mind:

- Something about combining two lambdas, which we've seen in functional composition
- Something about the parameters of a lambda, which we'll visit next

What could we do with a lambda's parameters? There are two things:

- Decompose a lambda with multiple arguments into more lambdas with one argument, an operation called **currying**
- Obtain a lambda with *N-1* arguments by binding an argument of a lambda with *N* arguments to a value, an operation called **partial application**

For reasons that will soon become apparent, the two operations are connected, so we'll discuss them together.

Partial application

If you have a lambda with *N* arguments, partial application means obtaining another lambda by binding one argument to a value, hence obtaining a new lambda with *N-1* arguments. We could, for example, take an add function and do a partial application to bind one of its parameters to the value 1, resulting in an increment function. In pseudo C++, it would look something like this:

```
auto add = [](const int first, const int second){return first + second;};
auto increment = partialApplication(add, /*first*/ 1);
/* equivalent with
auto increment = [](const int second){return 1 + second;};
*/
```

That's it! The idea of partial application is fairly simple. Let's look at the syntax in C++.

Partial application in C++

A basic implementation of partial application can be done manually. We can simply create a lambda called `increment` that calls the general `add` function, passing `1` as the second parameter:

```
auto add = [](const int first, const int second) { return first + second;
};
TEST_CASE("Increments using manual partial application"){
    auto increment = [](const int value) { return add(value, 1); };

    CHECK_EQ(43, increment(42));
}
```

This is not the neat operation we're looking for, but it can be useful when you can't use the generic method for some reason.

Fortunately, STL offers a better alternative in our friendly header file, `functional`—the `bind` function. It takes as parameters the function, the values you want to bind, and placeholder arguments that just forward the arguments. To obtain the `increment` function with a call to `bind`, we pass in the general `add` lambda; the argument value, `1`, for the first argument; and a placeholder that specifies an unbound parameter:

```
using namespace std::placeholders; // to allow _1, _2 etc.

TEST_CASE("Increments using bind"){
    // bind the value 1 to the first parameter of add
    // _1 is a placeholder for the first parameter of the increment
        lambda
    auto increment = bind(add, 1, _1);

    CHECK_EQ(43, increment(42));
}
```

While convenient, you should be aware that `bind` has a high compile-time overhead. When this is a problem, you can always revert to the previous option—calling the more general lambda directly from another manually written lambda.

Of course, nothing stops us from binding both parameters. Since programmers like the number `42`, I will bind both parameters of the `add` lambda to the values, `1` and `41`, in order to obtain another lambda, `number42`:

```
TEST_CASE("Constant using bind"){
    auto number42 = bind(add, 1, 41);
    CHECK_EQ(42, number42());
}
```

The `bind` syntax can be a bit tricky sometimes, so let's look at it in more detail. The key is to understand that the *parameter placeholder refers to the parameters of the resulting lambda and not of the initial lambda.*

To make this clearer, let's look at an example of a lambda that adds its three arguments:

```
auto addThree = [](const int first, const int second, const int
third){return first + second + third;};

TEST_CASE("Adds three"){
    CHECK_EQ(42, addThree(10, 20, 12));
}
```

If we want to obtain another lambda, `addTwoNumbersTo10`, from our `addThree` lambda, by binding its first parameter to the value `10`, what is the syntax of `bind`? Well, our resulting lambda, `addTwoNumbersTo10`, will receive two parameters. Their placeholders will be denoted with `_1` and `_2`. So, we need to tell bind that the first argument to our initial lambda, `addThree`, is `10`. The second argument will be forwarded from `addTwoNumbersTo10`, so it's `_1`. The third argument is forwarded as well, from the second argument of `addNumbersTo10`, so it's `_2`. We end up with this code:

```
TEST_CASE("Adds two numbers to 10"){
    auto addTwoNumbersTo10 = bind(addThree, 10, _1, _2);

    CHECK_EQ(42, addTwoNumbersTo10(20, 12));
}
```

Let's go forward. We want to obtain another lambda, `addTo10Plus20`, from our initial `addThree` lambda by using partial application. The resulting function will have only one argument, `_1`. The other arguments to bind will be the values, `10` and `20`. We end up with the following code:

```
TEST_CASE("Adds one number to 10 + 20"){
    auto addTo10Plus20 = bind(addThree, 10, 20, _1);

    CHECK_EQ(42, addTo10Plus20(12));
}
```

What if we wanted to bind the first and the third argument? It should be clear now that the parameters are exactly the same, but their order changes in the `bind` call:

```
TEST_CASE("Adds 10 to one number, and then to 20"){
    auto addTo10Plus20 = bind(addThree, 10, _1, 20);

    CHECK_EQ(42, addTo10Plus20(12));
}
```

What if we want to bind the second and third arguments instead? Well, the placeholder moves, but it's still the only argument of the resulting function, so _1:

```
TEST_CASE("Adds one number to 10, and then to 20"){
    auto addTo10Plus20 = bind(addThree, _1, 10, 20);

    CHECK_EQ(42, addTo10Plus20(12));
}
```

What if we want to do partial application on a class method?

Partial application on class methods

The bind function allows us to do partial application on a class method, but there's a catch—the first argument has to be the instance of the class. For this example, we'll use an AddOperation class that implements simple addition between two numbers:

```
class AddOperation{
    private:
        int first;
        int second;

    public:
        AddOperation(int first, int second): first(first),
            second(second){}
        int add(){ return first + second;}
};
```

We can create a new function, add, by binding an instance of the AddOperation class to the function:

```
TEST_CASE("Bind member method"){
    AddOperation operation(41, 1);
    auto add41And1 = bind(&AddOperation::add, operation);

    CHECK_EQ(42, add41And1());
}
```

More interestingly, and closer to the concept of partial application, we can forward the instance parameter from the caller:

```
TEST_CASE("Partial bind member method no arguments"){
    auto add = bind(&AddOperation::add, _1);
    AddOperation operation(41, 1);
    CHECK_EQ(42, add(operation));
}
```

The binding is possible as well if the method receives arguments. For example, let's say we have another class implementing AddToOperation:

```
class AddToOperation{
    private:
        int first;

    public:
        AddToOperation(int first): first(first) {}
        int addTo(int second){ return first + second;}
};
```

We can do a partial application of addTo with just an instance of the class, as shown in the following code:

```
TEST_CASE("Partial application member method"){
    AddToOperation operation(41);
    auto addTo41 = bind(&AddToOperation::addTo, operation, _1);

    CHECK_EQ(42, addTo41(1));
}
```

The partial application of the class methods shows that it's quite easy to move between the functional and the OOP world. We'll see in the next chapters how we can take advantage of this. Until then, let's rejoice in the fact that we now know what partial application is and how to use it in C++. It's time to talk about its close cousin, currying.

Currying

Let's try for a moment to name a few famous people from software development, without searching the internet. There's Alan Turing, Ada Lovelace (she has a fascinating story), Grace Hopper, Donald Knuth, Bjarne Stroustroup, Grady Booch, and probably many others. How many of them have given their name to not one, but two things that you hear about constantly in the industry? That's true for Alan Turing, definitely, with the Turing machine and the Turing test, but not so for many others.

It's therefore surprising to learn that both the name of the Haskell programming language and the name of the currying operation come from the same person—Haskell Curry. Haskell Curry was an American mathematician and logician. He worked on something called **combinatory logic**, which is the basis of part of functional programming.

But what is currying? And how does it connect to partial application?

What is currying?

Currying is a process of decomposing functions with N arguments into N functions with one argument. We can do this through variable capture or through partial application.

Let's take our add lambda again:

```
auto add = [](const int first, const int second) { return first +
    second; };

TEST_CASE("Adds values"){
    CHECK_EQ(42, add(25, 17));
}
```

How can we decompose it? The key is that a lambda is just a normal value, which means we can return it from a function. We can therefore pass in the first parameter and return a lambda that captures the first parameter and uses both first and second arguments. It's easier to understand in code than in words, so here it is:

```
auto curryAdd = [](const int first){
    return [first](const int second){
        return first + second;
    };
};

TEST_CASE("Adds values using captured curry"){
    CHECK_EQ(42, curryAdd(25)(17));
}
```

Let's unpack what happens:

- Our curryAdd lambda returns a lambda.
- The returned lambda captures the first parameter, takes a second argument, and returns their sum.

That's why, when calling it, we need to use double parentheses.

But this looks familiar, as if it has something to do with partial application.

Currying and partial application

Let's look again at how we did partial application previously. We created an `increment` function through partial application of the `add` function:

```
TEST_CASE("Increments using bind"){
    auto increment = bind(add, 1, _1);

    CHECK_EQ(43, increment(42));
}
```

However, let's curry our `add` function:

```
auto curryAdd = [](const int first){
    return [first](const int second){
        return first + second;
    };
};

TEST_CASE("Adds values using captured curry"){
    CHECK_EQ(42, curryAdd(25)(17));
}
```

Then, `increment` is very easy to write. Can you see how?

The `increment` lambda is just `curryAdd(1)`, as shown in the following code:

```
TEST_CASE("Increments value"){
    auto increment = curryAdd(1);
    CHECK_EQ(43, increment(42));
}
```

This shows us a trick that's commonly used by functional programming languages—the functions can be curried by default. In such a language, writing the following means that we apply the `add` function first to the `first` argument, and then the resulting function to the `second` argument:

```
add first second
```

It looks as if we are calling the function with a parameter list; in reality, it's a partially applied curried function. In such a language, the `increment` function can be derived from `add` simply by writing the following:

```
increment = add 1
```

The reverse is also true. Since C++ doesn't do currying by default, but offers an easy method for partial application, we can implement currying through partial application. Instead of returning the complex lambda with value capture, just bind to the single value and forward the single parameter of the resulting function:

```
auto curryAddPartialApplication = [](const int first){
    return bind(add, first, _1);
};

TEST_CASE("Adds values using partial application curry"){
    CHECK_EQ(42, curryAddPartialApplication(25)(17));
}
```

But how far can we take this? Is it easy to curry functions with multiple arguments?

Currying functions with multiple arguments

We have seen, in the previous section, how to curry functions with two arguments. When we move to three arguments, the curried function grows as well. We now need to return a lambda that returns a lambda. Once again, the code is easier to understand than any explanation, so let's see it:

```
auto curriedAddThree = [](const int first){
    return [first](const int second){
        return [first, second](const int third){
            return first + second + third;
        };
    };
};

TEST_CASE("Add three with curry"){
    CHECK_EQ(42, curriedAddThree(15)(10)(17));
}
```

There seems to be a recursive structure going on there. Maybe by using bind we can make sense of it?

It turns out it's not that simple, but it is possible. What I would like to write is something like this:

```
bind(bind(bind(addThree, _1),_1), _1)
```

However, `addThree` has three arguments, so we'd need to bind them to something. The next `bind` results in a function with two arguments, and again, we need to bind them to something. So, it would actually look like this:

```
bind(bind(bind(addThree, ?, ?, _1), ?,_1), _1)
```

The question marks should be replaced with the previously bound values, but that doesn't work with our current syntax.

However, there's a workaround. Let's implement multiple `simpleCurryN` functions that use `bind` on functions with *N* arguments and reduce them to *N-1*. For a function with one argument, the result is simply the following function:

```
auto simpleCurry1 = [](auto f){
    return f;
};
```

For two arguments, we bind the first and forward the next:

```
auto simpleCurry2 = [](auto f){
    return [f](auto x){ return bind(f, x, _1); };
};
```

Similar operations apply for three and four arguments:

```
auto simpleCurry3 = [](auto f){
    return [f](auto x, auto y){ return bind(f, x, y, _1); };
};
auto simpleCurry4 = [](auto f){
    return [f](auto x, auto y, auto z){ return bind(f, x, y, z, _1);
};
};
```

This set of `simpleCurryN` functions allow us to write our `curryN` functions that take one function with *N* arguments and return its curried form:

```
auto curry2 = [](auto f){
    return simpleCurry2(f);
};

auto curry3 = [](auto f){
    return curry2(simpleCurry3(f));
};

auto curry4 = [](auto f){
    return curry3(simpleCurry4(f));
};
```

Let's test them on `add` lambdas with two, three, and four arguments, as shown in the following code:

```
TEST_CASE("Add three with partial application curry"){
    auto add = [](int a, int b) { return a+b; };
    CHECK_EQ(3, curry2(add)(1)(2));

    auto addThreeCurryThree = curry3(addThree);
    CHECK_EQ(6, curry3(addThree)(1)(2)(3));

    auto addFour = [](int a, int b, int c, int d){return a + b + c +
        d;};
    CHECK_EQ(10, curry4(addFour)(1)(2)(3)(4));
}
```

It's likely that we can rewrite these functions with some imaginative use of templates. I will leave this exercise to the reader.

For now, it's important to see how partial application connects with currying. In programming languages that curry functions by default, partial application is very easy—just call the function with fewer arguments. For other programming languages, we can implement currying through partial application.

These concepts are very interesting, but you're probably wondering if they are useful in practice. Let's have a look at how to remove duplication using these techniques.

Removing duplication using partial application and currying

Programmers have long looked for solutions to write less code that does more things. Functional programming proposes one solution—build functions by deriving from other functions.

We've already seen this in action in the previous examples. Since `increment` is a particular case of addition, we can derive it from our addition function:

```
auto add = [](const auto first, const auto second) { return first + second;
};
auto increment = bind(add, _1, 1);

TEST_CASE("Increments"){
    CHECK_EQ(43, increment(42));
}
```

How does this help us? Well, imagine your customer comes in one day and tells you *we want to use another type of addition.* Imagine having to search for + and ++ everywhere in your code and figuring out ways to implement the new behavior.

Instead, with our add and increment functions, and a bit of template magic, this is what we can do:

```
auto add = [](const auto first, const auto second) { return first +
    second; };

template<typename T, T one>
auto increment = bind(add, _1, one);

TEST_CASE("Increments"){
    CHECK_EQ(43, increment<int, 1>(42));
}
```

Our add method doesn't care what type it gets, as long as it has a plus operator. Our increment function doesn't care what type it uses and how add works, just that you provide a value for one. And we've done this within three lines of code. I rarely say this about code, but isn't it beautiful?

Sure, you might say, but our clients don't really want to change the way we add things. You would be surprised how much you can do with a few simple operators. Let me give you just a simple example. Implement a game in which a character moves on a line that wraps, as shown in the following screenshot:

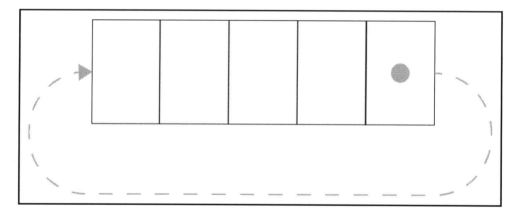

Isn't this just a modified version of addition? Let's have a look:

```
// Assume wrap at 20 for now
auto addWrapped = [](const auto first, const auto second) { return
    (first + second)%20; };

TEST_CASE("Adds values"){
    CHECK_EQ(7, addWrapped(10, 17));
}

template<typename T, T one>
auto incrementWrapped = bind<T>(addWrapped, _1, one);

TEST_CASE("Increments"){
    CHECK_EQ(1, incrementWrapped<int, 1>(20));
}
```

Hmm, this code looks very similar with `add`. Maybe we can use partial application? Let's see how:

```
auto addWrapped = [](const auto first, const auto second, const auto
    wrapAt) { return (first + second) % wrapAt; };

auto add = bind(addWrapped, _1, _2, 20);

template<typename T, T one>
    auto increment = bind<T>(add, _1, one);

TEST_CASE("Increments"){
    CHECK_EQ(1, increment<int, 1>(20));
}
```

Our `increment` function is exactly the same as before, while our `add` function has become a partial application of `addWrapped`. It's worth noting that, to make the code cleaner, I would still change the function names to make it very clear what the functions are doing. However, the main point is that partial application and currying help us to remove certain types of duplication from our code, empowering us to open the code to implementations we didn't necessarily know about when designing the initial solution. And while we can do this with OOP or templates, the functional solution limits complexity by removing side effects and requires just a few lines of code. That makes it a worthy choice when designing a program.

Summary

Look how far we've gone in our understanding of functional programming! We learned about all of the building blocks—pure functions and lambdas—and about the operations we can use on them—currying, partial application, and functional composition. We also saw how the operations relate to one another and how we can use currying to implement partial application and vice versa. We also saw ways to implement currying in C++.

But our quest is just beginning. The next stop is—starting to use these constructs in more interesting contexts. It's time to tackle the difficult question—how exactly do we design with functions?

Questions

1. What is a partial function application?
2. What is currying?
3. How does currying help us to implement partial application?
4. How can we implement partial application in C++?

Section 2: Design with Functions

So far, we have learned about the basic building blocks of functional programming. It's time to take them for a spin and visit the world of software design focused on functions.

First, we will look at a way of changing our mindset from **object-oriented programming (OOP)** written in an imperative manner to function-centric design. To do so, we need to understand how to transform input data into the desired output data, preferably with the help of existing higher-order functions. Then, we will look at the **Don't Repeat Yourself (DRY)** principle and how we can use functional operations (partial application, currying, and functional composition) to remove certain types of duplication from our code. We will then look at the relationship between functions and classes, how we can group pure functions into classes if we want to switch a design from function-focused to OOP, and how we can turn a class into a set of pure functions.

Armed with all these techniques, we will then learn about test-driven development and how it is simplified through the use of pure functions.

The following chapters will be covered in this section:

6
Thinking in Functions - from Data in to Data out

In my journey toward understanding functional programming, I hit a difficult hurdle—my mind was trained in a completely different style of programming. Let's call it imperative object-oriented programming. So, how could I shift my thought patterns from thinking in objects to thinking in functions? And how could I mix these two in a good way?

I first looked into functional programming resources. Unfortunately, most of them are focused on the mathematics and the inner beauty of the concepts—which is great for anyone who can already think in these terms. But what if you're just trying to learn them? Is going through mathematical theories the only way to learn? While I like math, I'm rusty at it, and I'd rather find more practical ways.

I've then been exposed to various ways of writing code through events such as Coderetreats, Coding Dojos, or pair programming with programmers from around Europe. And I realized, little by little, that there's a simple approach to fixing this problem—just focus on inputs and outputs instead of focusing on the model between them. That's a much more concrete and practical way to learn to think in functions, and this is what we'll explore next.

The following topics will be covered in this chapter:

- The basics of a functional mindset
- Relearning how to identify data in and data out for features and taking advantage of type inference
- Defining data transformations as pure functions
- How to use typical data transformations such as a map, reduce, filter, and more
- How to use the functional mindset to solve a problem
- Designing error management for code designed around functions

Technical requirements

You will need a compiler that supports C++ 17. I used GCC 7.3.0.

The code can be found on GitHub at `https://github.com/PacktPublishing/Hands-On-Functional-Programming-with-Cpp`, in the `Chapter06` folder. It includes and uses `doctest`, which is a single header open source unit testing library. You can find it on its GitHub repository at `https://github.com/onqtam/doctest`.

From data in to data out through functions

My computer programming education, and my focus as a programmer, was mostly on writing code rather than deeply understanding input and output data. This focus changed when I learned **test-driven development (TDD)**, since this practice forces the programmer to start from inputs and outputs. Through applying an extreme form called **TDD As If You Meant It**, I gained a new appreciation for the core definition of a program—something that takes input data and returns output data.

It wasn't easy, though. My training was pushing me back to thinking of the things that form the program. But then, I realized that those things can just be pure functions. After all, any program can be written as follows:

- A set of pure functions, as previously defined
- A set of functions that interact with **input/output (I/O)**

If we reduce the program to the minimum and separate everything that is I/O, figure out the I/O for the rest of the program, and write pure functions for everything we can, we've just made our first steps for thinking in functions.

The next question is—what should those functions be? In this chapter, we will look into the simplest way of designing with functions:

1. Start from data in.
2. Define the data out.
3. Define a series of transformations (pure functions) that turn the data in into the data out step by step.

Let's see a few examples contrasting the two approaches of writing the program.

A worked example of imperative versus functional style

To show the differences between approaches, we will need to use a problem. I like practicing new programming techniques using problems derived from games. On the one hand, it's a fun domain that I don't work with very often. On the other hand, games provide a lot of challenges that common business applications don't, thereby allowing us to explore new ideas.

In the following section, we will look at one problem that allows people to learn how to start thinking in functions—**the tic-tac-toe result problem**.

Tic-tac-toe result

The tic-tac-toe result problem has the following requirements—given a tic-tac-toe board that's either empty or already has moves, print out the result of the game, if the game has ended, or print out the game that is still in progress.

It looks as if the problem is fairly simple, yet it will show us a fundamental difference between the functional and imperative **object-oriented (OO)** approaches.

If we approach the problem from an OO perspective, we're already considering some objects to define—a game, a player, a board, maybe some representation for X and O (which I call tokens), and so on. We might then be looking at how to connect these objects—a game has two players and a board, and the board has tokens or empty fields on it and so on. As you can see, there's a lot of representation involved. Then, we need to implement a `computeResult` method somewhere that returns `GameState`, either `XWon`, `OWon`, `draw`, or `InProgress`. At first glance, it looks as if `computeResult` fits into the `Game` class. That method will probably need to loop inside `Board`, use some conditional statements, and return the corresponding `GameState`.

Instead of using the OO approach, we'll use a few strict steps to help us think differently about the code structure:

1. Clearly define the input; give examples.
2. Clearly define the output; give examples.
3. Identify a chain of functional transformations that you can apply to the input data to turn it into the output data.

Before we move on, please be aware that this mindset change requires a bit of knowledge and practice. We will look into the most common transformations to provide you with a good start, but you will need to try this method for yourself.

Inputs and outputs

The first lesson we learned as programmers is that any program has an input and an output. We then proceed to focus the rest of our careers on what happens between the input and the output, in the code itself.

Input and output deserve more attention from programmers, though, because they define the requirements of our software. And we know that the biggest waste in software is to implement something that works perfectly but doesn't do what it was supposed to.

I've noticed that it's very difficult for programmers to go back to thinking in terms of input and output. The seemingly simple question of what the input and what the output for a given feature should be often leaves them baffled and confused. So, let's look in detail at the input and output data for our problem.

At this point, we will do something unexpected. I've learned a neat trick from business analysts—it's best to start from the output when analyzing a feature because the output tends to be smaller and clearer than the input data. So, let's do that.

What is the output data?

What do we expect as outputs? Given that the board can have anything on it, or nothing at all, we are looking at the following possibilities:

- *Game not started*
- *Game in progress*
- X won
- O won
- Draw

See, the output is simple! Now, we can see how the input data relates with these possibilities.

What is the input data?

In this case, the input data is in the problem statement—our input is a board with moves on it. But let's look at some examples. The simplest example is an empty board:

```
_ _ _
_ _ _
_ _ _
```

For clarity, we use _ to represent an empty space on the board.

The empty board corresponds, of course, to the *game not started* output.

That's simple enough. Now, let's see one with a few moves on it:

```
X _ _
O _ _
_ _ _
```

Both X and O have made their moves, but the game is still in progress. There are many examples we can provide of *game in progress*:

```
X X _
O _ _
_ _ _
```

Here's another example:

```
X X O
O _ _
_ _ _
```

There are a few examples that could never happen in a tic-tac-toe game, such as this one:

```
X X _
O X _
X _ _
```

In this case, X has made four moves, while O has made only one, which is something the tic-tac-toe rules wouldn't allow. We will ignore this situation for now and just return a *game in progress*. You can, however, implement your own algorithm for this once we finish the rest of the code.

Let's see a game won by X:

```
X X X
O O _
_ _ _
```

X wins because the first line is filled. Are there other ways in which X can win? Yes, on a column:

```
X _ _
X O O
X _ _
```

It could also win on the main diagonal:

```
X O _
O X _
_ _ X
```

Here's a win for X on the secondary diagonal:

```
_ O X
O X _
X _ _
```

Similarly, we have examples where O wins by filling a line:

```
X X _
O O O
X _ _
```

Here's a win by filling a column:

```
X O _
X O X
_ O _
```

Here's a win by the main diagonal for O:

```
O X _
_ O X
X _ O
```

And here's a win via the secondary diagonal:

```
X X O
_ O X
O _ _
```

How about a game that ends in a draw? That's easy—all the squares are filled but there's no winner:

```
X X O
O X X
X O O
```

We've looked at examples for all possible outputs. Now, it's time to look at data transformations.

Data transformations

How can we transform the input into the output? To do this, we'll have to pick one of the possible outputs to tackle first. The easiest one for now is the case when X wins. So, how can X win?

According to the rules of the game, X wins if either a line, a column, or a diagonal in the board is filled with X. Let's write down all the possible cases. X wins if any of the following happen:

- Any line is filled with X OR
- Any column is filled with X OR
- The main diagonal is filled with X OR
- The secondary diagonal is filled with X

To implement this, we need a few things:

- Get all the lines from the board.
- Get all the columns from the board.
- Get the main and the secondary diagonal from the board.
- If any of them are filled with X, X won!

We can write this in another way:

```
board -> collection(all lines, all columns, all diagonals) ->
any(collection, filledWithX) -> X won
```

What does `filledWithX` mean? Let's take an example; we are looking for lines such as this:

```
X X X
```

We are not looking for lines such as X O X or X _ X.

It sounds like we are checking whether all the tokens on the line, column, or diagonal are 'X'. Let's visualize this check as a transformation:

```
line | column | diagonal -> all tokens equal X -> line | column | diagonal
filled with X
```

So, our set of transformations becomes this:

```
board -> collection(all lines, all columns, all diagonals) -> if
any(collection, filledWithX) -> X won

filledWithX(line|column|diagonal L) = all(token on L equals 'X')
```

One question remains—how can we get the lines, the columns, and the diagonals? We can look at this problem separately, in the same way we looked at the big problem. Our input is definitely the board. Our output is a list formed of first line, second line, and third line, first column, second column, and third column, main diagonal, and the secondary diagonal.

The next question is, what defines a line? Well, we know how to get the first line—we use the [0, 0], [0, 1], and [0, 2] coordinates. The second line has the [1, 0], [1, 1], and [1, 2] coordinates. What about a column? Well, the first column has the [1, 0], [1, 1], and [2, 1] coordinates. And, as we'll see, the diagonals are also defined by specific coordinate sets.

So, what did we learn? We learned that to get the lines, columns, and diagonals, we need the following transformation:

```
board -> collection of coordinates for lines, columns, diagonals -> apply
coordinates to the board -> obtain list of elements for lines, columns, and
diagonals
```

That concludes our analysis. It's time to move on to implementation. All the previous transformations can be expressed in code by using functional constructs. In fact, some of the transformations are so common that they're already implemented in the standard library. Let's see how we can use them!

Using all_of for filledWithX

The first transformation we'll look at is `all_of`. Given a collection and a function that returns a Boolean (also called a **logical predicate**), `all_of` applies the predicate to every element of the collection and returns the logical AND between the results. Let's see a few examples:

```
auto trueForAll = [](auto x) { return true; };
auto falseForAll = [](auto x) { return false; };
auto equalsChara = [](auto x){ return x == 'a';};
auto notChard = [](auto x){ return x != 'd';};

TEST_CASE("all_of"){
    vector<char> abc{'a', 'b', 'c'};

    CHECK(all_of(abc.begin(), abc.end(), trueForAll));
    CHECK(!all_of(abc.begin(), abc.end(), falseForAll));
    CHECK(!all_of(abc.begin(), abc.end(), equalsChara));
    CHECK(all_of(abc.begin(), abc.end(), notChard));
}
```

The `all_of` function takes two iterators defining the beginning and end of a range and a predicate as parameters. The iterators are useful when you want to apply the transformation to a subset of a collection. Since I usually use it on full collections, I find it annoying to write `collection.begin()` and `collection.end()` repeatedly. Thus, I implement my own simplified `all_of_collection` version that takes the whole collection and takes care of the rest:

```
auto all_of_collection = [](const auto& collection, auto lambda){
    return all_of(collection.begin(), collection.end(), lambda);
};

TEST_CASE("all_of_collection"){
    vector<char> abc{'a', 'b', 'c'};

    CHECK(all_of_collection(abc, trueForAll));
    CHECK(!all_of_collection(abc, falseForAll));
    CHECK(!all_of_collection(abc, equalsChara));
    CHECK(all_of_collection(abc, notChard));
}
```

Knowing this transformation, it's easy to write our `lineFilledWithX` function—we turn the collection of tokens into a collection of Booleans specifying whether the token is X:

```
auto lineFilledWithX = [](const auto& line){
    return all_of_collection(line, [](const auto& token){ return token ==
```

```
    'X';});
};

TEST_CASE("Line filled with X"){
    vector<char> line{'X', 'X', 'X'};

    CHECK(lineFilledWithX(line));
}
```

And that's it! We can ascertain whether our line is filled with x.

Before we move on, let's make a few simple adjustments. First, let's make the code clearer by naming our vector<char> type:

```
using Line = vector<char>;
```

Then, let's check that the code works fine for the negative scenarios as well. If Line is not filled with the X token, lineFilledWithX should return false:

```
TEST_CASE("Line not filled with X"){
    CHECK(!lineFilledWithX(Line{'X', 'O', 'X'}));
    CHECK(!lineFilledWithX(Line{'X', ' ', 'X'}));
}
```

Finally, an astute reader will notice that we will need the same function for the O wins condition. We now know how to do that—remember the power of argument binding. We just need to extract a lineFilledWith function and obtain the lineFilledWithX and lineFilledWithO functions by binding the tokenToCheck parameter to the X and O token values, respectively:

```
auto lineFilledWith = [](const auto line, const auto tokenToCheck){
    return all_of_collection(line, [&tokenToCheck](const auto token){
        return token == tokenToCheck;});
};

auto lineFilledWithX = bind(lineFilledWith, _1, 'X');
auto lineFilledWithO = bind(lineFilledWith, _1, 'O');
```

Let's recap—we have a Line data structure, and we have a function that can check whether the line is filled with X or O. We used the all_of function to do the heavy lifting for us; we just had to define the logic of our tic-tac-toe line.

It's time to move forward. We need to turn our board into a collection of lines, formed out of the three lines, the three columns, and the two diagonals. To do so, we need to visit another functional transformation, map, which is implemented in **Standard Template Library (STL)** as the transform function.

Using map/transform

We now need to write a function that turns the board into a list of lines, columns, and diagonals; therefore, we could use a transformation that takes a collection and turns it into another collection. This transformation is called map in general functional programming, and is implemented as transform in STL. To understand it, we will use a simple example; given a vector of characters, let's replace each character with 'a':

```
TEST_CASE("transform"){
    vector<char> abc{'a', 'b', 'c'};

// Not the best version, see below
vector<char> aaa(3);
transform(abc.begin(), abc.end(), aaa.begin(), [](auto element){return
    'a';});
CHECK_EQ(vector<char>{'a', 'a', 'a'}, aaa);
}
```

While it works, the previous code sample is naive because it initializes the aaa vector with values that are overwritten afterward. We can avoid this issue by first reserving 3 elements in the aaa vector, and then use back_inserter so that transform automatically calls push_back on the aaa vector:

```
TEST_CASE("transform-fixed") {
    const auto abc = vector{'a', 'b', 'c'};
    vector<char> aaa;
    aaa.reserve(abc.size());
    transform(abc.begin(), abc.end(), back_inserter(aaa),
            [](const char elem) { return 'a'; }
    );
    CHECK_EQ(vector{'a', 'a', 'a'}, aaa);
}
```

As you can see, transform is based on iterators in the same way all_of works. By now, you will have noticed that I like to keep things simple and focused on what we are trying to accomplish. There is no need to write this all the time; instead, we can implement our own simplified version that works on a full collection and takes care of all the rituals surrounding this function.

Simplifying transform

Let's try to implement the `transform_all` function in the simplest way possible:

```
auto transform_all = [](auto const source, auto lambda){
    auto destination; // Compilation error: the type is not defined
    ...
}
```

Unfortunately, we hit a snag when we try to implement it in this way—we need a type for the destination collection. The natural way of doing this is to use C++ templates and pass in the `Destination` type parameter:

```
template<typename Destination>
auto transformAll = [](auto const source,  auto lambda){
    Destination result;
    result.reserve(source.size());
    transform(source.begin(), source.end(), back_inserter(result),
        lambda);
    return result;
};
```

This works fine for any collection that has a `push_back` function. A nice side effect is that we can use it to concatenate the resulting characters in `string`:

```
auto turnAllToa = [](auto x) { return 'a';};

TEST_CASE("transform all"){
    vector abc{'a', 'b', 'c'};

    CHECK_EQ(vector<char>({'a', 'a', 'a'}), transform_all<vector<char>>
        (abc, turnAllToa));
    CHECK_EQ("aaa", transform_all<string>(abc,turnAllToa));
}
```

Using `transform_all` with `string` allows us to do things such as turning lowercase characters into uppercase characters:

```
auto makeCaps = [](auto x) { return toupper(x);};

TEST_CASE("transform all"){
    vector<char> abc = {'a', 'b', 'c'};

    CHECK_EQ("ABC", transform_all<string>(abc, makeCaps));
}
```

But that's not all—the output type doesn't necessarily have to be the same as the input:

```
auto toNumber = [](auto x) { return (int)x - 'a' + 1;};

TEST_CASE("transform all"){
    vector<char> abc = {'a', 'b', 'c'};
    vector<int> expected = {1, 2, 3};

    CHECK_EQ(expected, transform_all<vector<int>>(abc, toNumber));
}
```

The `transform` function is therefore very useful whenever we need to transform a collection into another, be it the same type or different types. With the support of `back_inserter`, it can also be used for `string` outputs, thereby enabling the implementation of string representations for any type of collection.

We now know how to use transform. So, let's go back to our problem.

Our coordinates

Our transformation starts by computing coordinates. So, let's define them first. The STL `pair` type is a simple representation for coordinates:

```
using Coordinate = pair<int, int>;
```

Getting a line from board and coordinates

Assuming we built the list of coordinates for a line, column, or diagonal, we need to transform the collection of tokens into the `Line` parameter. That's easily done with our `transformAll` function:

```
auto accessAtCoordinates = [](const auto& board, const Coordinate&
    coordinate){
        return board[coordinate.first][coordinate.second];
};

auto projectCoordinates = [](const auto& board, const auto&
    coordinates){
        auto boardElementFromCoordinates = bind(accessAtCoordinates,
        board, _1);
        return transform_all<Line>(coordinates,
            boardElementFromCoordinates);
};
```

The `projectCoordinates` lambda takes the board and a list of coordinates, and returns the list of elements from the board that corresponds to those coordinates. We use `transformAll` on the coordinates list, and a transformation that takes two parameters—the `board` parameter and a `coordinate` parameter. However, `transformAll` requires a lambda with a single parameter, a `Coordinate` value. Therefore, we have to either capture the value of the board or use partial application.

We now just have to build our list of coordinates for lines, columns, and diagonals!

Getting a line from the board

We can easily get a line from the board by using the previous function, `projectCoordinates`:

```
auto line = [](auto board, int lineIndex){
    return projectCoordinates(board, lineCoordinates(board, lineIndex));
};
```

The `line` lambda takes `board` and `lineIndex`, builds the line coordinates list, and uses `projectCoordinates` to return the line.

So, how do we build the line coordinates? Well, since we have `lineIndex` and `Coordinate` as a pair, we need to call `make_pair` on `(lineIndex, 0)`, on `(lineIndex, 1)`, and on `(lineIndex, 2)`. This looks like a `transform` call as well; the input is a `{0, 1, 2}` collection, and the transformation is `make_pair(lineIndex, index)`. Let's write it:

```
auto lineCoordinates = [](const auto board, auto lineIndex){
    vector<int> range{0, 1, 2};
    return transformAll<vector<Coordinate>>(range, [lineIndex](auto
        index){return make_pair(lineIndex, index);});
};
```

Ranges

But what is `{0, 1, 2}`? In other programming languages, we could use the concept of ranges; for example, in Groovy, we could write the following:

```
def range = [0..board.size()]
```

Ranges are very useful, and they were adopted in the C++ 20 standard. We will discuss them in `Chapter 14`, *Lazy Evaluation Using the Ranges Library*. Until then, we will write our own function, `toRange`:

```
auto toRange = [](auto const collection){
    vector<int> range(collection.size());
    iota(begin(range), end(range), 0);
    return range;
};
```

`toRange` takes a collection as input and creates `range` from 0 to `collection.size()`. So, let's use it in our code:

```
using Board = vector<Line>;
using Line = vector<char>;

auto lineCoordinates = [](const auto board, auto lineIndex){
    auto range = toRange(board);
    return transform_all<vector<Coordinate>>(range, [lineIndex](auto
        index){return make_pair(lineIndex, index);});
};

TEST_CASE("lines"){
    Board board {
        {'X', 'X', 'X'},
        {' ', 'O', ' '},
        {' ', ' ', 'O'}
    };

    Line expectedLine0 = {'X', 'X', 'X'};
    CHECK_EQ(expectedLine0, line(board, 0));
    Line expectedLine1 = {' ', 'O', ' '};
    CHECK_EQ(expectedLine1, line(board, 1));
    Line expectedLine2 = {' ', ' ', 'O'};
    CHECK_EQ(expectedLine2, line(board, 2));
}
```

We have all the elements in place, so it's time to look at the columns.

Getting the columns

The code for getting a column is very similar to the one for a line, except that we keep `columnIndex` instead of `lineIndex`. We just need to pass it as a parameter:

```
auto columnCoordinates = [](const auto& board, const auto columnIndex){
    auto range = toRange(board);
    return transformAll<vector<Coordinate>>(range, [columnIndex](const
        auto index){return make_pair(index, columnIndex);});
};

auto column = [](auto board, auto columnIndex){
    return projectCoordinates(board, columnCoordinates(board,
        columnIndex));
};

TEST_CASE("all columns"){
    Board board{
        {'X', 'X', 'X'},
        {' ', 'O', ' '},
        {' ', ' ', 'O'}
    };

    Line expectedColumn0{'X', ' ', ' '};
    CHECK_EQ(expectedColumn0, column(board, 0));
    Line expectedColumn1{'X', 'O', ' '};
    CHECK_EQ(expectedColumn1, column(board, 1));
    Line expectedColumn2{'X', ' ', 'O'};
    CHECK_EQ(expectedColumn2, column(board, 2));
}
```

Isn't this cool? With a few functions, and the help of standard functional transformations, we can build complex behavior in our code. The diagonals are a breeze now.

Getting the diagonals

The main diagonal is defined by equal line and column coordinates. It's pretty easy to use the same mechanic as before to read it; we build the pairs of equal indices and pass them to the `projectCoordinates` function:

```
auto mainDiagonalCoordinates = [](const auto board){
    auto range = toRange(board);
    return transformAll<vector<Coordinate>>(range, [](auto index)
        {return make_pair(index, index);});
};
auto mainDiagonal = [](const auto board){
```

```
        return projectCoordinates(board, mainDiagonalCoordinates(board));
};

TEST_CASE("main diagonal"){
    Board board{
        {'X', 'X', 'X'},
        {' ', 'O', ' '},
        {' ', ' ', 'O'}
    };

    Line expectedDiagonal = {'X', 'O', 'O'};

    CHECK_EQ(expectedDiagonal, mainDiagonal(board));
}
```

What about the secondary diagonal? Well, the sum of coordinates is always equal to the size of the board parameter. In C++, we also need to take into account the 0-based index, so we need a well-placed adjustment by 1 when building the list of coordinates:

```
auto secondaryDiagonalCoordinates = [](const auto board){
    auto range = toRange(board);
    return transformAll<vector<Coordinate>>(range, [board](auto index)
        {return make_pair(index, board.size() - index - 1);});
};

auto secondaryDiagonal = [](const auto board){
    return projectCoordinates(board,
        secondaryDiagonalCoordinates(board));
};

TEST_CASE("secondary diagonal"){
    Board board{
        {'X', 'X', 'X'},
        {' ', 'O', ' '},
        {' ', ' ', 'O'}
    };

    Line expectedDiagonal{'X', 'O', ' '};

    CHECK_EQ(expectedDiagonal, secondaryDiagonal(board));
}
```

Getting all lines, all columns, and all diagonals

With this being said, we can now build a collection of all lines, columns, and diagonals. There are multiple ways to do that; since I'm going for a general solution written in functional style, I will use transform again. We need to transform the (0..board.size()) range into the list of lines and the list of columns respectively. Then, we need to return a collection containing the main and secondary diagonals:

```
typedef vector<Line> Lines;

auto allLines = [](auto board) {
    auto range = toRange(board);
    return transform_all<Lines>(range, [board](auto index) { return
        line(board, index);});
};

auto allColumns = [](auto board) {
    auto range = toRange(board);
    return transform_all<Lines>(range, [board](auto index) { return
        column(board, index);});
};

auto allDiagonals = [](auto board) -> Lines {
    return {mainDiagonal(board), secondaryDiagonal(board)};
};
```

We just need one more thing—a way to concatenate the three collections. Since the vector doesn't have this implemented, the recommended solution is to use insert and move_iterator, thus moving the items from the second collection at the end of the first collection:

```
auto concatenate = [](auto first, const auto second){
    auto result(first);
    result.insert(result.end(), make_move_iterator(second.begin()),
        make_move_iterator(second.end()));
    return result;
};
```

Then, we just combine the three collections into two steps:

```
auto concatenate3 = [](auto first, auto const second, auto const third){
    return concatenate(concatenate(first, second), third);
};
```

We can now get the full list of lines, columns, and diagonals from the board, as you can see in the following tests:

```
auto allLinesColumnsAndDiagonals = [](const auto board) {
    return concatenate3(allLines(board), allColumns(board),
        allDiagonals(board));
};

TEST_CASE("all lines, columns and diagonals"){
    Board board {
        {'X', 'X', 'X'},
        {' ', 'O', ' '},
        {' ', ' ', 'O'}
    };

    Lines expected {
        {'X', 'X', 'X'},
        {' ', 'O', ' '},
        {' ', ' ', 'O'},
        {'X', ' ', ' '},
        {'X', 'O', ' '},
        {'X', ' ', 'O'},
        {'X', 'O', 'O'},
        {'X', 'O', ' '}
    };

    auto all = allLinesColumnsAndDiagonals(board);
    CHECK_EQ(expected, all);
}
```

There's only one more step left in finding out whether X has won. We have the list of all lines, columns, and diagonals. We know how to check that a line is filled with X. We just need to check whether any of the lines from the list are filled with X.

Using any_of to check whether X has won

Similar to all_of, another functional construct helps us to express an OR condition between predicates applied on a collection. In STL, this construct is implemented in the any_of function. Let's see it in action:

```
TEST_CASE("any_of"){
    vector<char> abc = {'a', 'b', 'c'};

    CHECK(any_of(abc.begin(), abc.end(), trueForAll));
    CHECK(!any_of(abc.begin(), abc.end(), falseForAll));
    CHECK(any_of(abc.begin(), abc.end(), equalsChara));
```

```
            CHECK(any_of(abc.begin(), abc.end(), notChard));
    }
```

Like the other higher-level functions we saw in this chapter, it uses iterators for the beginning and the end of the collection. As usual, I like to keep things simple; since I typically use any_of on full collections, I like to implement my helper function:

```
auto any_of_collection = [](const auto& collection, const auto& fn){
    return any_of(collection.begin(), collection.end(), fn);
};

TEST_CASE("any_of_collection"){
    vector<char> abc = {'a', 'b', 'c'};

    CHECK(any_of_collection(abc, trueForAll));
    CHECK(!any_of_collection(abc, falseForAll));
    CHECK(any_of_collection(abc, equalsChara));
    CHECK(any_of_collection(abc, notChard));
}
```

We just need to use it on our list to check whether X is the winner:

```
auto xWins = [](const auto& board){
    return any_of_collection(allLinesColumnsAndDiagonals(board),
        lineFilledWithX);
};

TEST_CASE("X wins"){
    Board board{
        {'X', 'X', 'X'},
        {' ', 'O', ' '},
        {' ', ' ', 'O'}
    };

    CHECK(xWins(board));
}
```

This concludes our solution for the winning condition for X. Before we move on, it would be nice to be able to display the board on the console. It's now time to use the close cousin of map/transform—reduce, or, as it's known in STL, accumulate.

Using reduce/accumulate to display the board

We would like to display the board on the console. Normally, we would use a mutable function such as `cout` to do that; however, remember how we discussed that while we need to keep parts of our program mutable, such as those calling `cout`, we should limit them to a minimum. So, what would the alternative be? Well, we need to think about inputs and outputs once again—we want to write a function that takes `board` as input and returns a `string` representation that we can display by using a mutable function such as `cout`. Let's write what we want in the form of a test:

```
TEST_CASE("board to string"){
    Board board{
        {'X', 'X', 'X'},
        {' ', 'O', ' '},
        {' ', ' ', 'O'}
    };
    string expected = "XXX\n O \n  O\n";

    CHECK_EQ(expected, boardToString(board));
}
```

To obtain this result, we first need to transform each line from `board` into its `string` representation. Our line is `vector<char>` and we need to turn it into `string`; while there are many ways of doing this, please allow me to use the `transformAll` function with a `string` output:

```
auto lineToString = [](const auto& line){
    return transformAll<string>(line, [](const auto token) -> char {
        return token;});
};

TEST_CASE("line to string"){
    Line line {
        ' ', 'X', 'O'
    };

    CHECK_EQ(" XO", lineToString(line));
}
```

With this function written, we can easily turn a board into `vector<string>`:

```
auto boardToLinesString = [](const auto board){
    return transformAll<vector<string>>(board, lineToString);
};

TEST_CASE("board to lines string"){
    Board board{
        {'X', 'X', 'X'},
        {' ', 'O', ' '},
        {' ', ' ', 'O'}
    };
    vector<string> expected{
        "XXX",
        " O ",
        "  O"
    };

    CHECK_EQ(expected, boardToLinesString(board));
}
```

The final step is to combine these strings with \n between them. We often need to combine elements of a collection in various ways; that's where `reduce` comes into play. In functional programming, `reduce` is an operation that takes a collection, an initial value (for example, empty strings), and an accumulation function. The function takes two parameters, performs an operation on them, and returns a new value.

Let's see a few examples. First, there's the classic example of adding a vector of numbers:

```
TEST_CASE("accumulate"){
    vector<int> values = {1, 12, 23, 45};

    auto add = [](int first, int second){return first + second;};
    int result = accumulate(values.begin(), values.end(), 0, add);
    CHECK_EQ(1 + 12 + 23 + 45, result);
}
```

The following shows us what to do if we need to add the vector with an initial value:

```
    int resultWithInit100 = accumulate(values.begin(), values.end(),
        100, add);
    CHECK_EQ(1oo + 1 + 12 + 23 + 45, resultWithInit100);
```

Similarly, we can concatenate `strings`:

```
    vector<string> strings {"Alex", "is", "here"};
    auto concatenate = [](const string& first, const string& second) ->
```

```
            string{
            return first + second;
    };
    string concatenated = accumulate(strings.begin(), strings.end(),
        string(), concatenate);
    CHECK_EQ("Alexishere", concatenated);
```

Alternatively, we can add a prefix:

```
    string concatenatedWithPrefix = accumulate(strings.begin(),
        strings.end(), string("Pre_"), concatenate);
    CHECK_EQ("Pre_Alexishere", concatenatedWithPrefix);
```

As usual, I prefer a simplified implementation that works on a full collection and uses a default value as an initial value. With a bit of `decltype` magic, it's easy to implement it:

```
auto accumulateAll = [](auto source, auto lambda){
    return accumulate(source.begin(), source.end(), typename
        decltype(source)::value_type(), lambda);
};
```

This just leaves us with one task—writing an implementation of concatenate that combines the `string` lines using a newline character:

```
auto boardToString = [](const auto board){
    auto linesAsString = boardToLinesString(board);
    return accumulateAll(linesAsString,
        [](string current, string lineAsString) { return current +
lineAsString + "\n"; }
    );
};
TEST_CASE("board to string"){
    Board board{
        {'X', 'X', 'X'},
        {' ', 'O', ' '},
        {' ', ' ', 'O'}
    };
    string expected = "XXX\n O \n  O\n";

    CHECK_EQ(expected, boardToString(board));
}
```

We can now use `cout << boardToString` to display our board. Once again, we used a few functional transformations and very little custom code to put everything together. That's quite nice.

The map/reduce combination, or, as it's known in STL, transform/accumulate, is very powerful and very common in functional programming. We often need to start from a collection, transform it into another collection multiple times, and then combine the elements of the collection. It's such a powerful concept that it's at the heart of big data analysis, using tools such as Apache Hadoop, albeit scaled at the level of machines. This shows that by mastering these transformations, you might end up applying them in unexpected situations, making you an indispensable problem solver. Cool, isn't it?

Using find_if to display specific win details

We are happy now that we have solved the tic-tac-toe result problem for X. However, as always, requirements change; we need now to not only say whether X won, but also how—on which line, or column, or diagonal.

Fortunately, we already have most of the elements in place. Since they are very small functions, we just need to recombine them in a way that helps us. Let's think again in terms of data—our input data is now a collection of lines, columns, and diagonals; our result should be something such as X won *on first line*. We just need to enhance our data structure to contain information about each line; let's use map:

```
map<string, Line> linesWithDescription{
    {"first line", line(board, 0)},
    {"second line", line(board, 1)},
    {"last line", line(board, 2)},
    {"first column", column(board, 0)},
    {"second column", column(board, 1)},
    {"last column", column(board, 2)},
    {"main diagonal", mainDiagonal(board)},
    {"secondary diagonal", secondaryDiagonal(board)},
};
```

We know how to find out where X won—through our lineFilledWithX predicate function. Now, we just need to search in the map for the line that fits the lineFilledWithX predicate and return the corresponding message.

Once again, this is a common operation in functional programming. In STL, it's implemented with the find_if function. Let's see it in action:

```
auto equals1 = [](auto value){ return value == 1; };
auto greaterThan11 = [](auto value) { return value > 11; };
auto greaterThan50 = [](auto value) { return value > 50; };

TEST_CASE("find if"){
    vector<int> values{1, 12, 23, 45};
```

```
    auto result1 = find_if(values.begin(), values.end(), equals1);
    CHECK_EQ(*result1, 1);

    auto result12 = find_if(values.begin(), values.end(),
        greaterThan11);
    CHECK_EQ(*result12, 12);

    auto resultNotFound = find_if(values.begin(), values.end(),
        greaterThan50);
    CHECK_EQ(resultNotFound, values.end());
}
```

find_if looks in a collection based on a predicate and returns a pointer to the result, or a pointer to the end() iterator if nothing is found.

As usual, let's do our wrapper implementation that allows a search in a whole collection. We need to represent the not found value in a way; fortunately, we can use the optional type from STL:

```
auto findInCollection = [](const auto& collection, auto fn){
    auto result = find_if(collection.begin(), collection.end(), fn);
    return (result == collection.end()) ? nullopt : optional(*result);
};

TEST_CASE("find in collection"){
    vector<int> values {1, 12, 23, 45};

    auto result1 = findInCollection(values, equals1);
    CHECK_EQ(result1, 1);

    auto result12 = findInCollection(values, greaterThan11);
    CHECK_EQ(result12, 12);

    auto resultNotFound = findInCollection(values, greaterThan50);
    CHECK(!resultNotFound.has_value());
}
```

Now, we can easily implement the new requirement. We can find the line that is filled with X by using our newly implemented findInCollection function and return the corresponding description. We can therefore tell the user how X won—on a line, on a column, or on a diagonal:

```
auto howDidXWin = [](const auto& board){
    map<string, Line> linesWithDescription = {
        {"first line", line(board, 0)},
        {"second line", line(board, 1)},
        {"last line", line(board, 2)},
```

```
            {"first column", column(board, 0) },
            {"second column", column(board, 1) },
            {"last column", column(board, 2) },
            {"main diagonal", mainDiagonal(board) },
            {"secondary diagonal", secondaryDiagonal(board) },
        };
        auto found = findInCollection(linesWithDescription, [] (auto value)
            {return lineFilledWithX(value.second); });
        return found.has_value() ? found->first : "X did not win";
    };
```

We should, of course, generate the map from the board instead of hardcoding it. I will leave this exercise to the reader; just use our favorite transform function again.

Completing our solution

While we have implemented the solution for X wins, we now need to look into the other possible outputs. Let's take the easiest one first—O wins.

Checking whether O has won

Checking whether O has won is easy—we just need a small change in our functions. We need a new function, oWins, that checks whether any line, column, or diagonal is filled with the O token:

```
auto oWins = [] (auto const board) {
    return any_of_collection(allLinesColumnsAndDiagonals(board),
        lineFilledWithO);
};
TEST_CASE("O wins") {
    Board board = {
            {'X', 'O', 'X'},
            {' ', 'O', ' '},
            {' ', 'O', 'X'}
    };

    CHECK(oWins(board));
}
```

We use the same implementation as for xWins, with just a slight change in the lambda that is passed as the parameter.

Checking for draw using none_of

What about `draw`? Well, a draw happens when the `board` parameter is full and neither X nor O has won:

```
auto draw = [](const auto& board){
    return full(board) && !xWins(board) && !oWins(board);
};

TEST_CASE("draw"){
    Board board {
        {'X', 'O', 'X'},
        {'O', 'O', 'X'},
        {'X', 'X', 'O'}
    };

    CHECK(draw(board));
}
```

What does a full board mean? It means that every line is full:

```
auto full = [](const auto& board){
    return all_of_collection(board, fullLine);
};
```

And how do we know whether the line is full? Well, we know that if none of the tokens from the line are the empty (' ') token, the line is full. As you probably expect by now, there is a function in STL called `none_of` that can check this for us:

```
auto noneOf = [](const auto& collection, auto fn){
    return none_of(collection.begin(), collection.end(), fn);
};

auto isEmpty = [](const auto token){return token == ' ';};
auto fullLine = [](const auto& line){
    return noneOf(line, isEmpty);
};
```

Checking for game in progress

The final case is when the game is still in progress. The simplest way is just to check that the game was not won and the board is not full yet:

```
auto inProgress = [](const auto& board){
    return !full(board) && !xWins(board) && !oWins(board);
};
```

```
TEST_CASE("in progress"){
    Board board {
        {'X', 'O', 'X'},
        {'O', ' ', 'X'},
        {'X', 'X', 'O'}
    };

    CHECK(inProgress(board));
}
```

Congratulations, we've done it! We've implemented the tic-tac-toe result problem using a number of functional transformations; a few lambdas of our own. But, more importantly, we've learned how to start thinking as a functional programmer—clearly defining the input data, clearly defining the output data, and figuring out the transformations that can turn the input data into the required output data.

Error management using optional types

By now, we have a small program written in functional style. But what about the error cases? How do we deal with them?

It's obvious that we can still use the C++ mechanisms—return values or exceptions. But functional programming also looks at another way—treating errors as data.

We already saw an example of this technique when we implemented our `find_if` wrapper:

```
auto findInCollection = [](const auto& collection, auto fn){
    auto result = find_if(collection.begin(), collection.end(), fn);
    return (result == collection.end()) ? nullopt : optional(*result);
};
```

Instead of throwing an exception or returning `collection.end()`, which is a local value, we used the `optional` type. As stated in its name, the optional type represents a variable that may, or may not, have a value. An optional value can be initialized, either with a value supported by the underlying type, or with `nullopt`—a default non-value, so to speak.

When encountering an optional value in our code, we need to take it into account, as we did in the function checking how X won:

```
return found.has_value() ? found->first : "X did not win";
```

Therefore, the *not found* condition is not an error; instead, it's a normal part of our code and of our data. Indeed, another way of dealing with this condition is to enhance `findInCollection` to return a specified value when nothing is found:

```
auto findInCollectionWithDefault = [](auto collection, auto
    defaultResult, auto lambda){
        auto result = findInCollection(collection, lambda);
        return result.has_value() ? (*result) : defaultResult;
};
```

We can now use `findInCollectionWithDefault` to obtain an `X did not win` message when we call `howDidXWin` on a board where `X` did not win:

```
auto howDidXWin = [](auto const board){
    map<string, Line> linesWithDescription = {
        {"first line", line(board, 0)},
        {"second line", line(board, 1)},
        {"last line", line(board, 2)},
        {"first column", column(board, 0)},
        {"second column", column(board, 1)},
        {"last column", column(board, 2)},
        {"main diagonal", mainDiagonal(board)},
        {"secondary diagonal", secondaryDiagonal(board)},
        {"diagonal", secondaryDiagonal(board)},
    };
    auto xDidNotWin = make_pair("X did not win", Line());
    auto xWon = [](auto value){
        return lineFilledWithX(value.second);
    };

    return findInCollectionWithDefault(linesWithDescription, xDidNotWin,
xWon).first;
};

TEST_CASE("X did not win"){
    Board board {
        {'X', 'X', ' '},
        {' ', 'O', ' '},
        {' ', ' ', 'O'}
    };

    CHECK_EQ("X did not win", howDidXWin(board));
}
```

My best advice is this—use exceptions for all exceptional situations, and make everything else part of your data structures. Use optional types, or transformations with default values. You'll be surprised by how easy and natural error management becomes.

Summary

We have covered a lot of ground in this chapter! We went through a journey of discovery—we started by listing the outputs and corresponding inputs for our problem, decomposed them, and figured out how to transform the inputs in the requisite outputs. We saw how small functions and the functional operations give us agility when new features are requested. We saw how to use any, all, none, find_if, map/transform, and reduce/accumulate, and how to use optional types or default values to support all possible cases in our code.

Now that we have an idea of how to write code in functional style, it's time to see how this approach fits with OO programming in the next chapter.

7
Removing Duplication with Functional Operations

A key principle in software design is reducing code duplication. Functional constructs provide additional opportunities for reducing code duplication through currying and functional composition.

The following topics will be covered in this chapter:

- How and why to avoid repeating code
- How to identify code similarities
- Using currying to remove certain types of code similarities
- Using composition to remove certain types of code similarities
- Using lambdas or composition to remove certain types of code similarities

Technical requirements

You will need a compiler that supports C++ 17. I used GCC 7.3.0.

The code can be found on GitHub at https://github.com/PacktPublishing/Hands-On-Functional-Programming-with-Cpp, in the Chapter07 folder. It includes and uses doctest, which is a single header open source unit testing library. You can find it on its GitHub repository at https://github.com/onqtam/doctest.

Removing duplication with functional operations

Maintaining code over long periods of time is much easier when we only need to change the code in one place, and when we can recombine existing pieces of code. One of the most effective ways to move toward this ideal is to identify and to remove duplication from code. The operations from functional programming—partial application, currying, and functional composition—offer many opportunities to make code cleaner and with limited duplication.

But first, let's understand what duplication is and why we need to reduce it. First, we'll look at the **Don't Repeat Yourself** (**DRY**) principle, and then at the relationship between duplication and code similarity. Finally, we'll look at ways to remove code similarity.

The DRY principle

The number of core books in software development is unexpectedly low. Sure, there are many books on details and on helping people understand the ideas better, but books on core ideas are remarkably few and old. Being on the list of core books is an honor for authors, as well as a hint that the topic is extremely important. Many programmers would place the book *Pragmatic Programmer*, by Andrew Hunt and David Thomas, on such a list. This book, published in 1999, details one principle that makes a lot of sense to anyone who's been working with large code bases for long periods of time—DRY.

At its core, the DRY principle operates on the understanding that code is a way to store knowledge. Every function and every data member represents knowledge about a problem. Ideally, we would like to avoid having knowledge duplicated around the system. In other words, whatever you're looking for should only be in one place. Unfortunately, most of the code bases are **WET** (an acronym for either **write everything twice**, **we enjoy typing**, or **waste everyone's time**), rather than DRY.

The idea of removing duplication is older, however. It was previously mentioned by Kent Beck in the 1990s as part of the **extreme programming** (**XP**) practices. Kent Beck described the four elements of simple design, a thinking tool for obtaining or improving software design.

Simple design means that it does the following:

- Passes the tests
- Reveals intention
- Reduces duplication
- Has fewer elements

I learned these rules from J.B. Rainsberger, who also worked on simplifying these rules. He taught me that in most situations, it's enough to focus on three things—testing the code, improving names, and reducing duplication.

But that's not the only place where removing duplication is mentioned. The principle has appeared in various ways in the Unix design philosophy, in the **domain-driven design (DDD)** techniques, as a help to **test-driven development (TDD)** practice, and many others. It's safe to say it's a universal principle of good software design, and it makes sense to use it whenever we talk about structuring the code within a module.

Duplication and similarity

Later in my journey toward learning good software design, I realized that the term **duplication** is very useful for expressing the philosophy of what we're trying to accomplish, but it's hard to understand how to put it in practice. I found a better name for the things I search for when trying to improve design—I look for **code similarities**. Once I find similarities, I ask whether they show a deeper duplication, or whether they're simply an accident.

I also noticed in time that I look for a few specific types of similarities. Here are a few examples:

- Similar names, either full names or names embedded inside longer names of functions, parameters, methods, variables, constants, classes, modules, namespaces, and so on
- Similar lists of parameters
- Similar function calls
- Different code trying to achieve similar results

In general, I follow these two steps:

1. First, notice similarities.
2. Second, decide whether to remove the similarity.

When unsure if the similarity says something deeper about the design, it's best to keep it. It's also best to start removing similarities once you've seen them around three times; this way, you know for sure that it violates the DRY principle rather than being just an accident.

Next, we will look at a few types of similarities that we can remove through functional operations.

Addressing parameter similarities with partial application

In our previous chapters, you have seen situations when a function is called multiple times with the same value for one of the parameters. See, for example, the code in our Tic-Tac-Toe result problem; we had one function responsible for checking whether a line is filled with a token:

```
auto lineFilledWith = [](const auto& line, const auto tokenToCheck){
    return all_of_collection(line, [&tokenToCheck](auto const token){
        return token == tokenToCheck;});
};
```

Since Tic-Tac-Toe uses two tokens, X and O, it's clear that we will have a repeated call of this function where tokenToCheck is either X or O. The usual way to remove this kind of similarity is to implement two new functions, lineFilledWithX and lineFilledWithO:

```
auto lineFilledWithX = [](const auto& line){
    return lineFilledWith(line, 'X');
};
```

This is a viable solution, but it still requires us to write a separate function and three lines of code. As we have seen, we have another option in functional programming; we can simply use partial application to obtain the same result:

```
auto lineFilledWithX = bind(lineFilledWith, _1, 'X');
auto lineFilledWithO = bind(lineFilledWith, _1, 'O');
```

I prefer to use partial application when possible because this type of code is just plumbing, and the fewer lines of plumbing I need to write, the better. However, you need to be careful when using partial application in a team. Every team member should be familiar with partial application and proficient in understanding this type of code. Otherwise, the use of partial application will just make the code more difficult to understand for the development team.

Replacing the call function on the output of another function similarity with functional composition

You may have noticed the pattern shown in the following code in the past:

```
int processA(){
     a   = f1(....)
     b = f2(a, ...)
     c = f3(b, ...)
}
```

Often, if you look hard enough, you will find another function in your code base that does something similar:

```
int processB(){
     a   = f1Prime(....)
     b = f2(a, ...)
     c = f3(b, ...)
}
```

There seems to be a deeper reason for this type of similarity, due to the way applications grow in complexity over time. We often start by implementing a simple flow that goes through multiple steps. We then implement variations of the same flow, with a few steps that repeat and others that change. Sometimes, a variation of the flow involves either changing the order of the steps, or adjusting a few of the steps.

In our implementation, the steps transform into functions that are combined in various ways within other functions. But if we use the output of the previous step and feed it into the next step, we have a similarity in the code that doesn't depend on what each of the steps does.

To remove this similarity, we would traditionally extract the similar parts of the code and pass the result, as shown in the following code:

```
int processA(){
     a   = f1(....)
     return doSomething(a)
}

int processB(){
     a = f1Prime(....)
     return doSomething(a)
}
```

```
int doSomething(auto a){
    b = f2(a, ...)
    return f3(b, ...)
}
```

However, the code often becomes more difficult to understand and more difficult to change when extracting functions, as shown in the previous code. Extracting the common part of the function doesn't take into account the fact that the code is, in reality, a chain call.

To make this visible, I tend to reformat this pattern of code to a single statement, as shown in the following code:

```
processA = f3(f2(f1(....), ...), ...)
processB = f3(f2(f1Prime(....), ...), ...)
```

While not everyone likes this format, the similarity and the difference between the two calls is clearer. It's also quite obvious that we have a solution using functional composition—we just need to compose f3 with f2, and compose the result with either f1 or f1Prime to get the result we want:

```
C = f3 ∘ f2
processA = C ∘ f1
processB  = C ∘ f1Prime
```

This is a very powerful mechanic! We can create countless combinations of chain calls just through functional composition, in a few lines of code. We can replace the hidden plumbing masquerading as the order of statements in a function with a few composition statements expressing the true nature of our code.

However, as we've seen in Chapter 4, *The Idea of Functional Composition*, this is not necessarily an easy task in C++, since we need to write our own compose functions that work for our specific situations. Until C++ offers better support for functional composition, we are forced to keep this mechanic to a minimum, and only use it where the similarity is not only obvious, but where we expect it to increase over time.

Removing structural similarity with higher-level functions

There's been a pattern in our discussion until now—functional programming helps us to remove the plumbing from our code and express the true structure of the code. Imperative programming uses a sequence of statements as a fundamental structure; functional programming reduces the sequences and focuses on the interesting play of the functions.

This is most visible when we discuss structural similarity. A widespread pattern, structural similarity refers to the situations when the structure of code repeats, although not necessarily through calling the same functions or using the same parameters. To see it in action, let's start from a very interesting similarity in our Tic-Tac-Toe code. This is code that we wrote in Chapter 6, *Thinking in Functions – from Data in to Data out*:

```
auto lineFilledWith = [](const auto& line, const auto& tokenToCheck){
    return allOfCollection(line, [&tokenToCheck](const auto& token){
        return token == tokenToCheck;});
};

auto lineFilledWithX = bind(lineFilledWith, _1, 'X');
auto lineFilledWithO = bind(lineFilledWith, _1, 'O');

auto xWins = [](const auto& board){
    return any_of_collection(allLinesColumnsAndDiagonals(board),
        lineFilledWithX);
};

auto oWins = [](const auto& board){
    return any_of_collection(allLinesColumnsAndDiagonals(board),
        lineFilledWithO);
};
```

The xWins and oWins functions look very similar, as they both call the same function as the first parameter, and a variation on the lineFilledWith function as their second parameter. Let's remove their similarity. First, let's remove lineFilledWithX and lineFilledWithO, and replace them with their lineFilledWith equivalent:

```
auto xWins = [](const auto& board){
    return any_of_collection(allLinesColumnsAndDiagonals(board), []
        (const auto& line) { return lineFilledWith(line, 'X');});
};

auto oWins = [](const auto& board){
    return any_of_collection(allLinesColumnsAndDiagonals(board), []
        (const auto& line) { return lineFilledWith(line, 'O');});
};
```

Now that the similarity is obvious, we can easily extract a common function:

```
auto tokenWins = [](const auto& board, const auto& token){
    return any_of_collection(allLinesColumnsAndDiagonals(board),
        [token](auto line) { return lineFilledWith(line, token);});
};
auto xWins = [](auto const board){
    return tokenWins(board, 'X');
```

```
};

auto oWins = [](auto const board){
    return tokenWins(board, 'O');
}
```

We also notice that xWins and oWins are just partial applications of tokenWins, so let's make this explicit:

```
auto xWins = bind(tokenWins, _1, 'X');
auto oWins = bind(tokenWins, _1, 'O');
```

Now, let's focus on tokenWins:

```
auto tokenWins = [](const auto& board, const auto& token){
    return any_of_collection(allLinesColumnsAndDiagonals(board),
        [token](auto line) { return lineFilledWith(line, token);});
};
```

First, we notice that the lambda we pass into any_of_collection is a partial application with a fixed token parameter, so let's replace it:

```
auto tokenWins = [](const auto& board, const auto& token){
    return any_of_collection(
            allLinesColumnsAndDiagonals(board),
            bind(lineFilledWith, _1, token)
    );
};
```

This is quite a small function now, packing a lot of power due to our partial applications. However, we can already extract a higher-level function that would allow us to create more similar functions without writing any code. I don't know what to call it yet, so I'll just call it foo:

```
template <typename F, typename G, typename H>
auto foo(F f, G g, H h){
    return [=](auto first, auto second){
    return f(g(first),
    bind(h, _1, second));
    };
}
auto tokenWins = compose(any_of_collection, allLinesColumnsAndDiagonals,
lineFilledWith);
```

Our `foo` function shows the structure of the code, but it's quite unreadable, so let's name things better:

```
template <typename CollectionBooleanOperation, typename CollectionProvider,
typename Predicate>
auto booleanOperationOnProvidedCollection(CollectionBooleanOperation
collectionBooleanOperation, CollectionProvider collectionProvider,
Predicate predicate){
    return [=](auto collectionProviderSeed, auto predicateFirstParameter){
        return
collectionBooleanOperation(collectionProvider(collectionProviderSeed),
            bind(predicate, _1, predicateFirstParameter));
    };
}
auto tokenWins = booleanOperationOnProvidedCollection(any_of_collection,
allLinesColumnsAndDiagonals, lineFilledWith);
```

We've introduced a higher level of abstraction, which can make code more difficult to understand. On the other hand, we've enabled the creation of functions of the `f(g(first), bind(h, _1, second))` form in one line of code.

Is the code better? That's up to context, your judgment, and how familiar you and your colleagues are with higher-level functions. Remember, however—abstractions, while very powerful, come with a price. An abstraction is more difficult to understand, but if you *speak* in abstractions, you can combine them in very powerful ways. Using these higher-level functions is like building a language from scratch—it enables you to communicate on a different level, but it also creates a barrier of entry for other people. Use abstractions with caution!

Removing hidden loops using higher-level functions

A particular example of structural duplication is often encountered in code, and I ended up calling it **hidden loops**. The idea of hidden loops is that we use the same code structure multiple times in a sequence. The trick, though, is that the functions called or the parameters don't have to be the same; since the basic idea of functional programming is that functions are data as well, we can see these structures as loops over data structures that might also store the functions that we call.

I usually see this pattern in a series of `if` statements. In fact, I started seeing them while facilitating hands-on sessions using the Tic-Tac-Toe result problem. The usual solution to the problem, in an **object-oriented programming (OOP)** or imperative language, looks something like what is shown in the following code:

```
enum Result {
    XWins,
    OWins,
    GameNotOverYet,
    Draw
};

Result winner(const Board& board){
    if(board.anyLineFilledWith(Token::X) ||
        board.anyColumnFilledWith(Token::X) ||
        board.anyDiagonalFilledWith(Token::X))
    return XWins;

    if(board.anyLineFilledWith(Token::O) ||
        board.anyColumnFilledWith(Token::O) ||
        board.anyDiagonalFilledWith(Token::O))
    return OWins;

    if(board.notFilledYet())
    return GameNotOverYet;

    return Draw;
}
```

In the previous example, the `enum` token contains three values:

```
enum Token {
    X,
    O,
    Blank
};
```

The `Board` class looks something like this:

```
using Line = vector<Token>;

class Board{
    private:
        const vector<Line> _board;

    public:
        Board() : _board{Line(3, Token::Blank), Line(3, Token::Blank),
            Line(3, Token::Blank)}{}
```

```
            Board(const vector<Line>& initial) : _board{initial}{}
    ...
    }
```

The implementations of `anyLineFilledWith`, `anyColumnFilledWith`, `anyDiagonalFilledWith`, and `notFilledYet` are quite similar; a very simplistic implementation of `anyLineFilledWith`, assuming a 3 x 3 board, is as follows:

```
        bool anyLineFilledWith(const Token& token) const{
            for(int i = 0; i < 3; ++i){
                if(_board[i][0] == token && _board[i][1] == token &&
                    _board[i][2] == token){
                    return true;
                }
            }
            return false;
        };
```

We are less interested in the underlying implementation however, and more interested in the similarities in the preceding winner function. First, the condition in the `if` statement repeats with a different parameter. But, more interestingly, there's a structure that repeats as follows:

```
    if(condition) return value;
```

If you saw a structure like this that uses data instead of different functions, you would immediately notice that it's a hidden loop. When function calls are involved, we don't notice this type of repetition since we're not trained to see functions as data. But that's exactly what they are.

Before we remove that similarity, let's simplify the conditions. I will make all conditions functions without parameters, through the magic of partial function application:

```
auto tokenWins = [](const auto board, const auto& token){
    return board.anyLineFilledWith(token) ||
board.anyColumnFilledWith(token) || board.anyDiagonalFilledWith(token);
};

auto xWins = bind(tokenWins, _1, Token::X);
auto oWins = bind(tokenWins, _1, Token::O);

auto gameNotOverYet = [](auto board){
    return board.notFilledYet();
};

Result winner(const Board& board){
    auto gameNotOverYetOnBoard = bind(gameNotOverYet, board);
```

```
    auto xWinsOnBoard = bind(xWins, board);
    auto oWinsOnBoard = bind(oWins, board);

    if(xWins())
        return XWins;

    if(oWins())
        return OWins;

    if(gameNotOverYetOnBoard())
        return GameNotOverYet;

    return Draw;
}
```

Our next step is to remove the variation between the four different conditions, and replace the similarity with a loop. We just need to have a list of pairs of *(lambda, result)* and use a higher-level function such as `find_if` to do the loop for us:

```
auto True = [](){
    return true;
};

Result winner(Board board){
    auto gameNotOverYetOnBoard = bind(gameNotOverYet, board);
    auto xWinsOnBoard = bind(xWins, board);
    auto oWinsOnBoard = bind(oWins, board);

    vector<pair<function<bool()>, Result>> rules = {
        {xWins, XWins},
        {oWins, OWins},
        {gameNotOverYetOnBoard, GameNotOverYet},
        {True, Draw}
    };

    auto theRule = find_if(rules.begin(), rules.end(), [](auto pair){
            return pair.first();
            });
    // theRule will always be found, the {True, Draw} by default.
    return theRule->second;
}
```

The last piece of the puzzle is ensuring that our code returns `Draw` if nothing else works. Since `find_if` returns the first element that fits the rule, we just need to have `Draw` at the end, associated with a function that always returns `true`. I named this function, appropriately, `True`.

How's this code working for us? Well, it has a few advantages. First, we can easily add a new pair of conditions and results, for example, if we ever get the request to implement variations of Tic-Tac-Toe in multiple dimensions or with more players. Second, the code is shorter. Third, with a few changes, we obtain a simple, albeit quite general, rule engine:

```
auto True = [](){
    return true;
};

using Rule = pair<function<bool()>, Result>;

auto condition = [](auto rule){
    return rule.first();
};

auto result = [](auto rule){
    return rule.second;
};

// assumes that a rule is always found
auto findTheRule = [](const auto& rules){
    return *find_if(rules.begin(), rules.end(), [](auto rule){
 return condition(rule);
 });
};

auto resultForFirstRuleThatApplies = [](auto rules){
    return result(findTheRule(rules));
};

Result winner(Board board){
    auto gameNotOverYetOnBoard = bind(gameNotOverYet, board);
    vector<Rule> rules {
        {xWins, XWins},
        {oWins, OWins},
        {gameNotOverYetOnBoard, GameNotOverYet},
        {True, Draw}
    };

    return resultForFirstRuleThatApplies(rules);
}
```

The only particular code in the previous sample is the list of rules. Everything else is quite general and can be reused on multiple problems.

As usual, there's a price to pay for going to a higher level of abstraction. We took the time to name things as clearly as possible, and I believe this code is very easy to read. However, it might not be familiar to many people.

Another possible issue is memory usage. The initial version of the code, while repeating the same code structure, doesn't need to allocate memory for a list of pairs of function and results; however, it's important to measure these things, since even the initial code will require some process memory for the extra instructions.

This example shows us how repeated structures can be turned into loops through a very simple code sample. This is just scratching the surface; this pattern is so widespread that I'm sure you'll notice it in your code once you start looking.

Summary

In this chapter, we looked at different types of code similarities and how we can reduce them through various functional programming techniques. From repeated parameters that can be replaced with partial application, to chained calls that can be turned into functional composition, all the way to the wonderfully complex world of structural similarities that can be removed through higher-level functions, you are now well armed to notice and reduce similarity in any code base you work with.

As you have noticed, we started to discuss code structures and software design. This leads us to another core principle of design—high cohesion and low coupling. How do we increase cohesion using functions? It turns out that that's where classes are very useful and this is what we will discuss in the next chapter.

8
Improving Cohesion Using Classes

We've previously discussed how we can use functions and operations on functions to organize our code. We can't ignore, however, the prevalent paradigm for software design of the past few decades—**object-oriented programming (OOP)**. Can OOP work with functional programming? Is there any compatibility between the two, or are they completely disjointed?

It turns out that we can easily convert between classes and functions. I learned through my friend and mentor, J.B. Rainsberger, that classes are nothing more than a set of partially applied, cohesive pure functions. In other words, we can use classes as a convenient location to group cohesive functions together. But, in order to do so, we need to understand the high cohesion principle and how to transform functions into classes and vice versa.

The following topics will be covered in this chapter:

- Understanding the connection between functional programming and OOP
- Understanding how classes are equivalent with sets of cohesive, partially-applied pure functions
- Understanding the need for high cohesion
- How to group pure functions into classes
- How to split a class into pure functions

Technical requirements

You will need a compiler that supports C++ 17. I used GCC 7.3.0.

The code can be found on GitHub at `https://github.com/PacktPublishing/Hands-On-Functional-Programming-with-Cpp` in the `Chapter08` folder. It includes and uses `doctest`, which is a single-header open source unit testing library. You can find it in its GitHub repository at `https://github.com/onqtam/doctest`.

Improving cohesion using classes

As a young software engineering student, I spent an inordinate amount of time reading about OOP. I was trying to understand how OOP works and why it's so important for modern software development. At that time, most books were mentioning that OOP is about organizing code into classes that have three important properties—encapsulation, inheritance, and polymorphism.

Almost 20 years later, I realized that this vision of OOP was quite limited. OOP was largely developed at Xerox PARC, the laboratory known for generating an amazing number of high-quality ideas, such as graphical user interfaces, point and click, the mouse, and the spreadsheet, to mention just a few. Alan Kay, one of the OOP originators, drew from his knowledge as a biology major while facing the problem of organizing large code bases in ways that supported the new GUI paradigm. He came up with the idea of objects and classes, but he stated years later that the main idea of this style of code organization is messaging. His view on objects was that they should communicate in a similar way to cells, with a simulation of their chemical messages in code. That's why a method call in an OOP language, from his view, should instead be a message that's passed from a cell or object to another cell or object.

Once we forget about ideas of encapsulation, inheritance, and polymorphism, and place more importance on objects instead of classes, the friction between the functional paradigm and OOP disappears. Let's see where this fundamental view of OOP takes us.

Classes from a functional perspective

There are multiple ways to look at classes. In terms of knowledge management, I conceptualize a *class* as a classification—it's a way of grouping instances (or objects) that have similar properties. If we think about classes in this way, then inheritance comes as a natural property—there are classes of objects that have similar properties, but they also differ in various ways; saying that they inherit from one another is a quick way to explain them.

However, this conception of classes works in domains where our knowledge is quasi-complete. In the software development sphere, we often work with limited knowledge of the application domain, and the domain keeps expanding over time. Therefore, we need to focus on code structures that have weak links between concepts, allowing us to change or replace them as we learn more about the domain. What should we do about classes then?

Even without their strong relationships, classes are a powerful construct in software design. They provide a neat way of grouping methods, and of combining methods with data. They can help us navigate larger domains better than functions, since we can end up with thousands of functions (if not more). So, how can we use classes with functional programming?

First, as you may have noticed from our previous examples, functional programming places complexity inside data structures. Classes are often a neat way of defining the data structures that we need, especially in a language such as C++, which allows us to override common operators. Common examples include imaginary numbers, measurable units (temperature, length, velocity, and so on), and currency data structures. Each of them requires data to be grouped with specific operators and conversions.

Second, the immutable functions we write tend to naturally group themselves into logical classifications. In our Tic-Tac-Toe example, we have a number of functions that work with a data structure that we call a **line**; our natural tendency is to group these functions together. While nothing stops us from grouping them in a header file, classes provide a natural place to combine functions so that we can find them later. This leads to another type of class—an immutable object that is initialized once, and whose every operation returns a value instead of mutating its state.

Let's look in more detail at the equivalence between an OOP design and a functional structure.

The equivalence OOP – functional

If we go back to our Tic-Tac-Toe result solution, you'll notice that there are a number of functions that receive `board` as a parameter:

```
auto allLines = [](const auto& board) {
...
};

auto allColumns = [](const auto& board) {
...
};

auto mainDiagonal = [](const auto& board){
...
};

auto secondaryDiagonal = [](const auto& board){
...
};

auto allDiagonals = [](const auto& board) -> Lines {
...
};

auto allLinesColumnsAndDiagonals = [](const auto& board) {
...
};
```

We can define a board as follows, for example:

```
Board board {
    {'X', 'X', 'X'},
    {' ', 'O', ' '},
    {' ', ' ', 'O'}
};
```

Then, when we pass it into the functions, it's like we're binding the board to the parameter of the functions. Now, let's do that for our `allLinesColumnsAndDiagonals` lambda:

```
auto bindAllToBoard = [](const auto& board){
    return map<string, function<Lines  ()>>{
        {"allLinesColumnsAndDiagonals",
            bind(allLinesColumnsAndDiagonals, board)},
    };
};
```

The preceding lambda and many other examples we have looked at in earlier chapters call other lambdas, yet they don't capture them. For example, how does the bindAllToBoard lambda know about the allLinesColumnsAndDiagonal lambda? The only reason this works is because the lambdas are in a global scope. Moreover, with my compiler, when trying to capture allLinesColumnsAndDiagonals, I get the following error message: <lambda> *cannot be captured because it does not have automatic storage duration*, so it actually will not compile if I try to capture the lambda I use.

 I hope what I am about to say is self-explanatory, but I will say it anyway—for production code, avoid having lambdas (and anything else, really) in the global scope. This will also force you to capture the variables, which is a good thing because it makes dependencies explicit.

Now, let's look at how we call it:

```
TEST_CASE("all lines, columns and diagonals with class-like structure"){
    Board board{
        {'X', 'X', 'X'},
        {' ', 'O', ' '},
        {' ', ' ', 'O'}
    };

    Lines expected{
        {'X', 'X', 'X'},
        {' ', 'O', ' '},
        {' ', ' ', 'O'},
        {'X', ' ', ' '},
        {'X', 'O', ' '},
        {'X', ' ', 'O'},
        {'X', 'O', 'O'},
        {'X', 'O', ' '}
    };

    auto boardObject = bindAllToBoard(board);
    auto all = boardObject["allLinesColumnsAndDiagonals"]();
    CHECK_EQ(expected, all);
}
```

Does this remind you of something? Let's look at how we would write this in a class. I will name it BoardResult for now, since I can't come up with a better name:

```
class BoardResult{
    private:
        const vector<Line> board;
```

```
    public:
        BoardResult(const vector<Line>& board) : board(board){
        };

        Lines allLinesColumnsAndDiagonals() const {
            return concatenate3(allLines(board), allColumns(board),
                allDiagonals(board));
        }
};

TEST_CASE("all lines, columns and diagonals"){
 BoardResult boardResult{{
 {'X', 'X', 'X'},
 {' ', 'O', ' '},
 {' ', ' ', 'O'}
 }};

 Lines expected {
 {'X', 'X', 'X'},
 {' ', 'O', ' '},
 {' ', ' ', 'O'},
 {'X', ' ', ' '},
 {'X', 'O', ' '},
 {'X', ' ', 'O'},
 {'X', 'O', 'O'},
 {'X', 'O', ' '}
 };

 auto all = boardResult.allLinesColumnsAndDiagonals();
 CHECK_EQ(expected, all);
 }
```

Let's recap what we did:

- We saw more functions taking board as a parameter.
- We decided to bind the board parameter to a value using a separate function, thereby obtaining a map between a string denoting the function name and the lambda bound to the value.
- To call it, we needed to first call the initializing function and then we could call the partially-applied lambda.
- *This looks extremely similar to a class*—use the constructor to pass in the value that's shared between the class methods, and then call the methods without passing in the parameter.

Therefore, *a class is just a set of partially applied lambdas*. But how do we group them?

The principle of high cohesion

In our previous example, we grouped the functions together in a class based on the fact that they took the same parameter, `board`. I have found this to be a good rule of thumb. However, we can encounter more complex situations.

To understand why, let's look into another set of functions (the implementation has been ignored for the purpose of this discussion):

```
using Coordinate = pair<int, int>;

auto accessAtCoordinates = [](const auto& board, const Coordinate&
coordinate)
auto mainDiagonalCoordinates = [](const auto& board)
auto secondaryDiagonalCoordinates = [](const auto& board)
auto columnCoordinates = [](const auto& board, const auto& columnIndex)
auto lineCoordinates = [](const auto& board, const auto& lineIndex)
auto projectCoordinates = [](const auto& board, const auto& coordinates)
```

Should these functions be part of the `BoardResult` class defined previously? Or should they be part of another class, `Coordinate`? Or should we split them, with some of them going to the `BoardResult` class, and others going to the `Coordinate` class?

Our previous method doesn't work for all the functions. If we look solely at their parameters, all of the preceding functions take `board`. However, some of them also take `coordinate` / `coordinates` as a parameter. Should `projectCoordinates` be part of the `BoardResult` class, or part of the `Coordinate` class?

More importantly, what's the base principle we can follow to group these functions into classes?

Since there's no clear answer regarding the static structure of the code, we need to think about the code evolution instead. The questions we need to ask are the following:

- Which of the functions do we expect to change together? Which of the functions do we expect to change separately?
- This line of reasoning leads us to the high cohesion principle. But, let's unpack it first. What do we mean by cohesion?

As an engineer and a science geek, I met cohesion in the physical world. When we talk about water, for example, the molecules composing the liquid tend to stick together. I also met cohesion as a social force. As a change agent working with customers who try to adopt modern software development practices, I've often had to deal with group cohesion—the tendency of people to cluster together around a point of view.

When we talk about cohesion for functions, there is no physical force that pushes them together, and they definitely don't stick to points of view. So, what are we talking about? We're talking about a neurological force, so to speak.

The human brain has a huge capacity for finding patterns and grouping related items in categories, combined with an uncannily fast way of navigating them. The force that binds functions together is in our brains—it's the finding of a unifying purpose that emerges from the combination of seemingly unrelated functions.

High cohesion is useful because it allows us to understand and navigate a few big concepts (such as board, line, and token) rather than tens or hundreds of small functions. Moreover, when (not if) we need to add a new behavior or change an existing one, high cohesion will allow us to find the place for a new behavior fast, and to add it with minimal changes to the remainder of the network.

Cohesion is a metric of software design, introduced by Larry Constantine in the 1960s as part of his *Structured Design* approach. Through experience, we have noticed that high cohesion correlates with a low cost of change.

Let's see how to apply this principle in order to group our functions in to classes.

Grouping cohesive functions into classes

As previously discussed, we can look at cohesion in terms of a unifying purpose or concept of the class. However, I usually find it more thorough to look at the evolution of code and decide on the function groups based on what might change in the future, and what other changes it might trigger.

You might not expect to learn many things from our Tic-Tac-Toe result problem. It is fairly simple, and seems quite contained. However, a quick search on the web leads us to a number of Tic-Tac-Toe variations, including the following:

- The *m x n* board, with the winner decided by *k* items in a row. An interesting variant is Gomoku, played on a *15 x 15* board, where the winner has to get 5 in a row.
- A 3D version.
- Using numbers as tokens, and the sum of the numbers as the win condition.
- Using words as tokens, and the winner has to place 3 words in a row with 1 common letter.
- Using 9 boards of *3 x 3* to play, where the winner must win 3 boards in a row.

These are not even the most weird variants, and, if you're interested, you can check the Wikipedia article on the topic at `https://en.wikipedia.org/wiki/Tic-tac-toe_variants`.

So, what could change in our implementation? Here are a few suggestions:

- Board size
- Number of players
- Tokens
- Winning rules (still in a row, but with different conditions)
- Board topology—rectangular, hexagonal, triangular, or 3D instead of square

Fortunately, if we just change the board size, nothing should really change in our code. In fact, we can pass in a larger board and everything will still work. Very small changes are required for changing the number of players; we will assume they have different tokens and we just need to bind the `tokenWins` function to different token values.

How about the winning rules? We will assume that the rules still take into account the lines, columns, and diagonals, since this is a basic requirement for Tic-Tac-Toe and all the variants use them. However, we might not take into account a full line, column, or diagonal; in Gomoku, for example, we need to look for 5 tokens in a row on a line, column, or diagonal that has the size 15. Looking at our code, this is merely a matter of selecting other groups of coordinates; instead of searching for a full line to be filled with token X, we need to select all possible sets of five-in-a-row coordinates. This means a change in our functions related to coordinates—`lineCoordinates`, `mainDiagonalCoordinates`, `columnCoordinates`, and `secondaryDiagonalCoordinates`. They will return a vector of five-in-a-row coordinates, which will result in changes in `allLines`, `allColumns`, and `allDiagonals`, and in the way we concatenate them.

What if the token is a word and the winning condition is about finding a common letter between the words? Well, the coordinates are the same, and the way we get the lines, columns, and diagonals stays the same. The only change is in the `fill` condition, so this is relatively easy to change.

This leads us to the final possible change—the board topology. Changing the board topology will require changing the board data structure, and all the coordinates and the corresponding functions. But will it require changes in the lines, columns, and diagonals rules? If we switch to 3D, then we have more lines, more columns, and a different way of addressing diagonals—all changes in coordinates. A rectangular board doesn't have a diagonal *per se*; we'll need to use partial diagonals such as in the Gomoku case. As for hexagonal or triangular boards, there is no clear variant, so we can ignore them for now.

This shows us that if we want to prepare for change, our functions should be grouped around the following lines:

- Rules (also known as the **fill condition**)
- Coordinates and projections—and prepare the code for multiple sets of lines, columns, and diagonals
- A basic board structure allowing access based on coordinates

That settles it—we need to separate the coordinates from the board itself. While the coordinate data type will change at the same time as the board data type, the functions providing the line, column, and diagonal coordinates might change due to the game rules. Thus, we need to separate the board from its topology.

In terms of **object-oriented design (OOD)**, we need to separate the responsibilities of the program between at least three cohesive classes—Rules, Topology, and Board. The Rules class contains the rules of the game—basically, how we compute the winning conditions, when we know it's a draw, or that the game has ended. The Topology class is about coordinates and the structure of the board. The Board class should be the structure we pass in to the algorithm.

So, how should our functions be structured? Let's make a list:

- **Rules**: xWins, oWins, tokenWins, draw, and inProgress
- **Topology**: lineCoordinates, columnCoordinates, mainDiagonalCoordinates, and secondaryDiagonalCoordinates
- **Board**: accessAtCoordinates and allLinesColumnsAndDiagonals
- **Undecided**: allLines, allColumns, allDiagonals, mainDiagonal, and secondaryDiagonal

There's always a list of functions that could be part of more structures. In our case, should allLines be part of the Topology class or the Board class? I can find equally good arguments for both. Therefore, the solution is left to the intuition of the programmer who writes the code.

This shows, however, the method you can use to group these functions into classes—think about what might change, and group them based on which functions will change together.

There is, however, a caveat for practicing this method—avoid the trap of over-analysis. Code is relatively easy to change; when you have little information about what might change, make it work and wait until a new requirement comes up in the same area of the code. Then, you'll have a better idea of the relationships between functions. This analysis shouldn't take you longer than 15 minutes; anything extra is most likely over-engineering.

Splitting a class into pure functions

We have learned how to group functions into a class. But how do we transform the code from a class to pure functions? It transpires that this is fairly straightforward—we just need to make the functions pure, move them out of the class, and then add an initializer that binds them to the data they need.

Let's take another example, a class that performs mathematical operations with two integer operands:

```
class Calculator{
    private:
        int first;
        int second;

    public:
        Calculator(int first, int second): first(first), second(second){}

        int add() const {
            return first + second;
        }

        int multiply() const {
            return first * second;
        }

        int mod() const {
            return first % second;
        }

};

TEST_CASE("Adds"){
    Calculator calculator(1, 2);

    int result = calculator.add();

    CHECK_EQ(result, 3);
}
```

```
TEST_CASE("Multiplies"){
    Calculator calculator(3, 2);

    int result = calculator.multiply();

    CHECK_EQ(result, 6);
}

TEST_CASE("Modulo"){
    Calculator calculator(3, 2);

    int result = calculator.mod();

    CHECK_EQ(result, 1);
}
```

To make it more interesting, let's add another function that reverts the first parameter:

```
class Calculator{
...
    int negateInt() const {
        return -first;
    }
...
}


TEST_CASE("Revert"){
    Calculator calculator(3, 2);

    int result = calculator.negateInt();

    CHECK_EQ(result, -3);
}
```

How can we split this class into functions? Fortunately, the functions are already pure. It's obvious that we can extract the functions as lambdas:

```
auto add = [](const auto first, const auto second){
    return first + second;
};

auto multiply = [](const auto first, const auto second){
    return first * second;
};

auto mod = [](const auto first, const auto second){
    return first % second;
```

```
};

auto negateInt = [](const auto value){
    return -value;
};
```

If you really need to, let's add the initializer:

```
auto initialize = [] (const auto first, const auto second) -> map<string,
function<int()>>{
    return  {
        {"add", bind(add, first, second)},
        {"multiply", bind(multiply, first, second)},
        {"mod", bind(mod, first, second)},
        {"revert", bind(revert, first)}
    };
};
```

Then, a check can be carried out to determine that everything works:

```
TEST_CASE("Adds"){
    auto calculator = initialize(1, 2);

    int result = calculator["add"]();

    CHECK_EQ(result, 3);
}

TEST_CASE("Multiplies"){
    auto calculator = initialize(3, 2);

    int result = calculator["multiply"]();

    CHECK_EQ(result, 6);
}

TEST_CASE("Modulo"){
    auto calculator = initialize(3, 2);

    int result = calculator["mod"]();

    CHECK_EQ(result, 1);
}

TEST_CASE("Revert"){
    auto calculator = initialize(3, 2);

    int result = calculator["revert"]();
```

```
        CHECK_EQ(result, -3);
}
```

This leaves us with only one open question—how can we turn impure functions into pure functions? We will discuss this question at length in `Chapter 12`, *Refactoring to and through Pure Functions*. For now, let's remember the important conclusion of this chapter—*a class is nothing more than a set of cohesive, partially applied functions*.

Summary

We had such an interesting journey in this chapter! We managed to link two styles of design that seem disjointed—OOP and functional programming, in a very elegant manner. Pure functions can be grouped into classes based on the principle of cohesion. We just need to exercise our imagination and think of scenarios in which functions might change, and decide which functions to group together. Reversely, we can always move functions from a class into multiple lambdas by making them pure and reversing the partial application.

There is no friction between OOP and functional programming; they are just two different ways of structuring the code that implements features.

Our journey into software design using functions has not finished yet. In the next chapter, we will discuss how to design functions using **test-driven development (TDD)**.

9

Test-Driven Development for Functional Programming

Test-driven development (TDD) is a very useful method for designing software. The method is as follows—we first write one single test that fails, then we implement the minimum code to make the test pass, and finally we refactor. We do this in small cycles in quick succession.

We will look at how pure functions simplify tests and provide an example of applying TDD with functions. Pure functions allow us to write simple tests because they always return the same values for the same input parameters; therefore, they are equivalent to big data tables. We can therefore write tests that emulate data tables for inputs and the expected outputs.

The following topics will be covered in this chapter:

- How to use data-driven tests to take advantage of pure functions
- Understanding the basics of the TDD cycle
- How to design a pure function using TDD

Technical requirements

You will need a compiler that supports **C++ 17**. I used **GCC 7.3.0**.

The code can be found on GitHub at `https://github.com/PacktPublishing/Hands-On-Functional-Programming-with-Cpp` in the `Chapter09` folder. It includes and uses `doctest`, which is a single header open source unit testing library. You can find it on its GitHub repository at `https://github.com/onqtam/doctest`.

TDD for functional programming

Programming in the 1950s was very different from what we know today. The job we now know as that of a programmer was split between three roles. The programmer would write the algorithm meant to be implemented. Then, a specialized typist would type it into punch cards using a special machine. The programmer then had to manually verify that the punch cards were correct—although there were hundreds of them. Once happy that the punch cards were correct, the programmer would take them to the mainframe operator. Since the only computers in existence were huge and very expensive, the time spent on the computer had to be protected. The mainframe operator took care of the computer, ensuring that the most important tasks took precedence, and thus a new program could wait for days until it was run. Once run, the program would print a full stack trace. If there was an error, the programmer had to look at a very long paper filled with weird symbols and figure out what might be wrong. The process was slow, error-prone, and unpredictable.

However, some of the engineers came up with an idea. What if, instead of getting the complex read-out from a failing program, they would get a clear indication of what was wrong? They decided to start writing additional code that would check the production code and produce an output of pass or fail. Instead of running the program, or in addition to running the program, they would run unit tests.

The practice of unit testing was forgotten once programmers had shorter feedback loops, with the invention of terminals and, later, personal computers and powerful debuggers. However, it never quite disappeared, and it suddenly came back in a different form.

It was in the 1990s that unit tests made a surprise re-appearance. A group of programmers, including Kent Beck, Ward Cunningham, and Ron Jeffries, experimented with taking development practices to the extreme. The result of their effort was called **extreme programming** (**XP**). One of these practices was unit testing, and the results were very interesting.

The common practice of unit testing was to write some tests after the code was written, as part of the testing period. These tests were often written by testers—a different group from the programmers who implemented the features.

However, the initial XPers tried unit testing in a different way. What if we were to write the tests along with the code? And, more interestingly, what if we were to write the tests *before* the implementation? This led to two different techniques—**test-first programming** (**TFP**), which consists of writing a few tests first, and then some code to make the tests pass, and TDD, which we'll discuss in more detail.

When I first heard about these techniques, I was both puzzled and fascinated. How could you write tests for something that doesn't exist? What would be the benefit? Fortunately, with the support of J.B. Rainsberger, I quickly realized the power of TFP/TDD. Our clients and our stakeholders want working features in software as soon as possible. Yet, all too often, they can't explain what features they want. Starting with the tests means that you fully understand what to implement and leads to useful and interesting conversations that clarify the requirements. Once the requirements are clear, we can focus on the implementation. Moreover, in TDD, we clean the code as soon as possible, so that we don't create a mess as time passes. It truly is an amazingly powerful technique!

But let's start from the beginning. How do we write a unit test? And, more importantly for our purpose, is it easier to write unit tests for pure functions?

Unit tests for pure functions

Let's first see what a unit test looks like. I have been using them already for a while in this book, and I'm sure you understand the code. But it's time to look at one particular example:

```
TEST_CASE("Greater Than"){
    int first = 3;
    int second = 2;

    bool result = greater<int>()(first, second);

    CHECK(result);
}
```

We first initialize the two variables with specific values (the *Arrange* part of the unit test). We then call the production code (the *Act* part of the unit test). Finally, we check that the result is the one we expected (the *Assert* part of the unit test). The library we're using, called `doctest`, provides implementation for the macros that allow us to write the unit tests. While more unit testing libraries exist for C++, notable examples including GTest and `Boost::unit_test`, the facilities they offer to programmers are quite similar.

When talking about unit tests, it's more important to figure out the characteristics that make them useful. The previous test is small, focused, fast, and can fail for only one reason. All these characteristics make the test useful since it's easy to write, easy to maintain, crystal clear, and provides useful and fast feedback if a bug is introduced.

In terms of technique, the previous test is example-based since it uses a very specific example to check a specific behavior of the code. We will look at a different method of unit testing called **property-based testing** in Chapter 11, *Property-Based Testing*. Since this is an example-based test, an interesting question crops up: if we want to test the greaterThan function, what other examples would be interesting?

Well, we want to look at all the possible behaviors of the functions. So, what would be its possible outputs? Here's a list:

- True, if the first value is greater than the second value
- False, if the first value is less than the second value

However, that's not enough. Let's add the edge case:

- False, if the first value equals the second value

And, let's not forget possible errors. What is the domain for the values passed in? Is it OK to pass negative values? Floating point values? Complex numbers? This is an interesting conversation to have with the stakeholders of this function.

Let's assume the simplest case for now—the function will accept only valid integers. This means that we need two more unit tests checking the situations when the first parameter is less than the second and when the two are equal:

```
TEST_CASE("Not Greater Than when first is less than second"){
    int first = 2;
    int second = 3;

    bool result = greater<int>()(first, second);

    CHECK_FALSE(result);
}

TEST_CASE("Not Greater Than when first equals second"){
    int first = 2;

    bool result = greater<int>()(first, first);

    CHECK_FALSE(result);
}
```

In Chapter 7, *Removing Duplication with Functional Operations*, we discussed code similarity and how to remove it. Here, we have a case of similarity between tests. One way to remove it is to write so-called **data-driven tests** (DDT). In DDT, we write a list of inputs and expected outputs and repeat the test over every line of data. Different testing frameworks offer different ways to write these tests; for now, doctest has limited support for DDT, but we can still write them as follows:

```
TEST_CASE("Greater than") {
    struct Data {
        int first;
        int second;
        bool expected;
  } data;

    SUBCASE("2 is greater than 1") { data.first = 2; data.second = 1;
        data.expected = true; }
    SUBCASE("2 is not greater than 2") { data.first = 2; data.second =
        2; data.expected = false; }
    SUBCASE("2 is not greater than 3") { data.first = 2; data.second =
        3; data.expected = false; }
    CAPTURE(data);
    CHECK_EQ(greaterThan(data.first, data.second), data.expected);
}
```

If we ignore the plumbing code (the struct Data definition and the call to the CAPTURE macro), this shows a very convenient way of writing tests—especially for pure functions. Given that pure functions return, by definition, the same output when they receive the same inputs, it's only natural to test them with a list of inputs/outputs.

Another convenience of DDT is that we can easily add a new test by just adding a new line to the list. This, in particular, helps us when doing TDD with pure functions.

The TDD cycle

TDD is a development cycle that is commonly presented as follows:

- **Red**: Write a test that fails.
- **Green**: Make the test pass by making the smallest change possible in the production code.
- **Refactor**: Reorganize the code to include the newly introduced behavior.

However, TDD practitioners (such as myself) will be keen to mention that the TDD cycle starts with another step—think. More precisely, before writing the first test, let's understand what we are trying to implement and find a good place in the existing code to add the behavior.

This cycle is deceptively simple. However, beginners often struggle with what the first test should be and what the test after that should be, as well as with writing code that is too complex. **Refactoring** is an art in itself, requiring knowledge of code smells, design principles, and design patterns. Overall, the biggest mistake is to think too much about the code structure that you'd like to obtain, and write the tests that lead to that.

Instead, TDD requires a mindset change. We start from the behaviors and, in small steps, polish the code structure that fits the behavior. A good practitioner will have steps smaller than 15 minutes. But that's not the only surprise of TDD.

The biggest surprise of TDD is that it can teach you about software design by allowing you to explore various solutions to the same problem. The more solutions you're willing to explore, the better you'll become at designing code. TDD is a continuous learning experience when practiced with the right amount of curiosity.

I hope I made you curious about TDD. There's a lot more to study about the topic, but, for our goals, it's enough to try out an example. And since we're talking about functional programming, we'll use TDD to design a pure function.

Example – designing a pure function using TDD

Once again, we need a problem to showcase TDD in action. Since I like to practice development practices using games, I went through the list from Coding Dojo Katas (http://codingdojo.org/kata/PokerHands/) and I picked the poker hands problem for this exercise.

The poker hands problem

A description of the problem is as follows—given two or more hands of poker, we need to compare them and return the one that has the higher rank and why it wins.

Each hand has five cards, and the cards are picked from a normal 52-card deck. The deck is formed of four suits—clubs, diamonds, hearts, and spades. Each suit starts with a 2 and ends with an ace, and is denoted as follows—2, 3, 4, 5, 6, 7, 8, 9, T, J, Q, K, A (T means 10).

The cards in a poker hand will create formations. The value of a hand is determined by those formations, in the following descending order:

- **Straight flush**: Five cards of the same suit with consecutive values. For example, 2♠, 3♠, 4♠, 5♠, and 6♠. The higher the starting value, the more valuable the straight flush is.
- **Four of a kind**: Four cards with the same value. The highest one is four aces—A♣, A♠, A♦, and A♥.
- **Full house**: Three cards of the same value, and another two cards with the same value (but different). The highest one is as follows—A♣, A♠, A♦, K♥, and K♠.
- **Flush**: Five cards of the same suit. For example—2♠, 3♠, 5♠, 6♠, and 9♠.
- **Straight**: Five cards of consecutive values. For example—2♣, 3♠, 4♥, 5♣, and 6♦.
- **Three of a kind**: Three cards with the same value. For example—2♣, 2♠, and 2♥.
- **Two pairs**: See pair. For example—2♣, 2♠, 3♥, and 3♣.
- **Pair**: Two cards of the same value. For example—2♣ and 2♠.
- **High card**: When no other formation is present, the highest cards from each hand are compared and the highest wins. If the highest cards have the same value, the next highest cards are compared, and so on.

Requirements

Our goal is to implement a program that compares two or more poker hands and returns both the winner and the reason. For example, let's use the following input:

- **Player 1**: *2♥ 4♦ 7♣ 9♠ K♦*
- **Player 2**: *2♠ 4♥ 8♣ 9♠ A♥*

For this input, we should get the following output:

- *Player 2 wins with their high card—an ace*

Step 1 – Think

Let's look at the problem in more detail. More precisely, we are trying to split the problem into smaller pieces without thinking too much about the implementation. I find it useful to look at possible examples of inputs and outputs, and to start with a simplified problem that allows me to implement something that works as fast as possible while preserving the nature of the problem.

It's obvious that we have a very large number of combinations to test for. So, what would be a useful simplification of the problem that limits our test cases?

One obvious way is to start from a shorter hand. Instead of having five cards, we could start with one card in hand. This limits our rules to high cards. The next step is to have two cards, which introduces the *pair > high card*, and *higher pair > lower pair*, and so on.

Another way is to start with five cards, but to limit the rules. Start with a high card, then implement one pair, then two pairs, and so on; or, the other way around, from the straight flush all the way down to the pair and high card.

The interesting thing about TDD is that any of these roads will lead to results that work in the same way, albeit often with different code structures. One of the powers of TDD is to help you visit multiple designs for the same problem by varying the order of your tests.

Needless to say, I've done this problem before, but I've always started from one card in hand. Let's have some fun and try a different way, shall we? I choose to go with five cards and start from the straight flush. To keep things simple, I'll just support two players for now, and since I like to name them, I'll use Alice and Bob.

Examples

What would be some interesting examples for this situation? Let's think about possible outputs first:

- Alice wins with a straight flush.
- Bob wins with a straight flush.
- Alice and Bob have equally good straight flushes.
- Undecided (as in not implemented yet).

Now, let's write some examples of inputs for these outputs:

Case 1: Alice wins

```
Inputs:
 Alice: 2♠, 3♠, 4♠, 5♠, 6♠
 Bob: 2♣, 4♦, 7♥, 9♠, A♥

Output:
 Alice wins with straight flush
```

Case 2: Bob wins

```
Inputs:
    Alice: 2♠, 3♠, 4♠, 5♠, 9♠
    Bob: 2♣, 3♣, 4♣, 5♣, 6♣

Output:
    Bob wins with straight flush
```

Case 3: Alice wins with a higher straight flush

```
Inputs:
    Alice: 3♠, 4♠, 5♠, 6♠, 7♠
    Bob: 2♣, 3♣, 4♣, 5♣, 6♣

Output:
    Alice wins with straight flush
```

Case 4: Draw

```
Inputs:
    Alice: 3♠, 4♠, 5♠, 6♠, 7♠
    Bob: 3♣, 4♣, 5♣, 6♣, 7♣

Output:
    Draw (equal straight flushes)
```

Case 5: Undecided

```
Inputs:
    Alice: 3♠, 3♣, 5♠, 6♠, 7♠
    Bob: 3♣, 4♣, 6♣, 6♥, 7♣

Output:
    Not implemented yet.
```

With these examples, we're ready to start writing our first test!

First test

Based on our previous analysis, our first test is the following:

Case 1: Alice wins

```
Inputs:
 Alice: 2♠, 3♠, 4♠, 5♠, 6♠
 Bob: 2♣, 4♦, 7♥, 9♠, A♥

Output:
 Alice wins with straight flush
```

Let's write it! We expect this test to fail, so we can do whatever we want at this point. We need to initialize two hands with the preceding card. For now, we will use `vector<string>` to represent each hand. Then, we will call a function (that doesn't exist yet) that we imagine will, at some point, implement the comparison between the two hands. Finally, we check the result against the expected output message that was previously defined:

```
TEST_CASE("Alice wins with straight flush"){
    vector<string> aliceHand{"2♠", "3♠", "4♠", "5♠", "6♠"};
    vector<string> bobHand{"2♣", "4♦", "7♥", "9♠", "A♥"};

    auto result = comparePokerHands(aliceHand, bobHand);

    CHECK_EQ("Alice wins with straight flush", result);
}
```

For now, this test doesn't compile because we haven't even created the `comparePokerHands` function. Time to move forward.

Making the first test pass

Let's first write the function. The function needs to return something, so we'll just return the empty string for now:

```
auto comparePokerHands = [](const auto& aliceHand, const auto& bobHand){
    return "";
};
```

What would be the simplest implementation that makes the test pass? This is the point where TDD gets weirder. The simplest implementation to make the test pass is to return the expected result as a hardcoded value:

```
auto comparePokerHands = [](const auto& aliceHand, const auto& bobHand){
    return "Alice wins with straight flush";
};
```

At this point, my compiler complains because I turned all warnings on, and I report all warnings as errors. The compiler notices that we don't use the two arguments and complains. This is a valid complaint, but I plan to start using the arguments soon. The C++ language gives us an easy fix—just remove or comment out the parameter names, as shown in the following code:

```
auto comparePokerHands = [](const auto& /*aliceHand*/, const auto&
    /*bobHand*/){
        return "Alice wins with straight flush";
};
```

We run the tests, and our first test passes! Cool, something works!

Refactoring

Is there anything to refactor? Well, we have two commented argument names, and I would normally remove them because commented code is just clutter. But, I've decided to keep them there for now, knowing that we will soon use them.

We also have a duplication—the same `Alice wins with straight flush` string appears in both the test and the implementation. Would it be worth extracting it as a constant or common variable? If this was the end of our implementation, then sure. But I know that the string is actually built from multiple things—the name of the winning player, and the rule based on which hand wins. I'd like to keep this as it is for a while.

Therefore, there is nothing to refactor. So, let's move on!

Think (again)

The current implementation feels underwhelming. Just returning a hardcoded value doesn't solve much. Or does it?

This is the mindset change needed when you're learning TDD. I know it because I went through it. I was so used to looking at the end result, comparing this solution with what I'm trying to accomplish feels underwhelming. However, there's a different way to look at it—we have something that works, and we have the simplest possible implementation. There's still a long time to go, but we can already demonstrate something to our stakeholders. Also, as we'll see, we'll always build on solid ground since the code we write is fully tested. These two things are incredibly liberating; I can only hope you will feel the same when trying out TDD.

But, what do we do next? We have a few options.

Firstly, we could write another test in which Alice wins with a straight flush. However, that won't change anything in the implementation, and the test will immediately pass. While this seems to go against the TDD cycle, there's nothing wrong with adding more tests for our piece of mind. Definitely a valid option.

Secondly, we could move to the next test in which Bob wins with a straight flush. This will definitely change a few things.

Both options are good, and you can pick either of them. But since we want to see DDT in practice, let's write more tests first.

More tests

It's quite easy to turn our test into a DDT and add more cases. We will just vary the values of the Alice hand, while keeping Bob's hand intact. The result is as follows:

```
TEST_CASE("Alice wins with straight flush"){
    vector<string> aliceHand;
    const vector<string> bobHand {"2♣", "4♦", "7♥", "9♠", "A♥"};

    SUBCASE("2 based straight flush"){
        aliceHand = {"2♠", "3♠", "4♠", "5♠", "6♠"};
    };
    SUBCASE("3 based straight flush"){
        aliceHand = {"3♠", "4♠", "5♠", "6♠", "7♠"};
    };
    SUBCASE("4 based straight flush"){
        aliceHand = {"4♠", "5♠", "6♠", "7♠", "8♠"};
    };
    SUBCASE("10 based straight flush"){
        aliceHand = {"T♠", "J♠", "Q♠", "K♠", "A♠"};
    };
```

```
CAPTURE(aliceHand);

auto result = comparePokerHands(aliceHand, bobHand);

CHECK_EQ("Alice wins with straight flush", result);
}
```

Once again, all these tests pass. Time to move on to our next test.

Second test

The second test we've described is when Bob wins with a straight flush:

```
Case: Bob wins

Inputs:
 Alice: 2♠, 3♠, 4♠, 5♠, 9♠
 Bob: 2♣, 3♣, 4♣, 5♣, 6♣

Output:
 Bob wins with straight flush
```

Let's write it! And this time, let's use the data-driven format from the start:

```
TEST_CASE("Bob wins with straight flush"){
    const vector<string> aliceHand{"2♠", "3♠", "4♠", "5♠", "9♠"};
    vector<string> bobHand;

    SUBCASE("2 based straight flush"){
        bobHand = {"2♣", "3♣", "4♣", "5♣", "6♣"};
    };

    CAPTURE(bobHand);

    auto result = comparePokerHands(aliceHand, bobHand);

    CHECK_EQ("Bob wins with straight flush", result);
}
```

When we run this test, it fails, for a simple reason—we have a hardcoded implementation that says that Alice wins. What now?

Making the test pass

Once again, we need to find the simplest way to make this test pass. Even if we won't like the implementation, the next step is about cleaning up the mess. So, what would the simplest implementation be?

We obviously need to introduce a conditional statement in our implementation. The question is, what should we check?

Once again, we have a few options. One option is to fake it once more, using something as simple as comparing Bob's hand with the exact hand we expect to win:

```
auto comparePokerHands = [](const vector<string>& /*aliceHand*/, const
vector<string>& bobHand){
    const vector<string> winningBobHand {"2♣", "3♣", "4♣", "5♣", "6♣"};
    if(bobHand == winningBobHand){
        return "Bob wins with straight flush";
    }
    return "Alice wins with straight flush";
};
```

To make it compile, we also had to make the type of the `vector<string>` hands appear everywhere. Once these changes are made, the tests pass.

Our second option is to start implementing the actual check for a straight flush. However, that is a small problem in itself, and to do it properly requires more tests.

I will go with the first option for now, refactor, and then start looking deeper into the implementation of the check for a straight flush.

Refactor

Is there anything to refactor? We still have a duplication in strings. Moreover, we've added a duplication to the vector containing Bob's hand. But we expect both to go away quite soon.

However, another thing is bothering me—`vector<string>` appears everywhere. Let's remove this duplication by naming the `vector<string>` type for what it is—`Hand`:

```
using Hand = vector<string>;

auto comparePokerHands = [](const Hand& /*aliceHand*/, const Hand&
bobHand){
    Hand winningBobHand {"2♣", "3♣", "4♣", "5♣", "6♣"};
    if(bobHand == winningBobHand){
```

```
            return "Bob wins with straight flush";
        }
        return "Alice wins with straight flush";
};

TEST_CASE("Bob wins with straight flush"){
    Hand aliceHand{"2♠", "3♠", "4♠", "5♠", "9♠"};
    Hand bobHand;

    SUBCASE("2 based straight flush"){
        bobHand = {"2♣", "3♣", "4♣", "5♣", "6♣"};
    };

    CAPTURE(bobHand);

    auto result = comparePokerHands(aliceHand, bobHand);

    CHECK_EQ("Bob wins with straight flush", result);
}
```

Think

Time to think again. We have two cases implemented with hardcoded values. That's not a big problem for Alice winning with a straight flush, but it is a problem if we add another test case for Bob with a different set of cards. We could go on for a few more tests, but inevitably, we'll need to actually check for the straight flush. I think now is as good a time as any.

So, what is a straight flush? It's a set of five cards that have the same suit and consecutive values. We need a function that can take a set of five cards and return `true` if it's a straight flush, or `false` if not. Let's write down a few examples:

- Input: 2♣ 3♣ 4♣ 5♣ 6♣ => Output: `true`
- Input: 2♠ 3♠ 4♠ 5♠ 6♠ => Output: `true`
- Input: T♠ J♠ Q♠ K♠ A♠ => Output: `true`
- Input: 2♣ 3♣ 4♣ 5♣ 7♣ => Output: `false`
- Input: 2♣ 3♣ 4♣ 5♣ 6♠ => Output: `false`
- Input: 2♣ 3♣ 4♣ 5♣ => Output: `false` (only four cards, need exactly five)
- Input: [empty vector] => Output: `false` (no cards, need exactly five)
- Input: 2♣ 3♣ 4♣ 5♣ 6♣ 7♣ => Output: `false` (six cards, need exactly five)

You will notice that we also considered edge cases and weird situations. We have enough information to continue, so let's write the next test.

Next test – simple straight flush

I prefer to start from the positive cases, since they tend to advance the implementation more. Let's see the simplest one:

- Input: 2♣ 3♣ 4♣ 5♣ 6♣ => Output: `true`

The test appears as follows:

```
TEST_CASE("Hand is straight flush"){
    Hand hand;

    SUBCASE("2 based straight flush"){
        hand = {"2♣", "3♣", "4♣", "5♣", "6♣"};
    };

    CAPTURE(hand);

    CHECK(isStraightFlush(hand));
}
```

Once again, the test doesn't compile because we have no `isStraightFlush` function implemented. But the test is right, and it's failing, so it's time to move on.

Making the test pass

Once again, the first step is to write the body of the function and to return the expected hardcoded value:

```
auto isStraightFlush = [](const Hand&){
    return true;
};
```

We ran the tests and they passed, so we're done for now!

Moving forward

Well, you can see where this is going. We can either add some more inputs for a correct straight flush, but they won't change the implementation. The first test that will force us to advance the implementation is our first example of a set of cards that isn't a straight flush.

For the goals of this chapter, I will fast forward. However, I strongly advise you to go through all the small steps by yourself and compare your result with mine. The only way to learn TDD is to practice it by yourself and reflect on your methods.

Implementing isStraightFlush

Let's look at what we're trying to accomplish again—a straight flush, which is defined by having exactly five cards with the same suit and consecutive values. We just need to express these three conditions in code:

```
auto isStraightFlush = [](const Hand& hand){
    return has5Cards(hand) &&
        isSameSuit(allSuits(hand)) &&
        areValuesConsecutive(allValuesInOrder(hand));
};
```

The implementation is helped by a number of different lambdas. First, to check the length of the formation, we use has5Cards:

```
auto has5Cards = [](const Hand& hand){
    return hand.size() == 5;
};
```

Then, to check that it has the same suit, we use allSuits to extract the suits from the hand, isSuitEqual to compare two suits, and isSameSuit to check that all suits from a hand are the same:

```
using Card = string;
auto suitOf = [](const Card& card){
    return card.substr(1);
};

auto allSuits = [](Hand hand){
    return transformAll<vector<string>>(hand, suitOf);
};

auto isSameSuit = [](const vector<string>& allSuits){
    return std::equal(allSuits.begin() + 1, allSuits.end(),
        allSuits.begin());
};
```

Finally, to verify that the values are consecutive, we use `valueOf` to extract the values from a card, `allValuesInOrder` to get all the values from a hand and sort them, `toRange` to create a range of consecutive values starting from an initial value, and `areValuesConsecutive` to check that the values from a hand are consecutive:

```
auto valueOf = [](const Card& card){
    return charsToCardValues.at(card.front());
};

auto allValuesInOrder = [](const Hand& hand){
    auto theValues = transformAll<vector<int>>(hand, valueOf);
    sort(theValues.begin(), theValues.end());
    return theValues;
};

auto toRange = [](const auto& collection, const int startValue){
    vector<int> range(collection.size());
    iota(begin(range), end(range), startValue);
    return range;
};

auto areValuesConsecutive = [](const vector<int>& allValuesInOrder){
    vector<int> consecutiveValues = toRange(allValuesInOrder,
        allValuesInOrder.front());

    return consecutiveValues == allValuesInOrder;
};
```

The final piece of the puzzle is a map from `char` to `int` that helps us to translate all the card values, including `T`, `J`, `Q`, `K`, and `A`, into numbers:

```
const std::map<char, int> charsToCardValues = {
    {'1', 1},
    {'2', 2},
    {'3', 3},
    {'4', 4},
    {'5', 5},
    {'6', 6},
    {'7', 7},
    {'8', 8},
    {'9', 9},
    {'T', 10},
    {'J', 11},
    {'Q', 12},
    {'K', 13},
    {'A', 14},
};
```

Let's also see our tests (which are obviously all passing). First, the ones for a valid straight flush; we'll check straight flushes starting with 2, 3, 4, and 10, and how they vary along the data interval:

```
TEST_CASE("Hand is straight flush"){
    Hand hand;

    SUBCASE("2 based straight flush"){
        hand = {"2♣", "3♣", "4♣", "5♣", "6♣"};
    };

    SUBCASE("3 based straight flush"){
        hand = {"3♣", "4♣", "5♣", "6♣", "7♣"};
    };

    SUBCASE("4 based straight flush"){
        hand = {"4♣", "5♣", "6♣", "7♣", "8♣"};
    };

    SUBCASE("4 based straight flush on hearts"){
        hand = {"4♥", "5♥", "6♥", "7♥", "8♥"};
    };

    SUBCASE("10 based straight flush on hearts"){
        hand = {"T♥", "J♥", "Q♥", "K♥", "A♥"};
    };


    CAPTURE(hand);

    CHECK(isStraightFlush(hand));
}
```

Finally, the tests for a set of cards that is not a valid straight flush. For input, we'll use hands that are almost a straight flush, except for being from another suit, not having enough cards, or having too many cards:

```
TEST_CASE("Hand is not straight flush"){
    Hand hand;

    SUBCASE("Would be straight flush except for one card from another
        suit"){
            hand = {"2♣", "3♣", "4♣", "5♣", "6♠"};
    };

    SUBCASE("Would be straight flush except not enough cards"){
        hand = {"2♣", "3♣", "4♣", "5♣"};
```

```
    };

    SUBCASE("Would be straight flush except too many cards"){
        hand = {"2♣", "3♣", "4♣", "5♣", "6♣", "7♠"};
    };

    SUBCASE("Empty hand"){
        hand = {};
    };

    CAPTURE(hand);

    CHECK(!isStraightFlush(hand));
}
```

It's now time to get back to our main problem—comparing the poker hands.

Plugging the check for straight flush back into comparePokerHands

Despite everything we have implemented hitherto, our implementation of comparePokerHands is still hardcoded. Let's remember its current status:

```
auto comparePokerHands = [](const Hand& /*aliceHand*/, const Hand&
bobHand){
    const Hand winningBobHand {"2♣", "3♣", "4♣", "5♣", "6♣"};
    if(bobHand == winningBobHand){
        return "Bob wins with straight flush";
    }
    return "Alice wins with straight flush";
};
```

But, we now have a way of checking for a straight flush! So, let's plug our implementation in:

```
auto comparePokerHands = [](Hand /*aliceHand*/, Hand bobHand){
    if(isStraightFlush(bobHand)) {
        return "Bob wins with straight flush";
    }
    return "Alice wins with straight flush";
};
```

All our tests pass, so we're almost done. Time to add a few more tests to our `Bob wins with straight flush` case to be certain that we haven't missed things. We'll keep the same hand for Alice, an almost straight flush, and vary Bob's hand from 2, 3, and 10-based straight flushes:

```
TEST_CASE("Bob wins with straight flush"){
    Hand aliceHand{"2♠", "3♠", "4♠", "5♠", "9♠"};
    Hand bobHand;

    SUBCASE("2 based straight flush"){
        bobHand = {"2♣", "3♣", "4♣", "5♣", "6♣"};
    };

    SUBCASE("3 based straight flush"){
        bobHand = {"3♣", "4♣", "5♣", "6♣", "7♣"};
    };

    SUBCASE("10 based straight flush"){
        bobHand = {"T♣", "J♣", "Q♣", "K♣", "A♣"};
    };

    CAPTURE(bobHand);

    auto result = comparePokerHands(aliceHand, bobHand);

    CHECK_EQ("Bob wins with straight flush", result);
}
```

All the previous tests pass. So, we're done with two cases—when either Alice or Bob have a straight flush and their competitor doesn't. Time to move to the next case.

Comparing two straight flushes

As we discussed in the beginning of this section, there's another case when both Alice and Bob have straight flushes, but Alice wins with a higher one:

```
Case: Alice wins with a higher straight flush

Inputs:
 Alice: 3♠, 4♠, 5♠, 6♠, 7♠
 Bob: 2♣, 3♣, 4♣, 5♣, 6♣

Output:
 Alice wins with straight flush
```

Let's write the test and run it:

```
TEST_CASE("Alice and Bob have straight flushes but Alice wins with higher
straight flush"){
    Hand aliceHand;
    Hand bobHand{"2♣", "3♣", "4♣", "5♣", "6♣"};

    SUBCASE("3 based straight flush"){
        aliceHand = {"3♠", "4♠", "5♠", "6♠", "7♠"};
    };

    CAPTURE(aliceHand);

    auto result = comparePokerHands(aliceHand, bobHand);

    CHECK_EQ("Alice wins with straight flush", result);
}
```

The test fails, because our `comparePokerHands` function returns that Bob won instead of Alice. Let's fix this with the simplest implementation:

```
auto comparePokerHands = [](const Hand& aliceHand, const Hand& bobHand){
    if(isStraightFlush(bobHand) && isStraightFlush(aliceHand)){
        return "Alice wins with straight flush";
    }

    if(isStraightFlush(bobHand)) {
        return "Bob wins with straight flush";
    }

    return "Alice wins with straight flush";
};
```

Our implementation decides that Alice always wins if both Alice and Bob have a straight flush. That's obviously not what we want, but the tests pass. So, what test can we write to push the implementation forward?

Think

It turns out that we missed one case from our previous analysis. We looked at what happens when both Alice and Bob have straight flushes and Alice wins; but what about when Bob has a higher straight flush? Let's write down an example:

Case: Bob wins with a higher straight flush

Inputs:

```
Alice: 3♠, 4♠, 5♠, 6♠, 7♠
Bob: 4♣, 5♣, 6♣, 7♣, 8♣
```

```
Output:
Bob wins with straight flush
```

Time to write another failing test.

Comparing two straight flushes (continued)

The test is fairly obvious to write by now:

```
TEST_CASE("Alice and Bob have straight flushes but Bob wins with higher
    straight flush"){
        Hand aliceHand = {"3♠", "4♠", "5♠", "6♠", "7♠"};
        Hand bobHand;

        SUBCASE("3 based straight flush"){
            bobHand = {"4♣", "5♣", "6♣", "7♣", "8♣"};
    };

    CAPTURE(bobHand);

    auto result = comparePokerHands(aliceHand, bobHand);

    CHECK_EQ("Bob wins with straight flush", result);
}
```

The test fails again, because our implementation assumes that Alice always wins when both Alice and Bob have straight flushes. It might be time to check which is the highest straight flush of them.

To do so, we will need once again to write down a few cases and go through our TDD cycles. Once again, I will fast forward to the implementation. We end up with the following helper function that compares two straight flushes. It returns 1 if the first hand has a higher straight flush, 0 if the two are equal, and −1 if the second hand is a higher straight flush:

```
auto compareStraightFlushes = [](const Hand& first, const Hand& second){
    int firstHandValue = allValuesInOrder(first).front();
    int secondHandValue = allValuesInOrder(second).front();
    if(firstHandValue > secondHandValue) return 1;
    if(secondHandValue > firstHandValue) return -1;
    return 0;
};
```

And, by changing our implementation, we can make the tests pass:

```
auto comparePokerHands = [](const Hand& aliceHand, const Hand& bobHand){
    if(isStraightFlush(bobHand) && isStraightFlush(aliceHand)){
        int whichIsHigher = compareStraightFlushes(aliceHand, bobHand);
        if(whichIsHigher == 1) return "Alice wins with straight flush";
        if(whichIsHigher == -1) return "Bob wins with straight flush";
    }

    if(isStraightFlush(bobHand)) {
        return "Bob wins with straight flush";
    }

    return "Alice wins with straight flush";
};
```

This leaves us with the final case—a draw. The test is once again quite clear:

```
TEST_CASE("Draw due to equal straight flushes"){
    Hand aliceHand;
    Hand bobHand;

    SUBCASE("3 based straight flush"){
        aliceHand = {"3♠", "4♠", "5♠", "6♠", "7♠"};
    };

    CAPTURE(aliceHand);
    bobHand = aliceHand;

    auto result = comparePokerHands(aliceHand, bobHand);

    CHECK_EQ("Draw", result);
}
```

And the change in implementation is fairly straightforward:

```
auto comparePokerHands = [](Hand aliceHand, Hand bobHand){
    if(isStraightFlush(bobHand) && isStraightFlush(aliceHand)){
        int whichIsHigher = compareStraightFlushes(aliceHand, bobHand);
        if(whichIsHigher == 1) return "Alice wins with straight flush";
        if(whichIsHigher == -1) return "Bob wins with straight flush";
        return "Draw";
    }

    if(isStraightFlush(bobHand)) {
        return "Bob wins with straight flush";
    }
```

```
      return "Alice wins with straight flush";
};
```

This is not the prettiest function, but it passes all our tests for straight flush comparison. We can definitely refactor it into smaller functions, but I'll stop here since we've reached our goal—we've designed not only one, but multiple, pure functions using TDD and DDT.

Summary

In this chapter, you've learned how to write unit tests, how to write data-driven tests, and how to use data-driven tests combined with TDD to design pure functions.

TDD is one of the core practices of effective software development. While it may seem weird and counterintuitive at times, it has a strong advantage—every few minutes, you have something working that you can demo. A passing test is not only a demo point, but also a save point. If anything wrong happens while trying to refactor or to implement the following test, you can always go back to the last save point. I find this practice even more valuable in C++, where so many things can go wrong. In fact, I wrote all the code since Chapter 3, *Deep Dive into Lambdas*, with a TDD approach. This has been immensely helpful, since I know that my code is working—something that is quite difficult to do when writing a technical book without this method. I strongly advise you to look more into TDD and practice it for yourself; it's the only way you'll become proficient.

TDD with functional programming is a perfect fit. When using it with imperative object-oriented code, we often need to take into account mutation and it makes things more difficult. With pure functions and data-driven tests, the practice of adding more tests becomes as simple as it can be, and allows us to focus on implementation. With the support of functional operations, making a test pass becomes easier in many situations. I personally find this combination incredibly rewarding; I hope you'll find it equally useful.

Now it's time to move forward and revisit another section of software design—design patterns. Do they change with functional programming? (Spoiler alert—they actually become much simpler.) This is what we will discuss in the next chapter.

Section 3: Reaping the Benefits of Functional Programming

3

We have learned a lot about the building blocks of functional programming, how to write them in C++, and how to use them to build function-centric design. It's time to look at a few specialized topics strongly related to functional programming.

First, we'll dive into the huge topic of performance optimization. We'll learn a few optimization techniques that fit particularly well with pure functions (for example, memoization and tail recursion optimization). We will look at both memory footprint and execution time optimization, carry out many measurements, and compare approaches.

Then, we will look into how functional programming enables parallel and asynchronous execution. Immutability leads to the avoidance of shared state, therefore, to simpler patterns of parallel execution.

But we can take advantage of more functional programming. Data generators and pure functions enable an automated testing paradigm called **property-based testing**, which allows us to check, with very little code, many possible scenarios. Then, if we need to refactor complex existing code, we will see that we can first refactor it to pure functions, quickly write tests for them, and then decide whether to redistribute them into classes or preserve them.

Finally, we'll go one level higher, to an architectural paradigm based on immutable state and, therefore, something that is closely connected to functional programming: event sourcing.

The following chapters will be covered in this section:

- Chapter 10, *Performance Optimization*
- Chapter 11, *Property-Based Testing*
- Chapter 12, *Refactoring to and through Pure Functions*
- Chapter 13, *Immutability and Architecture - Event Sourcing*

Performance Optimization **10**

Performance is one of the key drivers for choosing C++ as a programming language for a project. The time has come to discuss how we can improve performance when we're structuring code in a functional style.

While performance is a huge topic that we obviously can't completely cover in one chapter, we will look at key ideas for improving performance, how purely functional languages optimize performance, and how to translate these optimizations into C++.

The following topics will be covered in this chapter:

- A process for delivering performance
- How to use parallel/async to improve performance
- Understanding what tail recursion is and how to activate it
- How to improve memory consumption when using functional constructs
- Functional asynchronous code

Technical requirements

You will need a compiler that supports C++ 17. I used GCC 7.3.0.

The code can be found on GitHub at `https://github.com/PacktPublishing/Hands-On-Functional-Programming-with-Cpp` in the `Chapter10` folder. It includes and uses `doctest`, which is a single-header open source unit testing library. You can find it on its GitHub repository at `https://github.com/onqtam/doctest`.

Performance optimization

Talking about performance optimization is like talking about pizza. Some people like and search for pizza with pineapple. Others only eat traditional Italian pizzas (or from a specific region). Some only eat vegetarian pizza, while others like all kinds of pizza. The point is, performance optimization is contextual to your code base and your product. What kind of performance are you looking at? What is the most valuable part of performance for your users? And what constraints do you need to take into account?

The customers I work with usually have a few performance requirements, depending on the topic:

- *Embedded products* (for example, automotive, energy, or telecommunications) often need to work within memory constraints. The stack and the heap are often small, thus limiting the number of long-lived variables. The cost of increasing memory can be prohibitive (one customer told us they would need more than 10 million euros for an extra 1 MB of memory on all of their devices). Therefore, programmers need to work around these limitations by avoiding unnecessary memory allocation whenever possible. This can include initialization, passing arguments by copy (especially larger structures), and avoiding specific algorithms that require memory consumption, among others.
- *Engineering applications* (for example computer-aided design or CAD) need to use specific algorithms derived from math, physics, and engineering on very large datasets and return results as quickly as possible. Processing is usually done on modern PCs, so RAM is less of a problem; however, the CPU is. With the advent of multi-core CPUs, specialized GPUs that can take over part of the processing and cloud technologies that allow the distribution of workloads between multiple powerful or specialized servers, the job of developers often becomes optimizing for speed in a parallel and asynchronous world.
- *Desktop games and game engines* have their own particular concerns. The graphics have to look as good as possible to gracefully scale down on middle- or lower-end machines and avoid lag. Games usually take over the machine they run on, so they only need to fight for resources with the operating system and the system applications (such as antiviruses or firewalls). They can also assume a specific level of GPU, CPU, and RAM. Optimization becomes about parallelism (since multiple cores are expected) and about avoiding waste in order to keep a smooth experience throughout the gameplay.

- *Game servers*, however, are a different beast. Services such as Blizzard's Battle.net (the one I'm using a lot as a *Starcraft II* player) are required to respond quickly, even under stress. The number of servers used and their power doesn't really matter in the age of cloud computing; we can easily scale them up or down. The main concern is responding as quickly as possible to a mostly I/O workload.

- *The future is exciting*. The tendency in games is to move processing to the servers, thus allowing gamers to play even on lower-end machines. This will open up amazing opportunities for future games. (What could you do with 10 GPUs instead of one? What about with 100?)But will also lead to the need to optimize the game engine for server-side, multi-machine, parallel processing. To move away from gaming, the IoT industry opens up even more opportunities for embedded software and scalable server-side processing.

Given all these possibilities, what can we do to deliver performance in a code base?

A process for delivering performance

As you can see, performance optimization depends a lot on what you're trying to achieve. The next steps can be quickly summarized as such:

1. Define a clear goal for performance, including the metrics and how to measure them.
2. Define a few coding guidelines for performance. Keep them clear and tailored to specific parts of the code.
3. Make the code work.
4. Measure and improve performance where needed.
5. Monitor and improve.

Before we look into each of these steps in more detail, it's important to understand one important caveat of performance optimization—there are two types of optimization. The first comes from clean designs and clean code. For example, by removing certain types of similarity from your code, you may end up reducing the size of the executable, thus allowing more space for data; the data may end up traveling less through the code, thus avoiding unnecessary copies or indirections; or, it will allow the compiler to understand the code better and optimize it for you. From my experience, refactoring code towards simple design has also often improved performance.

The second way to improve performance is by using point optimizations. These are very specific ways in which we can rewrite a function or a flow that allows the code to work faster or with less memory consumption, usually for a specific compiler and platform. The resulting code often looks smart but is difficult to understand and difficult to change.

Point optimizations have a natural conflict with writing code that's easy to change and maintain. This has famously led to Donald Knuth saying that *premature optimization is the root of all evil*. This doesn't mean that we should write code that's obviously slow, such as passing large collections by copy. It does mean, however, that we should first optimize the design for changeability, then measure performance, then optimize it, and only use point optimizations if absolutely necessary. Quirks in the platform, a specific compiler version, or libraries that are used may require point optimizations from time to time; keep them separate and use them scarcely.

Let's look now into our process for optimizing performance.

Define a clear goal for performance, including the metrics and how to measure them

If we don't know where we're going, it doesn't matter in which direction we go—I'm paraphrasing from Alice in the Wonderland. We should, therefore, know where we're going. We need a list of performance metrics that fit the needs of our product. In addition, for each of the performance metrics, we need a range that defines what is a *good* value for the metric and what is an *acceptable* value. Let's look at a few examples.

If you're building an *embedded product* for a device with 4 MB of memory, you might look at metrics such as:

- Memory consumption:
    - Great: 1-3 MB
    - Good: 3-4 MB
- Device boot time:
    - Great: < 1s
    - Good: 1-3s

If you're building a *desktop CAD application* that models the sound waves through a building design, other metrics are interesting.

Computation time for modeling sound waves:

- For a small room:
    - Great: < 1 min
    - Good: < 5 min
- For a medium-sized room:
    - Great: < 2 min
    - Good: < 10 min

The numbers here are illustrative only; you'll need to find your own metrics for your product.

Having these metrics and the good/great ranges allows us to measure performance after a new feature is added and optimize accordingly. It also allows us to simply explain the performance of a product to stakeholders or business people.

Define a few coding guidelines for performance—keep them clear and tailored to specific parts of the code

If you ask 50 different C++ programmers about tips to optimize performance, you'll soon be overwhelmed with advice. If you start investigating the advice, it will turn out that some of it is dated, some of it is very specific, and some is great.

It is, therefore, important to have coding guidelines for performance, but there's a caveat. C++ code bases tend to be huge because they've been developed over many years. If you look critically at your code base, you'll realize that only some parts of the code are bottlenecks for performance. To give an example, computing a mathematical operation 1 ms faster only makes sense if that operation will be called many times; if it's only called once or twice, or very seldom, there's no need to optimize it. In fact, the next version of the compiler or CPU will probably do a better job than you at optimizing it.

Because of this fact, you should understand which parts of your code are critical for the performance criteria that you've defined. Figure out what design fits that particular piece of code best; have clear guidelines, and follow them. While `const&` is useful everywhere, maybe you could avoid wasting the developer's time sorting a very small collection that's only done once.

Make the code work

With these guidelines in mind, and with a new feature to implement, the first step should always be to make the code work. Also, structure it so it's easy to change within your constraints. Don't try to optimize for performance here; once again, the compiler and the CPU might be smarter than you think and do more work than you expect. The only way to know whether that's the case is to measure performance.

Measure and improve performance where needed

Your code works and is structured according to your guidelines and is optimized for change. It's time to write down a few hypotheses about optimizing it and then test them.

Since you have clear metrics for performance, it's relatively easy to verify them. Sure, it requires the correct infrastructure and a proper measurement process. With these in place, you can measure where you stand against your performance metrics.

Additional hypotheses should be welcome here. Something like—*if we restructure this code like this, I expect an improvement in the indicator X.* You can then move on and test your hypothesis—start a branch, change the code, build the product, take it through the performance metrics measurement process, and see the results. Sure, it's more complex than I make it sound—sometimes it may require builds with different compilers, with different optimization options, or statistics. All these are necessary if you want to make an informed decision. It's better to invest some time into metrics over changing the code and making it more difficult to understand. Otherwise, you'll end up with a technical debt on which you'll pay interest for a long time.

However, if you have to do point optimizations, there's no workaround. Just make sure to document them in as much detail as possible. Since you've tested your hypothesis before, you'll have a lot to write, won't you?

Monitor and improve

We started the loop by defining metrics for performance. It's time to close it—we need to monitor those metrics (and possibly others) and adjust our intervals and coding guidelines based on what we've learned. Performance optimization is a continuous process because the target devices evolve as well.

We've looked at a process for delivering performance, but how does this relate to functional programming? Which use cases make functional code structures shine, and which don't work so well? It's time to look deeper into our code structures.

Parallelism – taking advantage of immutability

Writing code that runs in parallel has been the source of much pain in software development. It seems like the problems arising from multithreaded, multi-process, or multi-server environments are fundamentally difficult to solve. Deadlocks, starvation, data races, locks, or debugging multi-threaded code are just a few terms that make those of us who've seen them afraid of ever meeting them again. However, we have to face parallel code because of multi-core CPUs, GPUs, and multiple servers. Can functional programming help with this?

Everyone agrees that this is one of the strong points of functional programming, specifically derived from immutability. If your data never changes, there are no locks and the synchronization is so simple that it can be generalized. If you just use pure functions and functional transformations (barring I/O, of course), you get parallelization (almost) for free.

In fact, the C++ 17 standard includes execution policies for the STL higher-level functions, allowing us to change the algorithm from sequential to parallel with just one parameter. Let's check whether all numbers from a vector are greater than 5 in parallel. We just need to use `execution::par` as the execution policy for `all_of`:

```
auto aVector = {1, 2, 3, 4, 5, 6, 7, 8, 9, 10};
auto all_of_parallel = [&aVector](){
    return all_of(execution::par, aVector.begin(), aVector.end(),
        [](auto value){return value > 5;});
};
```

We can then measure the difference between using the sequential and the parallel version of the algorithm with the high-resolution timer from the `chrono` namespace, as seen here:

```
auto measureExecutionTimeForF = [](auto f){
    auto t1 = high_resolution_clock::now();
    f();
    auto t2 = high_resolution_clock::now();
    chrono::nanoseconds duration = t2 - t1;
    return duration;
};
```

Normally, I would now show you the difference in execution based on my experiments. Unfortunately, in this case, I can't do this. At the time of writing, the only compilers implementing execution policies are MSVC and Intel C++, but neither of them met the standard. However, as shown in the following snippet, I wrote the code in the `parallelExecution.cpp` source file, allowing you to enable it by uncommenting a line when your compiler supports the standard, as shown here:

```
// At the time when I created this file, only MSVC had implementation
    for execution policies.
// Since you're seeing this in the future, you can enable the parallel
    execution code by uncommenting the following line
//#define PARALLEL_ENABLED
```

The code you will be running when you do this will display the comparative duration for running `all_of` sequentially and in parallel, like this:

```
TEST_CASE("all_of with sequential execution policy"){
    auto aVector = {1, 2, 3, 4, 5, 6, 7, 8, 9, 10};

    auto all_of_sequential = [&aVector](){
        return all_of(execution::seq, aVector.begin(), aVector.end(),
            [](auto value){return value > 5;});
    };

    auto sequentialDuration =
        measureExecutionTimeForF(all_of_sequential);
        cout << "Execution time for sequential policy:" <<
            sequentialDuration.count() << " ns" << endl;

    auto all_of_parallel = [&aVector](){
        return all_of(execution::par, aVector.begin(), aVector.end(),
            [](auto value){return value > 5;});
    };

    auto parallelDuration = measureExecutionTimeForF(all_of_parallel);
    cout << "Execution time for parallel policy:" <<
        parallelDuration.count() << " ns" << endl;
}
```

While I would have loved to analyze some execution data here, maybe it's for the best that I can't, since the most important message of this chapter is measure, measure, measure, and, only then, optimize. Hopefully, you'll do some measuring yourself when the time comes.

The C++ 17 standard supports the execution policies for many STL functions, including `sort`, `find`, `copy`, `transform`, and `reduce`. That is, if you're chaining these functions and using pure functions, you just need to pass an extra parameter to all calls (or `bind` the higher-level functions) to achieve parallel execution! I would go as far as to say that this is akin to magic for anyone who has tried managing threads by themselves or debugging weird synchronization issues. In fact, all the code we wrote for Tic-Tac-Toe and Poker Hands in the previous chapters can be easily switched to parallel execution, provided the compiler supports the full C++ 17 standard.

But how does this work? It's fairly easy for `all_of` to run in multiple threads; each of them executes the predicate on a specific element from the collection, a Boolean value is returned, and the process stops when the first predicate returns `False`. This is only possible if the predicate is a pure function; modifying the result or the vector in any way will create race conditions. The documentation specifically states that the programmer is responsible for keeping the predicate function pure—there will be no warning or compilation error. In addition to being pure, your predicate must not assume the order in which the elements are treated.

In case the parallel execution policy cannot be started (for example, due to a lack of resources), the execution will fall back to sequential calls. This is a useful thing to remember when measuring performance: if it's much lower than expected, check first whether the program can execute in parallel.

This option is useful for computation-heavy applications using multiple CPUs. If you're interested in its memory hit, you'll have to measure it, since it depends on the compiler and the standard library that you use.

Memoization

Pure functions have an interesting property. For the same input values, they return the same outputs. This makes them equivalent to a big table of values with an output value corresponding to every combination of values for the input arguments. Sometimes, it's faster to remember parts of this table rather than doing the computation. This technique is called **memoization**.

Pure functional programming languages, as well as languages such as Python and Groovy, have ways to enable memoization on specific function calls, thus providing a high level of control. Unfortunately, C++ doesn't have this facility, so we'll have to write it ourselves.

Implementing memoization

To start our implementation, we will need a function; ideally, computationally expensive. Let's pick the `power` function. A simple implementation is just a wrapper over the standard `pow` function, as shown in the following snippet:

```
function<long long(int, int)> power = [](auto base, auto exponent){
    return pow(base, exponent);
};
```

How do we start to implement memoization? Well, at its core, memoization is caching. Whenever a function is called for the first time, it runs normally but also stores the result in combination with the input values. On subsequent calls, the function will search through the map to see if the value is cached and return it if so.

This means that we'll need a cache that has, as key, the parameters, and, as value, the result of the computation. To group the parameters together, we can simply use a pair or a tuple:

```
tuple<int, int> parameters
```

Therefore, the cache will be:

```
map<tuple<int, int>, long long> cache;
```

Let's change our `power` function to use this cache. First, we need to look in the cache for a result:

```
function<long long(int, int)> memoizedPower = [&cache](int base,
    int exponent){
        tuple<int, int> parameters(base, exponent);
        auto valueIterator = cache.find(parameters);
```

If nothing is found, we compute the result and store it in the cache. If something is found, that's the value we return:

```
if(valueIterator == cache.end()){
    result = pow(base, exponent);
    cache[parameters] = result;
} else{
    result = valueIterator -> second;
}
return result;
```

To check that this method is working fine, let's run some tests:

```
CHECK_EQ(power(1, 1), memoizedPower(1, 1));
CHECK_EQ(power(3, 19), memoizedPower(3, 19));
CHECK_EQ(power(2, 25), memoizedPower(2, 25));
```

Everything works fine. Now let's compare the two versions of power, with and without memoization in the following snippet. The following code shows how we can extract a more generic way to memoize functions:

```
function<long long(int, int)> power = [](int base, int exponent){
    return pow(base, exponent);
};

map<tuple<int, int>, long long> cache;

function<long long(int, int)> memoizedPower = [&cache](int base,
    int exponent){
        tuple<int, int> parameters(base, exponent);
        auto valueIterator = cache.find(parameters);
        long long result;
        if(valueIterator == cache.end()){
        result = pow(base, exponent);
        cache[parameters] = result;
    } else{
        result = valueIterator -> second;
    }
    return result;
};
```

The first observation is that we can replace the bold line with a call to the original power function, so let's do that:

```
function<long long(int, int)> memoizedPower = [&cache, &power](int
    base, int exponent){
        tuple<int, int> parameters(base, exponent);
        auto valueIterator = cache.find(parameters);
        long long result;
        if(valueIterator == cache.end()){
        result = power(base, exponent);
        cache[parameters] = result;
    } else{
        result = valueIterator -> second;
    }
    return result;
};
```

If we pass in the function we need to call during memoization, we obtain a more general solution:

```
auto memoize = [&cache](int base, int exponent, auto
    functionToMemoize){
        tuple<int, int> parameters(base, exponent);
        auto valueIterator = cache.find(parameters);
        long long result;
        if(valueIterator == cache.end()){
        result = functionToMemoize(base, exponent);
        cache[parameters] = result;
    } else{
        result = valueIterator -> second;
    }
    return result;
};
```

```
CHECK_EQ(power(1, 1), memoize(1, 1, power));
CHECK_EQ(power(3, 19), memoize(3, 19, power));
CHECK_EQ(power(2, 25), memoize(2, 25, power));
```

But wouldn't it be nice to return a memoized function instead? We can modify our `memoize` function to receive a function and return a function that is memoized, which receives the same parameters as the initial function:

```
auto memoize = [](auto functionToMemoize){
    map<tuple<int, int>, long long> cache;
    return [&](int base, int exponent) {
        tuple<int, int> parameters(base, exponent);
        auto valueIterator = cache.find(parameters);
        long long result;
        if(valueIterator == cache.end()){
            result = functionToMemoize(base, exponent);
            cache[parameters] = result;
        } else{
            result = valueIterator -> second;
        }
        return result;
        };
};
auto memoizedPower = memoize(power);
```

This change doesn't work initially—I'm getting a segmentation fault. The reason is that we are changing the cache inside the lambda. To make it work, we need to make the lambda mutable and capture by value:

```
auto memoize = [](auto functionToMemoize){
    map<tuple<int, int>, long long> cache;
    return [=](int base, int exponent) mutable {
        tuple<int, int> parameters(base, exponent);
        auto valueIterator = cache.find(parameters);
        long long result;
        if(valueIterator == cache.end()){
            result = functionToMemoize(base, exponent);
            cache[parameters] = result;
        } else{
            result = valueIterator -> second;
        }
        return result;
    };
};
```

We now have a function that can memoize any function with two integer parameters. It's easy to make it more generic with the help of a few type arguments. We need a type for the return value, a type for the first argument, and a type for the second argument:

```
template<typename ReturnType, typename FirstArgType, typename
    SecondArgType>
auto memoizeTwoParams = [](function<ReturnType(FirstArgType,
SecondArgType)> functionToMemoize){
    map<tuple<FirstArgType, SecondArgType>, ReturnType> cache;
    return [=](FirstArgType firstArg, SecondArgType secondArg) mutable {
        tuple<FirstArgType, SecondArgType> parameters(firstArg,
    secondArg);
        auto valueIterator = cache.find(parameters);
        ReturnType result;
        if(valueIterator == cache.end()){
            result = functionToMemoize(firstArg, secondArg);
            cache[parameters] = result;
        } else{
            result = valueIterator -> second;
        }
        return result;
    };
};
```

We have achieved a memoization function for any function that has two arguments. We can do even better. C++ allows us to use templates with an unspecified number of type arguments—so-called **variadic templates**. Using their magic, we end up with an implementation for memoization that works with any function with any number of arguments:

```
template<typename ReturnType, typename... Args>
function<ReturnType(Args...)> memoize(function<ReturnType(Args...)> f){
    map<tuple<Args...>, ReturnType> cache;
    return ([=](Args... args) mutable   {
            tuple<Args...> theArguments(args...);
            auto cached = cache.find(theArguments);
            if(cached != cache.end()) return cached -> second;
            auto result = f(args...);
            cache[theArguments] = result;
            return result;
    });
};
```

This function is helpful for caching any other function; however, there's a catch. We have, until now, used the wrapped implementation of power. The following is an example of what it would look like if we wrote our own instead:

```
function<long long(int, int)> power = [&](auto base, auto exponent)
{
    return (exponent == 0) ? 1 : base * power(base, exponent - 1);
};
```

Memoizing this function will merely cache the final results. However, the function is recursive and the call to our `memoize` function will not memoize the intermediate results from the recursion. To do so, we need to tell our memoized power function not to call the power function but the memoized `power` function.

Unfortunately, there's no easy way to do this. We could pass, as an argument, the function to call recursively, but this would change the original function signature for implementation reasons. Or we could just rewrite the function to take advantage of memoization.

Still, we end up with quite a good solution. Let's put it to the test.

Using memoization

Let's use our `measureExecutionTimeForF` function to measure the time it takes to make various calls to our `power` function. It's time to also think about the results we expect. We do cache the values of repeated calls, but this requires its own processing and memory on every call to the function. So, maybe it will help, maybe it won't. We won't know until we try it:

```
TEST_CASE("Pow vs memoized pow"){
    function<int(int, int)> power = [](auto first, auto second){
        return pow(first, second);
    };

    cout << "Computing pow" << endl;
    printDuration("First call no memoization: ",  [&](){ return
        power(5, 24);});
    printDuration("Second call no memoization: ", [&](){return power(3,
        1024);});
    printDuration("Third call no memoization: ", [&](){return power(9,
        176);});
    printDuration("Fourth call no memoization (same as first call): ",
        [&](){return power(5, 24);});

    auto powerWithMemoization = memoize(power);
    printDuration("First call with memoization: ",  [&](){ return
        powerWithMemoization(5, 24);});
    printDuration("Second call with memoization: ", [&](){return
        powerWithMemoization(3, 1024);});
    printDuration("Third call with memoization: ", [&](){return
        powerWithMemoization(9, 176);});
    printDuration("Fourth call with memoization (same as first call):
        ", [&](){return powerWithMemoization(5, 24);});
    cout << "DONE computing pow" << endl;

    CHECK_EQ(power(5, 24),  powerWithMemoization(5, 24));
    CHECK_EQ(power(3, 1024),  powerWithMemoization(3, 1024));
    CHECK_EQ(power(9, 176),  powerWithMemoization(9, 176));
}
```

This code is calling the `power` function with the same values, with the last call returning to the first values. It then proceeds to do the same, but after creating the memoized version of `power`. Finally, a sanity check—the result of the `power` function and the memoized `power` function are compared to ensure that we don't have a bug in the `memoize` function.

The question is—has memoization improved the time it takes to execute the last call from the series (exactly the same as the first call from the series)? In my configuration, the results are mixed, as shown in the following snippet:

```
Computing pow
First call no memoization: 26421 ns
Second call no memoization: 5207 ns
Third call no memoization: 2058 ns
Fourth call no memoization (same as first call): 179 ns
First call with memoization: 2380 ns
Second call with memoization: 2207 ns
Third call with memoization: 1539 ns
Fourth call with memoization (same as first call): 936 ns
DONE computing pow
```

Alternatively, for a better view (calls without memoization are first), there is the following:

```
First call: 26421 ns > 2380 ns
Second call: 5207 ns > 2207 ns
Third call: 2058 ns > 1539 ns
Fourth call: 179 ns < 936 ns
```

Overall, the calls with memoization are better, except when we repeat the first call. Of course, the results vary when running the test repeatedly, but this shows that improving performance is not as easy as just using caching. What happens behind the scenes? I think that the most likely explanation is that another caching mechanism kicks in—CPU or otherwise.

If anything, this proves the importance of measurements. It's not a surprise that CPUs and compilers already do a fair share of optimizations, and we can only do so much in code.

What if we try recursive memoization? I rewrote the `power` function to use memoization recursively, and it mixes caching with the recursive call. Here's the code:

```
map<tuple<int, int>, long long> cache;
function<long long(int, int)> powerWithMemoization = [&](auto base,
    auto exponent) -> long long{
        if(exponent == 0) return 1;
        long long value;

        tuple<int, int> parameters(base, exponent);
        auto valueIterator = cache.find(parameters);
        if(valueIterator == cache.end()){
        value = base * powerWithMemoization(base, exponent - 1);
        cache[parameters] = value;
        } else {
        value = valueIterator->second;
```

```
    };
    return value;
};
```

When we run it, the results are as follows:

```
Computing pow
First call no memoization: 1761 ns
Second call no memoization: 106994 ns
Third call no memoization: 8718 ns
Fourth call no memoization (same as first call): 1395 ns
First call with recursive memoization: 30921 ns
Second call with recursive memoization: 2427337 ns
Third call with recursive memoization: 482062 ns
Fourth call with recursive memoization (same as first call): 1721 ns
DONE computing pow
```

Alternatively, in a compressed view (calls without memoization are first), there is the following:

```
First call: 1761 ns < 30921 ns
Second call: 106994 ns < 2427337 ns
Third call: 8718 ns < 482062 ns
Fourth call: 1395 ns < 1721 ns
```

As you can see, the time for building the cache is enormous. However, it pays off for repeated calls but it still can't beat the CPU and compiler optimizations in this case.

Does memoization help then? It does when we use a more complex function. Let's next try computing the difference between the factorial of two numbers. We'll use a naive implementation of the factorial, and we'll try to memoize the factorial function first, and then the function computing the difference. For the sake of consistency, we'll use the same pairs of numbers as before. Let's look at the code in the following snippet:

```
TEST_CASE("Factorial difference vs memoized") {
    function<int(int)> fact = [&fact](int n) {
        if(n == 0) return 1;
        return n * fact(n-1);
    };

    function<int(int, int)> factorialDifference = [&fact](auto first,
        auto second) {
            return fact(second) - fact(first);
    };
    cout << "Computing factorial difference" << endl;
    printDuration("First call no memoization: ", [&](){ return
        factorialDifference(5, 24);});
    printDuration("Second call no memoization: ", [&](){return
```

```
                factorialDifference(3, 1024);});
    printDuration("Third call no memoization: ", [&](){return
        factorialDifference(9, 176);});
    printDuration("Fourth call no memoization (same as first call): ",
        [&](){return factorialDifference(5, 24);});

    auto factWithMemoization = memoize(fact);
    function<int(int, int)> factorialMemoizedDifference =
        [&factWithMemoization](auto first, auto second){
        return factWithMemoization(second) -
            factWithMemoization(first);
    };
    printDuration("First call with memoized factorial: ",  [&](){
        return factorialMemoizedDifference(5, 24);});
    printDuration("Second call with memoized factorial: ", [&](){return
        factorialMemoizedDifference(3, 1024);});
    printDuration("Third call with memoized factorial: ", [&](){return
        factorialMemoizedDifference(9, 176);});
    printDuration("Fourth call with memoized factorial (same as first
        call): ", [&](){return factorialMemoizedDifference(5, 24);});

    auto factorialDifferenceWithMemoization =
        memoize(factorialDifference);
    printDuration("First call with memoization: ",  [&](){ return
        factorialDifferenceWithMemoization(5, 24);});
    printDuration("Second call with memoization: ", [&](){return
        factorialDifferenceWithMemoization(3, 1024);});
    printDuration("Third call with memoization: ", [&](){return
        factorialDifferenceWithMemoization(9, 176);});
    printDuration("Fourth call with memoization (same as first call):
        ", [&](){return factorialDifferenceWithMemoization(5, 24);});

    cout << "DONE computing factorial difference" << endl;

    CHECK_EQ(factorialDifference(5, 24),
        factorialMemoizedDifference(5, 24));
    CHECK_EQ(factorialDifference(3, 1024),
        factorialMemoizedDifference(3, 1024));
    CHECK_EQ(factorialDifference(9, 176),
        factorialMemoizedDifference(9, 176));

    CHECK_EQ(factorialDifference(5, 24),
        factorialDifferenceWithMemoization(5, 24));
    CHECK_EQ(factorialDifference(3, 1024),
        factorialDifferenceWithMemoization(3, 1024));
    CHECK_EQ(factorialDifference(9, 176),
        factorialDifferenceWithMemoization(9, 176));
}
```

What are the results? Let's first see the difference between the normal function, and the function using the memoized factorial:

```
Computing factorial difference
First call no memoization: 1727 ns
Second call no memoization: 79908 ns
Third call no memoization: 8037 ns
Fourth call no memoization (same as first call): 1539 ns
First call with memoized factorial: 4672 ns
Second call with memoized factorial: 41183 ns
Third call with memoized factrorial: 10029 ns
Fourth call with memoized factorial (same as first call): 1105 ns
```

Let's compare them side by side once again:

```
First call: 1727 ns < 4672 ns
Second call: 79908 ns > 41183 ns
Third call: 8037 ns < 10029 ns
Fourth call: 1539 ns > 1105 ns
```

Although the result is mixed for the other calls, there's a ~20% improvement with the memoized function over the non-memoized function when hitting the cached value. That seems a small improvement since factorial is recursive, so, in theory, the memoization should help immensely. However, *we did not memoize the recursion*. Instead, the factorial function is still calling the non-memoized version recursively. We'll come back to this later; for now, let's check what happens when memoizing the factorialDifference function:

```
First call no memoization: 1727 ns
Second call no memoization: 79908 ns
Third call no memoization: 8037 ns
Fourth call no memoization (same as first call): 1539 ns
First call with memoization: 2363 ns
Second call with memoization: 39700 ns
Third call with memoization: 8678 ns
Fourth call with memoization (same as first call): 704 ns
```

Let's look at the results side by side:

```
First call: 1727 ns < 2363 ns
Second call: 79908 ns > 39700 ns
Third call: 8037 ns < 8678 ns
Fourth call: 1539 ns > 704 ns
```

The memoized version is twice as fast as the non-memoized one on the cached value! This is huge! However, we pay for this improvement with a performance hit when we don't have the value cached. Also, something weird is going on at the second call; some kind of caching may interfere with our results.

Can we make this better by optimizing all the recursions of the factorial function? Let's see. We need to change our factorial function such that the cache applies to each call. In order to do this, we'll need to call the memoized factorial function recursively instead of the normal factorial function, as shown in the following:

```
map<int, int> cache;
function<int(int)> recursiveMemoizedFactorial =
    [&recursiveMemoizedFactorial, &cache](int n) mutable{
    auto value = cache.find(n);
    if(value != cache.end()) return value->second;
    int result;

    if(n == 0)
        result = 1;
    else
        result = n * recursiveMemoizedFactorial(n-1);

    cache[n] = result;
    return result;
};
```

We use the difference function, which recursively memoizes both calls to the factorial:

```
function<int(int, int)> factorialMemoizedDifference =
    [&recursiveMemoizedFactorial](auto first, auto second){
        return recursiveMemoizedFactorial(second) -
            recursiveMemoizedFactorial(first);
};
```

By running the initial function without memoization and the previous function with the same data side by side, I got the following output:

```
Computing factorial difference
First call no memoization: 1367 ns
Second call no memoization: 58045 ns
Third call no memoization: 16167 ns
Fourth call no memoization (same as first call): 1334 ns
First call with recursive memoized factorial: 16281 ns
Second call with recursive memoized factorial: 890056 ns
Third call with recursive memoized factorial: 939 ns
Fourth call with recursive memoized factorial (same as first call): 798 ns
```

We can look at this side by side:

```
First call: 1,367 ns < 16,281 ns
Second call: 58,045 ns < 890,056 ns
Third call: 16,167 ns > 939 ns
Fourth call: 1,334 ns > 798 ns
```

As we can see, the cache is building up, with a massive penalty hit for the first large computation; the second call involved 1024! However, the subsequent calls are much faster due to the cache hits.

In conclusion, we can say that memoization is useful for speeding up repeated complex computations when enough memory is available. It may require some tweaking since the cache size and cache hits depend on how many calls and how many repeated calls are made to the function. So, don't take this for granted—measure, measure, measure.

Tail recursion optimization

Recursive algorithms are very common in functional programming. In fact, many of our imperative loops can be rewritten as recursive algorithms using pure functions.

However, recursion is not very popular in imperative programming because it has a few issues. First, developers tend to have less practice with recursive algorithms compared to imperative loops. Second, the dreaded stack overflow—recursive calls are placed to the stack by default and if there are too many iterations, the stack overflows with an ugly error.

Fortunately, compilers are smart and can fix this problem for us, while at the same time optimizing recursive functions. Enter tail recursion optimization.

Let's take a look at a simple recursive function. We'll reuse the factorial from the previous section, as follows:

```
function<int(int)> fact = [&fact](int n){
    if(n == 0) return 1;
    return n * fact(n-1);
};
```

Normally, each call would be placed on the stack, so your stack will grow with each call. Let's visualize it:

```
Stack content
fact(1024)
1024 * fact(1023)
1023 * fact(1022)
...
1 * fact(0)
fact(0) = 1 => unwind the stack
```

We can avoid the stack by rewriting the code. We notice that the recursive call comes at the end; we can, therefore, rewrite the function similar to the following pseudocode:

```
function<int(int)> fact = [&fact](int n){
    if(n == 0) return 1;
    return n * (n-1) * (n-1-1) * (n-1-1-1) * ... * fact(0);
};
```

In a nutshell, this is what the compiler can do for us if we enable the correct optimization flag. Not only does this call take less memory and avoid stack overflows—but it is also faster.

By now, you should know not to trust anyone's claims—including mine—without measuring them. So, let's check this hypothesis.

First, we'll need a test that measures the timing for multiple calls to the factorial function. I picked some values to carry out the test:

```
TEST_CASE("Factorial"){
    function<int(int)> fact = [&fact](int n){
        if(n == 0) return 1;
        return n * fact(n-1);
    };

    printDuration("Duration for 0!: ", [&](){return fact(0);});
    printDuration("Duration for 1!: ", [&](){return fact(1);});
    printDuration("Duration for 10!: ", [&](){return fact(10);});
    printDuration("Duration for 100!: ", [&](){return fact(100);});
    printDuration("Duration for 1024!: ", [&](){return fact(1024);});
}
```

Then, we need to compile this function with optimization disabled and enabled. The **GNU Compiler Collection** (GCC) flag that optimizes tail recursion is `-foptimize-sibling-calls`; the name refers to the fact that the flag optimizes both sibling calls and tail calls. I will not go into detail about what sibling call optimization does; let's just say that it doesn't affect our test in any way.

Time to run the two programs. First, let's look at the raw output:

- This is the program without optimization:

```
Duration for 0!: 210 ns
Duration for 1!: 152 ns
Duration for 10!: 463 ns
Duration for 100!: 10946 ns
Duration for 1024!: 82683 ns
```

- This is the program with optimization:

```
Duration for 0!: 209 ns
Duration for 1!: 152 ns
Duration for 10!: 464 ns
Duration for 100!: 6455 ns
Duration for 1024!: 75602 ns
```

Let's see the results side by side now; the duration without optimization is on the left:

```
Duration for 0!: 210 ns > 209 ns
Duration for 1!: 152 ns  = 152 ns
Duration for 10!: 463 ns < 464 ns
Duration for 100!: 10946 ns > 6455 ns
Duration for 1024!: 82683 ns > 75602 ns
```

It seems that the optimization really kicks in for larger values on my machine. Once again, this proves the importance of metrics whenever performance matters.

In the following sections, we'll experiment with the code in various ways and measure the results.

Fully optimized calls

Out of curiosity, I've decided to run the same program with all of the safe optimization flags turned on. In GCC, this option is -O3. The results are staggering, to say the least:

```
Duration for 0!: 128 ns
Duration for 1!: 96 ns
Duration for 10!: 96 ns
Duration for 100!: 405 ns
Duration for 1024!: 17249 ns
```

Let's compare the results of enabling all of the optimization flags (the second value in the next snippet) with the results for just tail recursion optimization:

```
Duration for 0!: 209 ns > 128 ns
Duration for 1!: 152 ns > 96 ns
Duration for 10!: 464 ns > 96 ns
Duration for 100!: 6455 ns > 405 ns
Duration for 1024!: 75602 ns > 17249 ns
```

The difference is staggering, as you can see. The conclusion is that, while tail recursion optimization is useful, it's even better to have CPU cache hits and all the goodies enabled by compilers.

But we're using an `if` statement; will this work differently when we use the `?:` operator?

If vs ?:

For curiosity's sake, I decided to re-write the code using the `?:` operator instead of `if` statements, as follows:

```
function<int(int)> fact = [&fact](int n){
    return (n == 0) ? 1 : (n * fact(n-1));
};
```

I didn't know what to expect, and the results were interesting. Let's look at the raw output:

- Without optimization flags:

```
Duration for 0!: 633 ns
Duration for 1!: 561 ns
Duration for 10!: 1441 ns
Duration for 100!: 20407 ns
Duration for 1024!: 215600 ns
```

- With tail recursion flag turned on:

```
Duration for 0!: 277 ns
Duration for 1!: 214 ns
Duration for 10!: 578 ns
Duration for 100!: 9573 ns
Duration for 1024!: 81182 ns
```

Let's look at a comparison of the results; the duration without optimization comes first:

```
Duration for 0!: 633 ns > 277 ns
Duration for 1!: 561 ns > 214 ns
Duration for 10!: 1441 ns > 578 ns
Duration for 100!: 20407 ns > 9573 ns
Duration for 1024!: 75602 ns > 17249 ns
```

The difference is very great between the two versions, which is something I didn't quite expect. As always, this is most likely the result of the GCC compiler, and you should test it on your own. However, it seems that this version is better for tail optimization with my compiler—an intriguing result to say the least.

Double recursion

Does tail recursion work for double recursion? We need to come up with an example that passes recursion from one function to another to check for this. I decided to write two functions, f1 and f2, which recursively call each other. f1 multiplies the current parameter with f2(n - 1), while f2 adds f1(n) to f1(n-1). Here's the code:

```
function<int(int)> f2;
function<int(int)> f1 = [&f2](int n){
    return (n == 0) ? 1 : (n * f2(n-1));
};

f2 = [&f1](int n){
    return (n == 0) ? 2 : (f1(n) + f1(n-1));
};
```

Let's check the timing for calls to f1 with values from 0 to 8:

```
printDuration("Duration for f1(0): ", [&](){return f1(0);});
printDuration("Duration for f1(1): ", [&](){return f1(1);});
printDuration("Duration for f1(2): ", [&](){return f1(2);});
printDuration("Duration for f1(3): ", [&](){return f1(3);});
printDuration("Duration for f1(4): ", [&](){return f1(4);});
printDuration("Duration for f1(5): ", [&](){return f1(5);});
printDuration("Duration for f1(6): ", [&](){return f1(6);});
printDuration("Duration for f1(7): ", [&](){return f1(7);});
printDuration("Duration for f1(8): ", [&](){return f1(8);});
```

Here's what we obtain:

- Without tail call optimization:

```
Duration for f1(0): 838 ns
Duration for f1(1): 825 ns
Duration for f1(2): 1218 ns
Duration for f1(3): 1515 ns
Duration for f1(4): 2477 ns
Duration for f1(5): 3919 ns
Duration for f1(6): 5809 ns
Duration for f1(7): 9354 ns
Duration for f1(8): 14884 ns
```

- With call optimization:

```
Duration for f1(0): 206 ns
Duration for f1(1): 327 ns
Duration for f1(2): 467 ns
```

```
Duration for f1(3): 642 ns
Duration for f1(4): 760 ns
Duration for f1(5): 1155 ns
Duration for f1(6): 2023 ns
Duration for f1(7): 3849 ns
Duration for f1(8): 4986 ns
```

Let's look at the results side by side; the duration of calls without tail optimization is on the left:

```
f1(0): 838 ns > 206 ns
f1(1): 825 ns > 327 ns
f1(2): 1218 ns > 467 ns
f1(3): 1515 ns > 642 ns
f1(4): 2477 ns > 760 ns
f1(5): 3919 ns > 1155 ns
f1(6): 5809 ns > 2023 ns
f1(7): 9354 ns > 3849 ns
f1(8): 14884 ns > 4986 ns
```

The differences are very great indeed, showing that the code is greatly optimized. However, remember that, for GCC, we are using the `-foptimize-sibling-calls` optimization flag. This flag carries out two types of optimization: tail calls and sibling calls. Sibling calls are calls to functions that have a return type of the same size and a parameter list of the same total size, thus allowing the compiler to treat them similarly with tail calls. It's quite possible that, in our case, both optimizations are applied.

Optimizing execution time with asynchronous code

When we have multiple threads, we can use two close techniques to optimize the execution time: parallel execution and asynchronous execution. We've seen how parallel execution works in a previous section; what about asynchronous calls?

First, let's remind ourselves what asynchronous calls are. We would like to make a call, continue normally on the main thread, and get the result back at some point in the future. To me, this sounds like a perfect job for functions. We just need to call functions, let them execute, and talk to them again after a while.

Since we've talked about the future, let's talk about the `future` construct in C++.

Futures

We've already established that it's ideal to avoid managing threads in a program, except when doing very specialized work, but we need parallel execution and often need synchronization to obtain a result from another thread. A typical example is a long computation that would block the main thread unless we run it in its own thread. How do we know when the computation is done and how can we get the result of the computation?

In 1976–1977, two concepts were proposed in computer science to simplify the solution to this problem—futures and promises. While these concepts are often used interchangeably in various technologies, in C++ they have specific meanings:

- A future can retrieve a value from a provider while taking care of synchronization
- A promise stores a value for the future, offering, in addition, a synchronization point

Due to its nature, a `future` object has restrictions in C++. It cannot be copied, only moved, and it's only valid when associated with a shared state. This means that we can only create a valid future object by calling `async`, `promise.get_future()` or `packaged_task.get_future()`.

It's also worth mentioning that promises and futures use threading libraries in their implementation; therefore, you may need to add a dependency to another library. On my system (Ubuntu 18.04, 64 bits), when compiling with g++, I had to add a link dependency to the `pthread` library; I expect you'll need the same if you're using g++ on a mingw or cygwin configuration.

Let's first see how we use `future` and `promise` in tandem. First, we'll create a `promise` for a secret message:

```
promise<string> secretMessagePromise;
```

Then, let's create a `future` and start a new thread using it. The thread will use a lambda that simply prints the secret message:

```
future<string> secretMessageFuture =
    secretMessagePromise.get_future();
thread isPrimeThread(printSecretMessage, ref(secretMessageFuture));
```

Notice that we need to avoid copying the `future`; in this case, we use a reference wrapper over the future.

We'll stick with this thread for now; the next thing is to fulfill the promise, that is, to set a value:

```
secretMessagePromise.set_value("It's a secret");
isPrimeThread.join();
```

In the meantime, the other thread will do some stuff and then will request that we keep our promise. Well, not quite; it will ask for the value of the promise, which blocks it until join() is called:

```
auto printSecretMessage = [](future<string>& secretMessageFuture) {
    string secretMessage = secretMessageFuture.get();
    cout << "The secret message: " << secretMessage << '\n';
};
```

As you may notice, this method sets the responsibility for computing the value in the main thread. What if we want it to be on the secondary thread? We just need to use async.

Let's say we'd like to check whether a number is prime. We first write a lambda that will check for this in a naive way, for each possible divisor from 2 to x-1, and check whether x is divisible by it. If it's not divisible by any value, it is a prime number:

```
auto is_prime = [](int x) {
    auto xIsDivisibleBy = bind(isDivisibleBy, x, _1);
    return none_of_collection(
            rangeFrom2To(x - 1),
            xIsDivisibleBy
        );
};
```

A few helping lambdas are used. One for generating a range like this:

```
auto rangeFromTo = [](const int start, const int end){
    vector<int> aVector(end);
    iota(aVector.begin(), aVector.end(), start);
    return aVector;
};
```

This is then specialized for generating a range that starts with 2:

```
auto rangeFrom2To = bind(rangeFromTo, 2, _1);
```

Then, a predicate that checks whether two numbers are divisible or not:

```
auto isDivisibleBy = [](auto value, auto factor){
    return value % factor == 0;
};
```

To run this function in a separate thread from the main one, we need to declare a `future` using `async`:

```
future<bool> futureIsPrime(async(is_prime, 2597));
```

The second argument of `async` is the input argument for our function. Multiple arguments are allowed.

Then, we can do other stuff, and finally, ask for the result:

```
TEST_CASE("Future with async"){
    future<bool> futureIsPrime(async(is_prime, 7757));
    cout << "doing stuff ..." << endl;
    bool result = futureIsPrime.get();

    CHECK(result);
}
```

The bold line of code marks the point when the main thread stops to wait for a result from the secondary thread.

If you need more than one `future`, you can use them. In the following example, we'll run `is_prime` with four different values in four different threads, as shown here:

```
TEST_CASE("more futures"){
    future<bool> future1(async(is_prime, 2));
    future<bool> future2(async(is_prime, 27));
    future<bool> future3(async(is_prime, 1977));
    future<bool> future4(async(is_prime, 7757));

    CHECK(future1.get());
    CHECK(!future2.get());
    CHECK(!future3.get());
    CHECK(future4.get());
}
```

Functional asynchronous code

We've seen that the simplest implementation of a thread is a lambda, but we can do even more. The last example, which uses multiple threads to run the same operation asynchronously on different values, can be turned into a functional high-order function.

But let's start with a few simple loops. First, we will transform the input values and the expected results into vectors:

```
vector<int> values{2, 27, 1977, 7757};
vector<bool> expectedResults{true, false, false, true};
```

Then, we need a `for` loop to create the futures. It's important not to call the `future()` constructor, because this will fail due to trying to copy the newly constructed `future` object into a container. Instead, add the result of `async()` directly into the container:

```
vector<future<bool>> futures;
for(auto value : values){
    futures.push_back(async(is_prime, value));
}
```

Then, we need to get the results back from the threads. Once again, we need to avoid copying the `future`, so we will use a reference when iterating:

```
vector<bool> results;
for(auto& future : futures){
    results.push_back(future.get());
}
```

Let's see the whole test:

```
TEST_CASE("more futures with loops"){
    vector<int> values{2, 27, 1977, 7757};
    vector<bool> expectedResults{true, false, false, true};

    vector<future<bool>> futures;
    for(auto value : values){
        futures.push_back(async(is_prime, value));
    }

    vector<bool> results;
    for(auto& future : futures){
        results.push_back(future.get());
    }

    CHECK_EQ(results, expectedResults);
}
```

It's quite obvious that we can turn this into a few transform calls. However, we need to pay special attention to avoid the copying of futures. First, I created a lambda that helps with creating a `future`:

```
auto makeFuture = [](auto value){
    return async(is_prime, value);
};
```

The first `for` loop then turns into a `transformAll` call:

```
vector<future<bool>> futures = transformAll<vector<future<bool>>>
    (values, makeFuture);
```

The second part is trickier than expected. Our implementation of `transformAll` doesn't work, so I will call `transform` inline instead:

```
vector<bool> results(values.size());
transform(futures.begin(), futures.end(), results.begin(), []
    (future<bool>& future){ return future.get();});
```

We end up with the following test, which passes:

```
TEST_CASE("more futures functional"){
    vector<int> values{2, 27, 1977, 7757};

    auto makeFuture = [](auto value){
        return async(is_prime, value);
    };

    vector<future<bool>> futures = transformAll<vector<future<bool>>>
        (values, makeFuture);
    vector<bool> results(values.size());
    transform(futures.begin(), futures.end(), results.begin(), []
        (future<bool>& future){ return future.get();});

    vector<bool> expectedResults{true, false, false, true};

    CHECK_EQ(results, expectedResults);
}
```

I have to be honest with you, this was the most difficult code to implement correctly so far. So many things can go wrong when working with futures and it's not obvious why. The error messages are quite unhelpful, at least for my version of g++. The only way I managed to make this work was by going step by step, as I showed you in this section.

However, this code sample show an important fact; with the thoroughly thought out and tested use of futures, we can parallelize higher-order functions. It is, therefore, a possible solution if you need better performance, can use multiple cores, and can't wait for the implementation of a parallel running policy in the standard. If only for this, I think my efforts were useful!

Since we're talking about asynchronous calls, we could also do a quick pass through the world of reactive programming.

A taste of reactive programming

Reactive programming is a paradigm for writing code that focuses on processing data streams. Imagine having to analyze a stream of temperature values, values coming from sensors mounted on self-driving cars, or share values for specific companies. In reactive programming, we receive this continuous stream of data and run functions that analyze it. Since new data can arrive unpredictably on stream, the programming model has to be asynchronous; that is, the main thread is continuously waiting for new data, and, when it arrives, the processing is delegated to secondary streams. The results are usually collected asynchronously as well—either pushed to the user interface, saved in data stores, or passed to other data streams.

We've seen that the main focus of functional programming is on data. Therefore, it shouldn't be any surprise that functional programming is a good candidate for processing real-time data streams. The composability of higher-order functions such as `map`, `reduce`, or `filter`, plus the opportunities for parallel processing, make the functional style of design a great solution for reactive programming.

We won't go into much detail about reactive programming. Usually, specific libraries or frameworks are used that facilitate the implementation of such data flow processing, but with the elements we have up to now, we can write a small-scale example.

We need a few things. First, a data stream; second, a main thread that receives data and immediately passes it to a processing pipeline; and third, a way to get the output.

For the goal of this example, I will simply use the standard input as an input stream. We will input numbers from the keyboard and check whether they are prime in a reactive manner, thus keeping the main thread responsive at all times. This means we'll use the `async` function to create a `future` for every number we read from the keyboard. The output will simply be written to the output stream.

We will use the same `is_prime` function as before, but add another function that prints to the standard output whether the value is prime or not:

```
auto printIsPrime = [](int value){
    cout << value << (is_prime(value) ? " is prime" : " is not prime")
    << endl;
};
```

The `main` function is an infinite cycle that reads data from the input stream and starts a `future` every time a new value comes in:

```
int main(){
    int number;

    while(true){
        cin >> number;
        async(printIsPrime, number);
    }
}
```

Running this code with some randomly typed values results in the following output:

```
23423
23423 is not prime
453576
453576 is not prime
53
53 is prime
2537
2537 is not prime
364544366
5347
54
534532
436
364544366 is not prime
5347 is prime
54 is not prime
534532 is not prime
436 is not prime
```

As you can see, the results are returned as soon as possible, but the program allows new data to be introduced at all times.

I have to mention that, in order to avoid infinite cycles every time I compile the code for this chapter, the reactive example can be compiled and run with `make reactive`. You'll have to stop it with an interrupt since it's an infinite loop.

This is a basic reactive programming example. It can obviously become more complex with higher volumes of data, complex pipelines, and the parallelization of each pipeline among others. However, we achieved our goal for this section—to give you a taste of reactive programming and how we can use functional constructs and asynchronous calls to make it work.

We've discussed a lot about optimizing execution time, looking at various ways that help us accomplish faster performance. It's now time to look at a situation where we want to reduce the memory usage of our programs.

Optimizing memory usage

The method we've discussed so far, for structuring code in a functional way, involves passing multiple times through a collection that is treated as immutable. As a result, this can lead to copies of the collection. Let's look, for example, at a simple code sample that uses `transform` to increment all the elements of a vector:

```cpp
template<typename DestinationType>
auto transformAll = [](const auto source, auto lambda){
    DestinationType result;
    transform(source.begin(), source.end(), back_inserter(result),
        lambda);
    return result;
};

TEST_CASE("Memory"){
    vector<long long> manyNumbers(size);
    fill_n(manyNumbers.begin(), size, 1000L);

    auto result = transformAll<vector<long long>>(manyNumbers,
        increment);

    CHECK_EQ(result[0], 1001);
}
```

This implementation leads to a lot of memory allocations. First, the `manyNumbers` vector is copied into `transformAll`. Then, `result.push_back()` is automatically called, potentially resulting in memory allocation. Finally, the `result` is returned, but the initial `manyNumbers` vector is still allocated.

We can improve some of these problems immediately, but it's also worth discussing how they compare with other possible optimizations.

In order to carry out the tests, we will need to work with large collections and a way to measure the memory allocation for a process. The first part is easy—just allocate a lot of 64-bit values (the long, long type on my compiler); enough to allocate 1 GB of RAM:

```
const long size_1GB_64Bits = 125000000;
TEST_CASE("Memory"){
    auto size = size_1GB_64Bits;
    vector<long long> manyNumbers(size);
    fill_n(manyNumbers.begin(), size, 1000L);

    auto result = transformAll<vector<long long>>(manyNumbers,
        increment);

    CHECK_EQ(result[0], 1001);
}
```

The second part is a bit more difficult. Fortunately, on my Ubuntu 18.04 system, I can watch the memory for a process in a file in `/proc/PID/status`, in which PID is the process identifier. With a bit of Bash magic, I can create a `makefile` recipe that outputs memory values taken every 0.1 s into a file, like this:

```
memoryConsumptionNoMoveIterator: .outputFolder
    g++ -DNO_MOVE_ITERATOR -std=c++17 memoryOptimization.cpp -Wall -
        Wextra -Werror -o out/memoryOptimization
    ./runWithMemoryConsumptionMonitoring memoryNoMoveIterator.log
```

You'll notice the `-DNO_MOVE_ITERATOR` argument; this is a compilation directive that allows me to compile the same file for different goals, in order to check the memory footprint of multiple solutions. This means that our previous test is written within an `#if` NO_MOVE_ITERATOR directive.

There's only one caveat—since I used the bash `watch` command to generate the output, you will need to press a key after running `make memoryConsumptionNoMoveIterator`, as well as for every other memory logs recipe.

With this set up, let's improve `transformAll` to use less memory, and look at the output. We need to use reference types and allocate memory for the result from the beginning, as shown in the following:

```
template<typename DestinationType>
auto transformAll = [](const auto& source, auto lambda){
    DestinationType result;
    result.resize(source.size());
    transform(source.begin(), source.end(), result.begin(), lambda);
    return result;
};
```

As expected, the result of the improvement is that the maximum allocation starts from 0.99 GB, but jumps to 1.96 GB, which is roughly double.

We need to put this value in context. Let's first measure what a simple `for` loop can do, and compare the result with the same algorithm implemented with `transform`.

Measuring memory for a simple for loop

The solution with a `for` loop is very simple:

```
TEST_CASE("Memory"){
    auto size = size_1GB_64Bits;
    vector<long long> manyNumbers(size);
    fill_n(manyNumbers.begin(), size, 1000L);

    for(auto iter = manyNumbers.begin(); iter != manyNumbers.end();
        ++iter){
            ++(*iter);
    };

    CHECK_EQ(manyNumbers[0], 1001);
}
```

When measuring the memory, there's no surprise—the footprint stays at 0.99 GB during the whole process. Can we achieve this result with `transform` as well? Well, there's one version of `transform` that can modify the collection in place. Let's put it to the test.

Measure memory for in-place transform

To use `transform` in place, we need to provide the destination iterator parameter, `source.begin()`, as follows:

```
auto increment = [](const auto value){
    return value + 1;
};

auto transformAllInPlace = [](auto& source, auto lambda){
    transform(source.begin(), source.end(), source.begin(), lambda);
};

TEST_CASE("Memory"){
    auto size = size_1GB_64Bits;
    vector<long long> manyNumbers(size);
```

```
        fill_n(manyNumbers.begin(), size, 1000L);

        transformAllInPlace(manyNumbers, increment);

        CHECK_EQ(manyNumbers[0], 1001);
    }
```

According to the documentation, this is supposed to change in the same collection; therefore, it shouldn't allocate any more memory. As expected, it has the same behavior as a simple `for` loop and the memory footprint stays at 0.99 GB for the whole duration of the program.

However, you may notice that we're not returning the value now to avoid a copy. I like transform-to-return values though, and we have another option, using move semantics:

```
template<typename SourceType>
auto transformAllInPlace = [](auto& source, auto lambda) -> SourceType&& {
    transform(source.begin(), source.end(), source.begin(), lambda);
    return move(source);
};
```

To make the call compile, we need to pass in the type of the source when calling `transformAllInPlace`, so our test changes to:

```
TEST_CASE("Memory"){
    auto size = size_1GB_64Bits;
    vector<long long> manyNumbers(size);
    fill_n(manyNumbers.begin(), size, 1000L);

    auto result = transformAllInPlace<vector<long long>>(manyNumbers,
        increment);

    CHECK_EQ(result[0], 1001);
}
```

Let's measure to see if the move semantics helps in any way. The result is as expected; the memory footprint stays at 0.99 GB during the whole runtime.

This leads to an interesting idea. What if we use move semantics in the call to `transform`?

Transform with the move iterator

We can rewrite our `transform` function to use move iterators as follows:

```
template<typename DestinationType>
auto transformAllWithMoveIterator = [](auto& source, auto lambda){
    DestinationType result(source.size());
    transform(make_move_iterator(source.begin()),
        make_move_iterator(source.end()), result.begin(), lambda);
    source.clear();
    return result;
};
```

In theory, what this should do is move values to the destination rather than copying them, thus keeping the memory footprint low. To put it to the test, we run the same test while recording the memory:

```
TEST_CASE("Memory"){
    auto size = size_1GB_64Bits;
    vector<long long> manyNumbers(size);
    fill_n(manyNumbers.begin(), size, 1000L);

    auto result = transformAllWithMoveIterator<vector<long long>>
        (manyNumbers, increment);

    CHECK_EQ(result[0], 1001);
}
```

The result is unexpected; the memory starts at 0.99 GB, rises to 1.96 GB (probably after the `transform` call), and then goes back to 0.99 GB (most likely, the result of `source.clear()`). I tried multiple variants to avoid this behavior, but couldn't find a solution to keep the memory footprint at 0.99 GB. This appears to be a problem with the implementation of move iterators; I advise you to test it on your compiler to find out whether it works or not.

Comparing the solutions

The solutions using in-place or move semantics, while reducing the memory footprint, only work when the source data is not required for additional computations. If you plan to reuse the data for other computations, there's no way around preserving the initial collection. Moreover, it's unclear whether these calls can run in parallel; since g++ doesn't yet implement parallel execution policies I can't test them, so I will leave this question as an exercise for the reader.

But what do functional programming languages do in order to reduce memory footprint? The answer is very interesting.

Immutable data structures

Purely functional programming languages use a combination of immutable data structures and garbage collection. Each call to modify a data structure creates, what seems to be, a copy of the initial data structure, with only one element changed. The initial structure is not affected in any way. However, this is done using pointers; basically, the new data structure is the same as the initial one, except there is a pointer towards the changed value. When discarding the initial collection, the old value is no longer used and the garbage collector automatically removes it from memory.

This mechanism takes full advantage of immutability, allowing optimizations that are unavailable to C++. Moreover, the implementation is usually recursive, which also takes advantage of tail recursion optimization.

However, it is possible to implement such data structures in C++. An example is a library called **immer**, which you can find on GitHub at `https://github.com/arximboldi/immer`. Immer implements a number of immutable collections. We will look at `immer::vector`; every time we call an operation that would normally modify the vector (such as `push_back`), `immer::vector` returns a new collection. Each value returned can be constant, since it never changes. I wrote a small test using immer 0.5.0 in the chapter code, showcasing the usage of `immer::vector`, which you can see in the following code:

```
TEST_CASE("Check immutable vector"){
    const auto empty = immer::vector<int>{};
    const auto withOneElement = empty.push_back(42);

    CHECK_EQ(0, empty.size());
    CHECK_EQ(1, withOneElement.size());
    CHECK_EQ(42, withOneElement[0]);
}
```

I will not go into more detail regarding immutable data structures; however, I strongly advise you to take a look at the documentation on the *immer* website (`https://sinusoid.es/immer/introduction.html`) and play with the library.

Summary

We've seen that performance optimization is a complex topic. As C++ programmers, we are primed to require more performance from our code; the question we asked in this chapter was: is it possible to optimize code written in a functional style?

The answer is—yes, if you measure and if you have a clear goal. Do we need a specific computation to finish more quickly? Do we need to reduce the memory footprint? What area of the application requires the most performance improvements? How much do we want to do weird point optimizations that might need rewriting with the next compiler, library, or platform version? These are all questions you need to answer before moving on to optimize your code.

However, we have seen that functional programming has a huge benefit when it comes to using all the cores on a computer. While we're waiting for the standard implementation of parallel execution for higher-order functions, we can take advantage of immutability by writing our own parallel algorithms. Recursion is another staple of functional programming and we can take advantage of tail recursion optimization whenever we use it.

As for memory consumption, immutable data structures implemented in third-party libraries, and carefully optimizing the higher-order functions we're using depending on their goal, can help us maintain the simplicity of the code, while the complexity happens in specific places in the code. Move semantics can be used when we throw away the source collections, but remember to check it works with parallel execution.

Above all, I hope you've learned that measuring is the most important part of performance optimization. After all, if you don't know where you are and where you need to go, how can you make the trip?

We will continue our journey with functional programming by taking advantage of data generators for our tests. It's time to look at property-based testing.

11
Property-Based Testing

We've seen that pure functions have one important property—they return the same output for the same inputs. We've also seen that this property allows us to easily write example-based unit tests for pure functions. Moreover, we can write data-driven tests, allowing one test function to be reused with multiple inputs and outputs.

It turns out that we can do even better. Instead of, or in addition to, writing many lines of data-driven tests, we can take advantage of mathematical properties of pure functions. This technique is possible due to data generators that are enabled by functional programming. These tests are confusingly named **property-based tests**; you'll have to remember that the name comes from mathematical properties of pure functions, and not from properties implemented in classes or objects.

The following topics will be covered in this chapter:

- Understanding the idea of property-based tests
- How to write generators and take advantage of them
- How to get to property-based tests from example-based tests
- How to write good properties

Technical requirements

You will need a compiler that supports C++ 17. I used GCC 7.4.0.

The code can be found on GitHub at `https://github.com/PacktPublishing/Hands-On-Functional-Programming-with-Cpp` in the `Chapter11` folder. It includes and uses `doctest`, which is a single header open source unit testing library. You can find it on its GitHub repository at `https://github.com/onqtam/doctest`.

Property-based testing

Unit tests are an extremely useful software development technique. A good suite of unit tests can do the following:

- Speed up deployments by automating the boring parts of regression testing.
- Enable professional testers to find the hidden issues rather than running the same test plan again and again.
- Remove bugs very early in the development process, thereby reducing the cost of finding and fixing them.
- Improve the software design by providing feedback as a first client of the code structure (if tests are complicated, most likely your design is complicated), as long as the developers know how to see and interpret the feedback.
- Increase the trust in the code, hence allowing for more changes, and thereby facilitating refactoring that speeds up development or removes risks from the code.

I love writing unit tests. I love figuring out the interesting test cases, and I love using tests to drive my code—as you've seen in Chapter 9, *Test-Driven Development for Functional Programming*. At the same time, I'm always looking for better ways to write the tests, since it would be great if we could speed up the process.

We've seen in Chapter 9, *Test-Driven Development for Functional Programming*, that pure functions allow us to more easily identify test cases, because, by definition, their outputs are constrained. It turns out that we can go further than that if we venture into the realm of mathematical properties associated with these pure functions.

If you've been writing unit tests for a while, you probably had the feeling that some of the tests are a bit redundant. If only we could write tests like this—for inputs in a certain interval of values, the expected outputs must have a certain property. It turns out that, with the help of data generators and a bit of abstract thinking, we can make this work.

Let's compare approaches.

Example-based tests versus property-based tests

Let's take an example of the power function:

```
function<int(int, int)> power = [](auto first, auto second){
    return pow(first, second);
};
```

How would you test it using example-based tests? We need to figure out a few interesting values for first and second and combine them. We'll limit ourselves to positive integers for the goal of this exercise. In general, interesting values for integers are—0, 1, many, and maximum. This leads to the following possible cases:

- 0^0 -> *undefined* (* the `pow` implementation in C++ returns 1 unless specific errors are enabled)
- $0^{any\ integer\ from\ 0\ to\ max}$ -> *0*
- $1^{any\ integer}$ -> *1*
- *(any integer except 0)^0 -> 1*
- 2^2 -> *4*
- $2^{max\ integer\ that\ doesn't\ overflow}$ -> *value to be computed*
- 10^5 -> *100000*
- $10^{max\ integer\ that\ doesn't\ overflow}$ -> *value to be computed*

This list is by no means complete, but it shows an interesting analysis of the problem. So, let's write these tests:

```
TEST_CASE("Power"){
    int maxInt = numeric_limits<int>::max();
    CHECK_EQ(1, power(0, 0));
    CHECK_EQ(0, power(0, 1));
    CHECK_EQ(0, power(0, maxInt));
    CHECK_EQ(1, power(1, 1));
    CHECK_EQ(1, power(1, 2));
    CHECK_EQ(1, power(1, maxInt));
    CHECK_EQ(1, power(2, 0));
    CHECK_EQ(2, power(2, 1));
    CHECK_EQ(4, power(2, 2));
    CHECK_EQ(maxInt, power(2, 31) - 1);
    CHECK_EQ(1, power(3, 0));
    CHECK_EQ(3, power(3, 1));
    CHECK_EQ(9, power(3, 2));
    CHECK_EQ(1, power(maxInt, 0));
    CHECK_EQ(maxInt, power(maxInt, 1));
}
```

This is obviously not the full list of tests we would need to check to establish that the power function works, but it's a good start. While looking at this list, I'm wondering, what do you think—would you write more or fewer tests? I would definitely want to write more, but I lost the drive in the process. Sure, one of the issues is that I wrote these tests after the code; I'm much more motivated to write them along with the code as in **Test-Driven Development (TDD)**. But maybe there's a better way?

Let's think differently for a moment. Are there properties we can test that hold for some or all of the expected outputs? Let's write a list:

- 0^0 -> undefined (1 by default in pow function in C++)
- $0^{[1 .. maxInt]}$ -> 0
- value: $[1 .. maxInt]^0$ -> 1
- value: $[0 .. maxInt]^1$ -> value

These are some obvious properties. They cover, however, only a small subset of the values. We still need to cover the general case of x^y, where both x and y are neither 0 nor 1. Can we find any property here? Well, think about the mathematical definition of integer power—it's a repeated multiplication. We can therefore infer, for any x and y value greater than 1, the following:

$$X^Y = X^{y-1} \times X$$

We do have a boundary issue here, since the computation might overflow. So, the values of x and y need to be picked so that x^y is smaller than `maxInt`. One way to deal with this issue is to pick x first and pick y between $y=2$ and `maxy=floor(log`$_x$`maxInt)`. To make it as close to boundaries as possible, we should always pick `maxy` as a value. To check for the overflow case, we just need to test that x to the power of `maxy + 1` overflows.

The preceding approach implies, of course, that we trust the result of the logarithm function from the standard library. If your *tester paranoia* is larger than mine, I suggest using a verified logarithm table for all bases from 2 to `maxInt` and the value `maxInt`. I will, however, use the STL logarithm function.

We now have a list of the mathematical properties of the power function. But we'd like to implement them as previously seen, with intervals. Can we even do that? Enter data generators.

Generators

Generators are a staple feature of functional programming languages. They are usually implemented through a combination of lambdas and lazy evaluation, allowing code like the following:

```
// pseudocode
vector<int> values = generate(1, maxInt, [](){/*generatorCode*/}).pick(100)
```

The generator function usually generates an infinite number of values, but because it is lazy evaluated, the `100` values materialize only when `pick` is called.

C++ doesn't yet have standard support for lazy evaluation and data generators, so we'll have to implement our own generator. It's worth noting that C++ 20 has adopted the inclusion of the awesome ranges library in the standard, which enables both these features. For the goals of this chapter, we'll stick to the standard available today, but you'll find the basic usage of ranges library in the final chapters of this book.

First, how can we generate data? STL offers us a nice way to generate uniformly distributed random integers by using the `uniform_int_distribution` class. Let's first look at the code; I've added comments to explain what happens:

```
auto generate_ints = [](const int min, const int max){
    random_device rd; // use for generating the seed
    mt19937 generator(rd()); // used for generating pseudo-random
        numbers
    uniform_int_distribution<int> distribution(min, max); // used to
        generate uniformly distributed numbers between min and max
    auto values = transformAll<vector<int>>(range(0, 98), // generates
        the range [0..98]
            [&distribution, &generator](auto){
                return distribution(generator); // generate the random
                    numbers
        });
    values.push_back(min); // ensure that min and max values are
        included
    values.push_back(max);
    return values;
};
```

This function will generate uniformly distributed numbers from `min` to `max`. I prefer to always include the edges of the intervals, since these are always interesting values for tests.

We're also using a function called `range` that you haven't seen yet. Its goal is to fill a vector with the values from `minValue` to `maxValue` to allow simpler transformations. Here it is:

```
auto range = [](const int minValue, const int maxValue){
    vector<int> range(maxValue - minValue + 1);
    iota(range.begin(), range.end(), minValue);
    return range;
};
```

It's worth noting that ranges are usually lazy-evaluated in functional programming languages, which highly reduces their memory footprint. For the goals of our example though, this works fine.

The previous `generator` function allows us to create input data for our tests, uniformly distributed between one and the maximum integer value. It just takes a simple bind:

```
auto generate_ints_greater_than_1 = bind(generate_ints, 1,
numeric_limits<int>::max());
```

Let's use this for our property-based tests.

Putting the properties to the test

Let's see again the list of properties that we'd like to check:

- 0^0 -> *undefined (1 by default in pow function in C++)*
- $0^{[1 .. maxInt]}$ -> *0*
- *value:* $[1 .. maxInt]^0$ -> *1*
- *value:* $[0 .. maxInt]^1$ -> *value*
- $x^y = x^{y-1} * x$

We will now implement each of the properties in turn. For every property, we will use either a normal example-based test, or the data generators inspired by the `generate_ints_greater_than_1` function. Let's start with the simplest property—0^0 should be undefined—or actually 1 in its standard implementation.

Property: 0^0 -> *undefined*

The first one is quite simple to implement using a normal example-based test. We'll extract it in a function for the sake of consistency:

```
auto property_0_to_power_0_is_1 = []() {
    return power(0, 0) == 1;
};
```

In our test, we will write a description of the property, as well, in order to obtain an informative output:

```
TEST_CASE("Properties") {
    cout << "Property: 0 to power 0 is 1" << endl;
    CHECK(property_0_to_power_0_is_1);
}
```

When run, this results in the following output, passing the test:

```
g++ -std=c++17 propertyBasedTests.cpp -o out/propertyBasedTests
./out/propertyBasedTests
[doctest] doctest version is "2.0.1"
[doctest] run with "--help" for options
Property: 0 to power 0 is 1
=========================================================================
====
[doctest] test cases:    1 |       1 passed |      0 failed |       0
skipped
[doctest] assertions:    1 |       1 passed |      0 failed |
[doctest] Status: SUCCESS!
```

This was easy enough! We now have a basic structure for property-based test. The next test will require a data generator, but we already have it. Let's see how it will work for the 0 property to any power, except 0 equals 0.

Property: $0^{[1 .. maxInt]} \rightarrow 0$

We need our number generator from 1 to maxInt, which we've already implemented. We then need a property function that checks that, for any exponent from 1 to maxInt, 0 raised to the exponent equals 0. The code is quite easy to write:

```
auto prop_0_to_any_nonzero_int_is_0= [](const int exponent){
    CHECK(exponent > 0); // checking the contract just to be sure
    return power(0, exponent) == 0;
};
```

Next, we need to check this property. Since we have a list of generated values, we can use the `all_of` function to check all of them against the property. To make things more informative, I decided to display the list of values we're using:

```
auto printGeneratedValues = [](const string& generatorName, const auto&
    values){
        cout << "Check generator " << generatorName << endl;
        for_each(values.begin(), values.end(), [](auto value) { cout <<
            value << ", ";});
        cout << endl;
};

auto check_property = [](const auto& generator, const auto& property, const
string& generatorName){
    auto values = generator();
    printGeneratedValues(generatorName, values);
```

```
        CHECK(all_of_collection(values, property));
};
```

Finally, we can write our test. We once again display the property name before the test:

```
TEST_CASE("Properties"){
    cout << "Property: 0 to power 0 is 1" << endl;
    CHECK(property_0_to_power_0_is_1);

    cout << "Property: 0 to [1..maxInt] is 0" << endl;
    check_property(generate_ints_greater_than_1,
        prop_0_to_any_nonzero_int_is_0, "generate ints");
}
```

Running the test gives the following output:

```
Property: 0 to power 0 is 1
Property: 0 to [1..maxInt] is 0
Check generator generate ints
1073496375, 263661517, 1090774655, 590994005, 168796979, 1988143371,
1411998804, 1276384966, 252406124, 111200955, 775255151, 1669887756,
1426286501, 1264685577, 1409478643, 944131269, 1688339800, 192256171,
1406363728, 1624573054, 2654328, 1025851283, 1113062216, 1099035394,
624703362, 1523770105, 1243308926, 104279226, 1330992269, 1964576789,
789398651, 453897783, 1041935696, 561917028, 1379973023, 643316376,
1983422999, 1559294692, 2097139875, 384327588, 867142643, 1394240860,
2137873266, 2103542389, 1385608621, 2058924659, 1092474161, 1071910908,
1041001035, 582615293, 1911217125, 1383545491, 410712068, 1161330888,
1939114509, 1395243657, 427165959, 28574042, 1391025789, 224683120,
1222884936, 523039771, 1539230457, 2114587312, 2069325876, 166181790,
1504124934, 1817094271, 328329837, 442231460, 2123558414, 411757963,
1883062671, 1529993763, 1645210705, 866071861, 305821973, 1015936684,
2081548159, 1216448456, 2032167679, 351064479, 1818390045, 858994762,
2073835547, 755252854, 2010595753, 1882881401, 741339006, 1080861523,
1845108795, 362033992, 680848942, 728181713, 1252227588, 125901168,
1212171311, 2110298117, 946911655, 1, 2147483647,
========================================================================
====
[doctest] test cases:      1 |      1 passed |      0 failed |      0
skipped
[doctest] assertions:    103 |    103 passed |      0 failed |
[doctest] Status: SUCCESS!
```

As you can see, a bunch of random values are used for the test, and the final two values are 1 and maxInt.

It's time to pause and reflect for a minute. These tests are unusual. One of the key ideas in unit testing is to have repeatable tests, but here, we have a bunch of random values. Do these count? And what do we do when one value leads to a failure?

These are great questions! First, using property-based tests doesn't exclude example-based tests. In fact, we are mixing the two right now—0^0 is an example rather than a property. So, don't hesitate to check for any specific values when it makes sense.

Second, libraries that support property-based testing allow the collection of specific failure values and retesting for those automatically. It's simple enough—whenever there's a failure, save the values somewhere, and include them in the generation the following occasions when the tests are run. Not only does this allow you to test more thoroughly, but you also discover the behaviors of the code.

We have, therefore, to look at example-based testing and property-based testing as complementary techniques. The first helps you to drive the code using **Test-Driven Development** (**TDD**) and check the interesting cases. The second allows you to find the cases you haven't considered and retest for the same mistakes. Both are useful, just in different ways.

Let's go back to writing our properties, then. The next one is about any number to the power 0 equals 1.

Property: *value: [1 .. maxInt]^0 -> 1*

We have everything in place, and we just need to write it:

```
auto prop_anyIntToPower0Is1 = [](const int base){
    CHECK(base > 0);
    return power(base, 0) == 1;
};
```

The test then becomes the following:

```
TEST_CASE("Properties"){
    cout << "Property: 0 to power 0 is 1" << endl;
    CHECK(property_0_to_power_0_is_1);

    cout << "Property: 0 to [1..maxInt] is 0" << endl;
    check_property(generate_ints_greater_than_1,
        prop_0_to_any_nonzero_int_is_0, "generate ints");

    cout << "Property: any int to power 0 is 1" << endl;
    check_property(generate_ints_greater_than_1,
```

```
                    prop_anyIntToPower0Is1, "generate ints");
}
```

And running the test leads to the following output (a few lines are omitted for brevity):

```
Property: 0 to power 0 is 1
Check generator generate ints
1673741664, 1132665648, 342304077, 936735303, 917238554, 1081591838,
743969276, 1981329112, 127389617,
. . .
  1, 2147483647,
Property: any int to power 0 is 1
Check generator generate ints
736268029, 1304281720, 416541658, 2060514167, 1695305196, 1479818034,
699224013, 1309218505, 302388654, 765083344, 430385474, 648548788,
1986457895, 794974983, 1797109305, 1131764785, 1221836230, 802640954,
. . .
1543181200, 1, 2147483647,
=========================================================================
====
[doctest] test cases:        1 |        1 passed |        0 failed |        0
skipped
[doctest] assertions:      205 |      205 passed |        0 failed |
[doctest] Status: SUCCESS!
```

You can see from the preceding samples that the numbers are indeed random, while always including 1 and maxInt.

We're getting the hang of this! The next property is that any value to the power of 1 is the value.

Property: *value: [0 .. maxInt]^1 -> value*

We need another generator method, starting from 0. We just need to use the bind magic again to obtain the required result:

```
auto generate_ints_greater_than_0 = bind(generate_ints, 0,
numeric_limits<int>::max());
```

This property is easy enough to write:

```
auto prop_any_int_to_power_1_is_the_value = [](const int base){
    return power(base, 1) == base;
};
```

The test is obvious:

```
TEST_CASE("Properties"){
    cout << "Property: 0 to power 0 is 1" << endl;
    CHECK(property_0_to_power_0_is_1);

    cout << "Property: 0 to any non-zero power is 0" << endl;
    check_property(generate_ints_greater_than_1,
        prop_0_to_any_nonzero_int_is_0, "generate ints");

    cout << "Property: any int to power 0 is 1" << endl;
    check_property(generate_ints_greater_than_1,
        prop_anyIntToPower0Is1, "generate ints");

    cout << "Property: any int to power 1 is the value" << endl;
    check_property(generate_ints_greater_than_0,
        prop_any_int_to_power_1_is_the_value, "generate ints");
}
```

Running the test leads once again to a pass.

Let's take a moment to reflect once again:

- How many values do we check? The answer is 301.
- How many lines of test code are there? The test code is just 23 lines of code, while the *library* functions that we reuse for our tests are roughly 40 lines of code.

Isn't this amazing? Doesn't this make a worthy investment in your testing?

We know how to do this. It's time for the most complex property from our exercise—any number raised to power *y* equals the number raised to the power *y-1* multiplied by the number.

Property: $x^y = x^{y-1} * x$

This will require us to generate two sets of values, *x* and *y*, so that $x^y < maxInt$. It took me some fiddling with the data generators, but I figured out that any *x* that's larger than $\sqrt{maxInt}$ can only be tested for *y=1*. I will therefore use two generators; the first one will generate numbers between 2 and $\sqrt{maxInt}$, while the second generates numbers greater than $\sqrt{maxInt}$ and smaller than maxInt:

```
auto generate_ints_greater_than_2_less_sqrt_maxInt = bind(generate_ints, 2,
sqrt(numeric_limits<int>::max()));
```

The first part of the property becomes the following:

```
cout << "Property: next power of x is previous power of x multiplied by
    x" << endl;
check_property(generate_ints_greater_than_2_less_sqrt_maxInt,
    prop_nextPowerOfXIsPreviousPowerOfXMultipliedByX, "generate greater
        than 2 and less than sqrt of maxInt");
```

In order to implement the property, we also need to generate exponents for the x base, so that we can write the property as follows:

```
auto prop_nextPowerOfXIsPreviousPowerOfXMultipliedByX = [](const int x){
    auto exponents = bind(generate_exponent_less_than_log_maxInt, x);
    return check_property(exponents, [x](auto y){ return power(x, y) ==
        power(x, y - 1) * x;}, "generate exponents for " + to_string(x));
};
```

As you can see from the name of the generator function, we need to generate numbers between 1 and $log_x maxInt$. Any number above this value will overflow when computing x^y. Since we don't have a general logarithm function in STL, we need to implement one. To compute $log_x maxInt$, we just need to use a mathematical equality:

```
auto logMaxIntBaseX = [](const int x) -> int{
    auto maxInt = numeric_limits<int>::max() ;
    return floor(log(maxInt) / log(x));
};
```

And our generator function becomes the following:

```
auto generate_exponent_less_than_log_maxInt = [](const int x){
    return generate_ints(1, logMaxIntBaseX(x));
};
```

With this in place, we can run our tests. Here's a brief portion of the output:

```
Check generator generate exponents for 43740
1, 2,
Check generator generate exponents for 9320
1, 2,
Check generator generate exponents for 2
1, 2, 3, 4, 5, 6, 7, 8, 9, 10, 11, 12, 13, 14, 15, 16, 17, 18, 19, 20, 21,
22, 23, 24, 25, 26, 27, 28, 29, 30,
Check generator generate exponents for 46340
1, 2,
```

The final part of the test is to add the interval from $\sqrt{maxInt} + 1$ to `maxInt`:

```
check_property(generate_ints_greater_than_sqrt_maxInt,
    prop_nextPowerOfXIsPreviousPowerOfXMultipliedByX, "generate greater
    than sqrt of maxInt");
```

This also leads to an update in the generation function to support a few edge cases; refer to the comments for explanations in the following code:

```
auto generate_ints = [](const int min, const int max){
    if(min > max) { // when lower range is larger than upper range,
        just return empty vector
            return vector<int>();
    }
    if(min == max){ // if min and max are equal, just return {min}
        return range(min, min);
    }

    if(max - min <= 100){ // if there not enough int values in the
        range, just return it fully
            return range(min, max);
    }
    ...
}
```

And with this, we've implemented our final property!

Conclusion

We're now checking all of the following things with just a few lines of code:

- 0^0 -> undefined (1 by default in pow function in C++)
- $0^{[1 \ .. \ maxInt]}$ -> 0
- value: $[1 \ .. \ maxInt]^0$ -> 1
- value: $[0 \ .. \ maxInt]^1$ -> value
- $x^y = x^{y-1} * x$

How does this compare with the more commonly used approach of having example-based tests? We test more with less code. We can find hidden issues in code. But the properties are more difficult to identify than examples. We've also established that property-based tests work very well together with example-based tests.

So, let's tackle now the problem of finding the properties. This requires a bit of analysis, and we'll explore a practical way in which you can evolve the properties from examples through data-driven tests.

From examples to data-driven tests to properties

When I first heard about property-based tests, I had two issues. First, I thought they were meant to replace example tests—and we know now that they are not; just use the two techniques side by side. Second, I had no idea how to come up with good properties.

I had, however, a good idea on how to come with good examples and how to remove duplication between tests. We've seen a sample on how to come up with good examples for the power function; let's recap them:

- 0^0 -> *undefined (* the pow implementation in C++ returns 1 unless specific errors are enabled)*
- $0^{any\ integer\ from\ 0\ to\ max}$ -> 0
- $1^{any\ integer}$ -> 1
- *(any integer except 0)*^{0} -> 1
- 2^2 -> 4
- $2^{max\ int\ that\ doesn't\ overflow}$ -> *value to be computed*
- 10^5 -> 100000
- $10^{max\ int\ that\ doesn't\ overflow}$ -> *value to be computed*

We've also seen that it's easy enough to write the example-based tests for these situations:

```
TEST_CASE("Power"){
    int maxInt = numeric_limits<int>::max();
    CHECK_EQ(1, power(0, 0));
    CHECK_EQ(0, power(0, 1));
    CHECK_EQ(0, power(0, maxInt));
    CHECK_EQ(1, power(1, 1));
    CHECK_EQ(1, power(1, 2));
    CHECK_EQ(1, power(1, maxInt));
    CHECK_EQ(1, power(2, 0));
    CHECK_EQ(2, power(2, 1));
    CHECK_EQ(4, power(2, 2));
    CHECK_EQ(maxInt, power(2, 31) - 1);
    CHECK_EQ(1, power(3, 0));
```

```
        CHECK_EQ(3, power(3, 1));
        CHECK_EQ(9, power(3, 2));
        CHECK_EQ(1, power(maxInt, 0));
        CHECK_EQ(maxInt, power(maxInt, 1));
    }
```

These examples exhibit code similarity. The 0, 1, 2, and 3 bases repeat a number of times. We've seen in `Chapter 9`, *Test-Driven Development for Functional Programming*, that we can remove this similarity with data-driven tests by specifying multiple input values:

```
    TEST_CASE("1 raised to a power is 1"){
        int exponent;

        SUBCASE("0"){
            exponent = 0;
        }
        SUBCASE("1"){
            exponent = 1;
        }
        SUBCASE("2"){
            exponent = 1;
        }
        SUBCASE("maxInt"){
            exponent = maxInt;
        }

        CAPTURE(exponent);
        CHECK_EQ(1, power(1, exponent));
    }
```

After I worked to remove these similarities for some time, I started to see the properties. It's quite obvious, in this case, that we can add a test that checks the same mathematical property by using random inputs rather than specific examples. Indeed, we wrote it in the previous section, and it looks like this:

```
    cout << "Property: any int to power 1 is the value" << endl;
    check_property(generate_ints_greater_than_0,
        prop_any_int_to_power_1_is_the_value, "generate ints");
```

So my advice is—if you reflect for a few minutes on the problem and find the mathematical properties to check, perfect! (Write the property-based tests and add as many example-based tests to feel confident that you have covered the situations.) If you can't see them, no worries; keep adding example-based tests, remove duplication between tests by using data-driven tests, and eventually you will reveal the properties. Then, add property-based tests and decide what to do with the existing example-based tests.

Good properties, bad properties

Since properties are an abstraction level higher than the examples, it's easy to implement them in a confusing or unclear manner. You already need to pay a lot of attention to example-based tests; you now need to up your efforts in relation to the property-based tests.

First of all, good properties are like good unit tests. We want, therefore to have properties that are as follows:

- Small
- Named appropriately and clearly
- Giving a very clear message when they fail
- Fast
- Repeatable

There's one caveat with property-based tests though—since we're using random values, shouldn't we expect random failures? Well, when a property-based test fails, we learn something new about our code, so it's a reason for celebration. We should expect, however, to have fewer failures as time passes by and we remove our bugs. If your property-based tests fail every day, something is definitely wrong—maybe the property is too large, or the implementation has many holes in it. If your property-based tests fail from time to time, and they show a possible bug in the code—that's great.

One of the difficult things with property-based tests is to keep the generators and the property checks free of bugs. This is code too, and any code can have bugs. In example-based tests, we deal with this problem by simplifying the unit tests to a level where it's virtually impossible to make mistakes. Be aware that properties are more complex, and so may require more attention. The old principle *keep it simple, stupid* is even more valuable when it comes to property-based tests. So, favor smaller properties over larger ones, make your analysis, and review your code with colleagues—both the names and the implementation.

A few words regarding implementation

In this chapter, we've used a custom set of functions for implementing data generators in order to keep the code standard C++ 17. However, these functions are optimized for learning the technique, and are not production ready. You could already see that they are not optimized for memory footprint or performance. We could already make them better with a smart use of iterators, but there's a better way.

If you can use the range library or compile your tests using C++ 20, it's quite easy to implement infinite data generators (due to lazy evaluation). I also advise you to research for property-based tests libraries, or for generator libraries, since some of the generators have already been written by other people and it's much faster to use them in your code once you understand the concept.

Summary

Property-based tests are a welcome addition to the example-based tests we've known and used for many years. They show us how we can combine data generation with a bit of analysis to both remove duplication from tests and find cases we hadn't considered.

Property-based tests are enabled by data generators that are very easy to implement using pure functions. Things will become even easier with lazy evaluation coming in C++ 20 or with the ranges library.

But the core technique in property-based testing is to identify the properties. We've seen two ways to do that—the first by analyzing the examples, and the second by writing the example-based tests, removing duplication to turn them into data-driven tests, and then replacing the rows of data with properties.

Finally, remember that property-based tests are code, and they need to be very clean, easy to change, and easy to understand. Favor small properties whenever possible, and make them very understandable by naming them clearly.

In the next chapter, we will look at how we can use pure functions to support our refactoring effort and at how design patterns can be implemented as functions.

12
Refactoring to and through Pure Functions

Programmers often hit code they are afraid to change. By extracting pure functions, using currying and composition, and taking advantage of the compiler, you can refactor existing code in a safer manner. We'll see an example of refactoring through pure functions, and then we'll look at a few design patterns, how they are implemented in functional programming, and how to use them in your refactoring.

The following topics will be covered in this chapter:

- How to think about legacy code
- How to use the compiler and pure functions to identify and separate dependencies
- How to extract lambdas from any piece of code
- How to remove duplication between lambdas using currying and composition, and group them into classes
- How to implement a few design patterns (strategy, command, and dependency injection) using functions
- How to use design patterns based on functions to refactor toward them

Technical requirements

You will need a compiler that supports C++ 17. I used GCC 7.4.0c.

The code is on GitHub at `https://github.com/PacktPublishing/Hands-On-Functional-Programming-with-Cpp` in the `Chapter12` folder. It includes and uses `doctest`, which is a single-header, open source, unit testing library. You can find it on its GitHub repository at `https://github.com/onqtam/doctest`.

Refactoring to and through pure functions

Refactoring is an important and continuous part of software development. The main reason is the continuous change in requirements, driven by the changes in the world around the applications that we build. Our clients keep learning about the ecosystem in which products work, and need us to adapt these products to the new reality they discover. As a result, our code, even when perfectly structured, is almost always behind our current understanding of the problems that we're solving.

Structuring our code perfectly is no easy feat either. Programmers are people, so we make mistakes, lose focus, and sometimes fail to find the best solutions. The only way to deal with this complex situation is by using merciless refactoring; that is, after we make things work, we improve the code structure until the code is as good as it can be under the constraints we have.

That's easy to say and do, as long as we refactor very early and we write the tests. But what if we inherit a code base that has no tests? What do we do then? We'll visit this problem, along with a promising idea that uses pure functions to refactor the legacy code later.

First, let's define our terms. What is refactoring?

What is refactoring?

Refactoring is one of the terms that's universally used in the industry, but is not well understood. Unfortunately, the term is often used to justify big redesigns. Consider the following common story about a given project:

- When the project starts, features are added at a fast pace.
- Soon enough (months, one year, or even weeks), the speed decreases, but the demand is the same.
- Years later, it's so difficult to add new features that the clients are annoyed and pressure the team.
- Finally, a decision is made to rewrite or change the whole structure of the code in the hope it will speed things up.
- Six months later, the rewrite or redesign (usually) fails and the management faces an impossible situation—should we try to redesign, restart the project, or do something else?

The **big redesign** phase of this cycle is often erroneously called refactoring, but that's not what refactoring is.

Instead, to understand the true meaning of refactoring, let's start by thinking about what changes we can make to a code base. We can usually classify these changes into categories as follows:

- Implementing a new requirement
- Fixing a bug
- Reorganizing the code in various ways—refactoring, re-engineering, re-designing, and/or re-architecting

We can roughly classify these changes into two big categories as follows:

- Changes that impact on the behavior of the code
- Changes that don't impact on the behavior of the code

When we talk about behavior, we talk about inputs and outputs, such as "when I introduce these values in a **user interface** (**UI**) form and click this button, then I see this output and these things are saved". We don't usually include cross-functional concerns such as performance, scalability, or security in the behaviors.

With these terms clear, we can define refactoring—it is simply making changes to the code structure that don't affect the external behavior of the program. Big redesigns or rewrites rarely fit into this definition, because usually, teams doing big redesigns don't prove that the result has the same behaviors as the original (including the known bugs, since someone may depend on them).

Any change to the program that modifies its behavior is not refactoring. This includes fixing bugs or adding a feature. However, we can split these changes into two phases—first, refactor to *make space* for the change, and then make the change in behavior.

This definition raises a few questions, as follows:

- How can we prove we haven't changed the behavior? There's only one way we know to do this: automated regression tests. If we have a suite of automated tests that we trust and that are fast enough, we can easily make a change without changing any tests and see if they pass.

- How small is the refactoring? The larger a change is, the more difficult it is to prove that nothing is affected, since programmers are humans and make mistakes. We prefer to have very small steps in refactoring. Here are a few examples of small behavior-preserving code changes: rename, add a parameter to a function, change the order of parameters for a function, and extract a group of statements into a function, among others. Each small change can be easily made and the tests run to prove that no behavioral change happened. Whenever we need to make a bigger refactoring, we just make a series of these small changes.
- How can we prove that we haven't changed the behavior of code when we have no tests? This is when we need to talk about legacy code and the legacy code dilemma.

The legacy code dilemma

Programming is probably the only domain in which the word *legacy* has a negative connotation. In any other context, legacy means something that someone leaves behind and something that someone is usually proud of. In programming, legacy code refers to exclusive code that we inherit and is a pain to maintain.

Too often, programmers think that legacy code is inevitable and there's nothing that can be done about it. We can, however, do a lot of things. The first is to clarify what we mean by legacy code. Michael Feathers, in his book on legacy code, defines it as code that doesn't have tests. However, I like to use a more general definition: *code that you're afraid to change*. Code that you are afraid to change will slow you down, reduce your options, and make any new development an ordeal. But this is, by no means, inevitable: we can change it and we'll see how.

The second thing we can do is understand the dilemma of legacy code. To be less afraid of change, we need to refactor it, but in order to refactor the code, we need to write tests. To write tests, we need to adjust the code to make it testable; this looks like a circle—in order to change the code, we need to change the code! How do we do that if we're afraid to change the code in the first place?

Fortunately, this dilemma has a resolution. If we could just make safe changes to the code—changes that leave us very little opportunity for error and allows us to test the code—then we could slowly, but surely, improve the code. These changes are, indeed, refactoring, but they're even smaller and safer than the refactoring steps. Their main goal is to break the dependency between the design elements in your code, enabling us to write tests so we can continue refactoring afterward.

Since our focus is on using pure functions and functional constructs to refactor code, we won't look at the full list of techniques. I can give one simple example called **extract and override**. Let's say you need to write tests for a very large function. It would be ideal if we could just write tests for a small part of the function instead. The way we could do this is by extracting the code that we want to test into another function. However, the new function depends on old code, so we'll have a hard time figuring out all the dependencies. To solve this issue, we can create a derived class that overrides all the dependencies of our function with dummy functions. In unit testing, this is called a *partial mock*. This allows us to cover, with tests, all the code from our extracted function, while assuming that all the other parts of the class work as expected. Once we cover it with tests, we can then move to refactoring; we often end up extracting a new class that is fully mocked or stubbed by the end of this exercise.

These techniques were written before we had such widespread support for functional programming in our languages. We can now take advantage of pure functions to safely refactor the code we write. But, to do that, we need to understand how dependencies affect our ability to test and change code.

Dependencies and change

Our users and customers want more and more features, for as long as the project is successful. Yet, we often fail to deliver, because code tends to become more rigid over time. Adding new features gets slower and slower as time passes, and, when adding a feature, new bugs pop up.

This leads to the one-billion question—what makes code difficult to change? How can we write code that maintains the speed of change, or even increases it?

This is a complex problem, with many facets and with various solutions. One of them is fundamentally agreed in the industry—dependencies tend to slow down development. Code structures with fewer dependencies are generally easier to change, thus making it easier to add features.

We can look at dependencies on many levels. At a higher level, we can talk about executables that depend on other executables; for example, a web service that directly calls another web service. Reducing dependencies at this level can be done by using event-based systems instead of direct calls. At a lower level, we can talk about dependencies on libraries or OS routines; for example, a web service that depends on the existence of a specific folder or specific library version.

While all the other levels are interesting, for our goals we will focus on the class/function level, and specifically on how classes and functions depend on one another. Since it's impossible to avoid dependencies in any non-trivial code bases, we will focus instead on the strength of dependencies.

We'll use as an example a small piece of code I wrote that computes salaries based on a list of employees and parameters such as role, seniority, continuity in the organization, and bonus level. It reads the list of employees from a CSV file, computes salaries based on a few rules, and prints the computed salary list. The first version of the code is naively written, using just the main function and putting everything together in the same file, as shown in the following code example:

```cpp
#include <iostream>
#include <fstream>
#include <string>
#include <cmath>

using namespace std;

int main(){
    string id;
    string employee_id;
    string first_name;
    string last_name;
    string seniority_level;
    string position;
    string years_worked_continuously;
    string special_bonus_level;

    ifstream employeesFile("./Employees.csv");
    while (getline(employeesFile, id, ',')) {
        getline(employeesFile, employee_id, ',') ;
        getline(employeesFile, first_name, ',') ;
        getline(employeesFile, last_name, ',') ;
        getline(employeesFile, seniority_level, ',') ;
        getline(employeesFile, position, ',') ;
        getline(employeesFile, years_worked_continuously, ',') ;
        getline(employeesFile, special_bonus_level);
        if(id == "id") continue;

        int baseSalary;
        if(position == "Tester") baseSalary= 1500;
        if(position == "Analyst") baseSalary = 1600;
        if(position == "Developer") baseSalary = 2000;
        if(position == "Team Leader") baseSalary = 3000;
        if(position == "Manager") baseSalary = 4000;
        double factor;
```

```
        if(seniority_level == "Entry") factor = 1;
        if(seniority_level == "Junior") factor = 1.2;
        if(seniority_level == "Senior") factor = 1.5;

        double continuityFactor;
        int continuity = stoi(years_worked_continuously);
        if(continuity < 3) continuityFactor = 1;
        if(continuity >= 3 && continuity < 5) continuityFactor = 1.2;
        if(continuity >= 5 && continuity < 10) continuityFactor = 1.5;
        if(continuity >=10 && continuity <= 20) continuityFactor = 1.7;
        if(continuity > 20) continuityFactor = 2;

        int specialBonusLevel = stoi(special_bonus_level);
        double specialBonusFactor = specialBonusLevel * 0.03;

        double currentSalary = baseSalary * factor * continuityFactor;
        double salary = currentSalary + specialBonusFactor *
            currentSalary;

        int roundedSalary = ceil(salary);

        cout  << seniority_level << position << " " << first_name << "
            " << last_name << " (" << years_worked_continuously <<
            "yrs)" <<  ", " << employee_id << ", has salary (bonus
            level  " << special_bonus_level << ") " << roundedSalary <<
            endl;
    }
}
```

The input file was generated with random values using a specialized tool and looks like this:

```
id,employee_id,First_name,Last_name,Seniority_level,Position,Years_worked_c
ontinuously,Special_bonus_level
1,51ef10eb-8c3b-4129-b844-542afaba7eeb,Carmine,De Vuyst,Junior,Manager,4,3
2,171338c8-2377-4c70-bb66-9ad669319831,Gasper,Feast,Entry,Team Leader,10,5
3,807e1bc7-00db-494b-8f92-44acf141908b,Lin,Sunley,Medium,Manager,23,3
4,c9f18741-cd6c-4dee-a243-00c1f55fde3e,Leeland,Geraghty,Medium,Team
Leader,7,4
5,5722a380-f869-400d-9a6a-918beb4acbe0,Wash,Van der
Kruys,Junior,Developer,7,1
6,f26e94c5-1ced-467b-ac83-a94544735e27,Marjie,True,Senior,Tester,28,1
```

When we run the program, `salary` is computed for each employee and the output looks like this:

```
JuniorManager Carmine De Vuyst (4yrs), 51ef10eb-8c3b-4129-
b844-542afaba7eeb, has salary (bonus level  3) 6279
```

```
EntryTeam Leader Gasper Feast (10yrs), 171338c8-2377-4c70-
bb66-9ad669319831, has salary (bonus level  5) 5865
MediumManager Lin Sunley (23yrs), 807e1bc7-00db-494b-8f92-44acf141908b, has
salary (bonus level  3) 8720
MediumTeam Leader Leeland Geraghty (7yrs), c9f18741-cd6c-4dee-
a243-00c1f55fde3e, has salary (bonus level  4) 5040
JuniorDeveloper Wash Van der Kruys (7yrs), 5722a380-
f869-400d-9a6a-918beb4acbe0, has salary (bonus level  1) 3708
SeniorTester Marjie True (28yrs), f26e94c5-1ced-467b-ac83-a94544735e27, has
salary (bonus level  1) 4635
EntryAnalyst Muriel Dorken (10yrs), f4934e00-9c01-45f9-bddc-2366e6ea070e,
has salary (bonus level  8) 3373
SeniorTester Harrison Mawditt (17yrs), 66da352a-100c-4209-
a13e-00ec12aa167e, has salary (bonus level  10) 4973
```

So, does this code have dependencies? Yes, and they are hidden in plain sight.

One way to find dependencies is to look for constructor calls or global variables. In our case, we have one constructor call to `ifstream`, and one use of the `cout`, as shown in the following example:

```
ifstream employeesFile("./Employees.csv")
cout  << seniority_level << position << " " << first_name << " " <<
    last_name << " (" << years_worked_continuously << "yrs)" <<  ", "
    << employee_id << ", has salary (bonus level  " <<
    special_bonus_level << ") " << roundedSalary << endl;
```

Another way to identify dependencies is to create an imagination exercise. Imagine what requirements could produce changes in the code. There are a few. If we decide to switch to an employee database, we'll need to change the way we read data. If we want to output to a file, we'll need to change the lines of code that print the salaries. If the rules for computing salaries change, we will need to change the lines that compute `salary`.

Both methods lead to the same conclusion; we have dependencies on the file system and on the standard output. Let's focus on the standard output and ask one question; how can we change the code so that we can output the salaries both to standard output and to a file? The answer is quite easy, due to the polymorphic nature of the **Standard Template Library** (**STL**) streams, just extract a function that receives an output stream and writes the data. Let's see what such a function would look like; for simplicity, we've also introduced a structure called `Employee` that contains all the fields we need, as shown in the following example:

```
void printEmployee(const Employee& employee, ostream& stream, int
    roundedSalary){
        stream << employee.seniority_level << employee.position <<
        " " << employee.first_name << " " << employee.last_name <<
```

```
            " (" << employee.years_worked_continuously << "yrs)" <<   ",
            " << employee.employee_id << ", has salary (bonus level  " <<
            employee.special_bonus_level << ") " << roundedSalary << endl;
    }
```

This function doesn't depend on the standard output anymore. In terms of dependencies, we can say that *we broke the dependency* between the employee printing and the standard output. How did we do that? Well, we passed the `cout` stream as an argument of the function from the caller:

```
        printEmployee(employee, cout, roundedSalary);
```

This seemingly minor change makes the function polymorphic. The caller of `printEmployee` now controls the output of the function without changing anything inside the function.

Moreover, we can now write tests for the `printEmployee` function that never touch the filesystem. This is important, since file system access is slow and errors can appear when testing the happy path due to things such as a lack of disk space or corrupted sections. How can we write such tests? Well, we just need to call the function using an in-memory stream, and then compare the output written into the in-memory stream with what we expect.

Therefore, breaking this dependency leads to a huge improvement in the changeability and testability of our code. This mechanism is so useful and widespread that it gained a name—**dependency injection (DI)**. In our case, the caller of the `printEmployee` function (the `main` function, the `test` function, or another future caller) injects the dependency to the output stream into our function, thus controlling its behavior.

It's important to clarify one thing about DI—it is a design pattern, not a library. Many modern libraries and MVC frameworks enable DI, but you don't need anything external to inject dependencies. You just need to pass the dependency into a constructor, property, or function argument and you're all set.

We learned how to identify dependencies and how we can use DI to break them. It's time to look at how we can refactor this code by taking advantage of pure functions.

Pure functions and the structure of programs

A few years ago, I learned a fundamental law about computer programs that has led me to study how to use pure functions in refactoring:

Any computer program can be built from two types of classes/functions—some that do I/O and some that are pure.

Searching for similar ideas afterward, I found Gary Bernhardt's concise naming for such structures: *functional core, imperative shell* (https://www.destroyallsoftware.com/screencasts/catalog/functional-core-imperative-shell).

Regardless of what you call it, the consequences of this idea on refactoring are fundamental. If any program can be written as two separate types of classes/functions, some immutable and some I/O, then we can take advantage of this property to refactor legacy code. The high-level process would look like this:

- Extract pure functions (and we'll see that these steps identify dependencies).
- Test and refactor them.
- Regroup them into classes according to the high-cohesion principle.

I would like to add an axiom to this law. I believe we can apply this at any level of the code, be it a function, class, group of lines of code, group of classes, or whole module, except for those lines of code that are pure I/O. In other words, this law is fractal; it applies at any level of code except the most basic ones.

The importance of this axiom is huge. What it tells us is that we can apply the same method we previously described on any level of the code, except the most basic. In other words, it doesn't matter where we start applying the method because it will work anywhere.

In the following sections, we will explore each step of the method. First, let's extract some pure functions.

Use the compiler and pure functions to identify dependencies

It can feel risky to try to change code that we don't understand and that doesn't have tests. Any mistake can lead to ugly bugs, and any change can lead to a mistake.

Fortunately, the compiler and pure functions can help reveal the dependencies. Remember what pure functions are—functions that return the same outputs for the same inputs. This means, by definition, that all dependencies of pure functions are visible, passed either as parameters, global variables, or through variable capture.

This leads us to a simple way to identify dependencies in code: pick a few lines of code, extract them into a function, make it pure, and let the compiler tell you what the dependencies are. In addition, the dependencies will have to be injected, thus leading us to a testable function.

Let's look at a few examples. A simple start is the following few lines of code that compute the base salary based on a given employee's position in the company:

```
int baseSalary;
if(position == "Tester") baseSalary = 1500;
if(position == "Analyst") baseSalary = 1600;
if(position == "Developer") baseSalary = 2000;
if(position == "Team Leader") baseSalary = 3000;
if(position == "Manager") baseSalary = 4000;
```

Let's extract this as a pure function. The name doesn't matter for now, so we'll temporarily call it doesSomething and I'll just copy and paste the lines of code into the new function, without removing them from the old function, as shown in the following example:

```
auto doesSomething = [](){
        int baseSalary;
        if(position == "Tester") baseSalary = 1500;
        if(position == "Analyst") baseSalary = 1600;
        if(position == "Developer") baseSalary = 2000;
        if(position == "Team Leader") baseSalary = 3000;
        if(position == "Manager") baseSalary = 4000;
};
```

My compiler immediately complains that the position is not defined, so it did my work for me in figuring out the dependency. Let's add it as an argument as shown in the following example:

```
auto doesSomething = [](const string& position){
        int baseSalary;
        if(position == "Tester") baseSalary = 1500;
        if(position == "Analyst") baseSalary = 1600;
        if(position == "Developer") baseSalary = 2000;
        if(position == "Team Leader") baseSalary = 3000;
        if(position == "Manager") baseSalary = 4000;
};
```

This function is missing something; pure functions always return values, but this does not. Let's add the return statement as shown in the following code example:

```
auto doesSomething = [](const string& position){
        int baseSalary;
        if(position == "Tester") baseSalary = 1500;
        if(position == "Analyst") baseSalary = 1600;
        if(position == "Developer") baseSalary = 2000;
        if(position == "Team Leader") baseSalary = 3000;
        if(position == "Manager") baseSalary = 4000;
```

```
            return baseSalary;
    };
```

The function is now simple enough to test in isolation. But first, we need to extract it into a separate .h file and give it a proper name. baseSalaryForPosition sounds good; let's see its tests in the following code:

```
TEST_CASE("Base salary"){
    CHECK_EQ(1500, baseSalaryForPosition("Tester"));
    CHECK_EQ(1600, baseSalaryForPosition("Analyst"));
    CHECK_EQ(2000, baseSalaryForPosition("Developer"));
    CHECK_EQ(3000, baseSalaryForPosition("Team Leader"));
    CHECK_EQ(4000, baseSalaryForPosition("Manager"));
    CHECK_EQ(0, baseSalaryForPosition("asdfasdfs"));
}
```

The tests are fairly simple to write. They also duplicate many things from the function, the position strings and salary values included. There are better ways to organize the code, but that is expected from legacy code. For now, we are happy that we covered part of the initial code with tests. We can also show these tests to a domain expert and check that they are correct, but let's continue with our refactoring. We need to start calling the new function from main(), as shown in the following:

```
while (getline(employeesFile, id, ',')) {
    getline(employeesFile, employee_id, ',') ;
    getline(employeesFile, first_name, ',') ;
    getline(employeesFile, last_name, ',') ;
    getline(employeesFile, seniority_level, ',') ;
    getline(employeesFile, position, ',') ;
    getline(employeesFile, years_worked_continuously, ',') ;
    getline(employeesFile, special_bonus_level);
    if(id == "id") continue;

    int baseSalary = baseSalaryForPosition(position);
    double factor;
    if(seniority_level == "Entry") factor = 1;
    if(seniority_level == "Junior") factor = 1.2;
    if(seniority_level == "Senior") factor = 1.5;
    ...
}
```

While this was an easy case, it shows the basic process, as listed in the following:

- Pick a few lines of code.
- Extract them into a function.
- Make the function pure.

- Inject all dependencies.
- Write tests for the new pure function.
- Validate the behaviors.
- Repeat until the whole code is covered in tests.

If you follow this process, the risk of introducing bugs becomes extremely small. From my experience, what you need to be most careful about is making the function pure. Remember—if it's in a class, make it static with `const` parameters, but if it's outside of a class, pass all parameters as `const` and make it a lambda.

If we repeat this process a few more times, we end up with more pure functions. First, `factorForSeniority` computes the factor based on the seniority level, as shown in the following example:

```
auto factorForSeniority = [](const string& seniority_level){
    double factor;
    if(seniority_level == "Entry") factor = 1;
    if(seniority_level == "Junior") factor = 1.2;
    if(seniority_level == "Senior") factor = 1.5;
    return factor;
};
```

Then, `factorForContinuity` computes the factor based on—you guessed it—continuity:

```
auto factorForContinuity = [](const string& years_worked_continuously){
    double continuityFactor;
    int continuity = stoi(years_worked_continuously);
    if(continuity < 3) continuityFactor = 1;
    if(continuity >= 3 && continuity < 5) continuityFactor = 1.2;
    if(continuity >= 5 && continuity < 10) continuityFactor = 1.5;
    if(continuity >=10 && continuity <= 20) continuityFactor = 1.7;
    if(continuity > 20) continuityFactor = 2;
    return continuityFactor;
};
```

Finally, the `bonusLevel` function reads the bonus level:

```
auto bonusLevel = [](const string& special_bonus_level){
    return stoi(special_bonus_level);
};
```

Each of these functions can be easily tested with example-based, data-driven, or property-based tests. With all these functions extracted, our main method looks like the following example (a few lines were omitted for brevity):

```
int main() {
...
    ifstream employeesFile("./Employees.csv");
    while (getline(employeesFile, id, ',')) {
        getline(employeesFile, employee_id, ',') ;
...
        getline(employeesFile, special_bonus_level);
        if(id == "id") continue;

        int baseSalary = baseSalaryForPosition(position);
        double factor = factorForSeniority(seniority_level);

        double continuityFactor =
            factorForContinuity(years_worked_continuously);

        int specialBonusLevel =  bonusLevel(special_bonus_level);
        double specialBonusFactor = specialBonusLevel * 0.03;

        double currentSalary = baseSalary * factor * continuityFactor;
        double salary = currentSalary + specialBonusFactor *
            currentSalary;

        int roundedSalary = ceil(salary);

        cout  << seniority_level << position << " " << first_name << "
            " << last_name << " (" << years_worked_continuously << "yrs)"
            <<  ", " << employee_id << ", has salary (bonus level  " <<
            special_bonus_level << ") " << roundedSalary << endl;
    }
```

This is a bit cleaner and better covered with tests. Lambdas can be used for much more though; let's see how we can do this.

From legacy code to lambdas

Besides purity, lambdas offer us many operations we can use: functional composition, partial application, currying, and higher-level functions. We can take advantage of these operations while refactoring legacy code.

The easiest way to show this is by extracting the whole `salary` computation from the `main` method. These are the lines of code that compute the `salary`:

```
...
        int baseSalary = baseSalaryForPosition(position);
        double factor = factorForSeniority(seniority_level);

        double continuityFactor =
            factorForContinuity(years_worked_continuously);

        int specialBonusLevel =  bonusLevel(special_bonus_level);
        double specialBonusFactor = specialBonusLevel * 0.03;

        double currentSalary = baseSalary * factor * continuityFactor;
        double salary = currentSalary + specialBonusFactor *
            currentSalary;

        int roundedSalary = ceil(salary);
...
```

We can extract this pure function in two ways—one is by passing in every value needed as a parameter, the result of which is shown in the following:

```
auto computeSalary = [](const string& position, const string
seniority_level, const string& years_worked_continuously, const string&
special_bonus_level){
    int baseSalary = baseSalaryForPosition(position);
    double factor = factorForSeniority(seniority_level);

    double continuityFactor =
        factorForContinuity(years_worked_continuously);

    int specialBonusLevel =  bonusLevel(special_bonus_level);
    double specialBonusFactor = specialBonusLevel * 0.03;

    double currentSalary = baseSalary * factor * continuityFactor;
    double salary = currentSalary + specialBonusFactor * currentSalary;

    int roundedSalary = ceil(salary);
    return roundedSalary;
};
```

The second option is much more interesting. Instead of passing the variables, how about we pass the functions and bind them to the needed variables beforehand?

That's an intriguing idea. The result is a function that receives multiple functions as a parameter, each of them without any arguments:

```
auto computeSalary = [](auto baseSalaryForPosition, auto
factorForSeniority, auto factorForContinuity, auto bonusLevel){
    int baseSalary = baseSalaryForPosition();
    double factor = factorForSeniority();
    double continuityFactor = factorForContinuity();
    int specialBonusLevel = bonusLevel();

    double specialBonusFactor = specialBonusLevel * 0.03;

    double currentSalary = baseSalary * factor * continuityFactor;
    double salary = currentSalary + specialBonusFactor * currentSalary;

    int roundedSalary = ceil(salary);
    return roundedSalary;
};
```

The `main` method needs to bind the functions first and then inject them into our method, as follows:

```
auto roundedSalary = computeSalary(
        bind(baseSalaryForPosition, position),
        bind(factorForSeniority, seniority_level),
    bind(factorForContinuity, years_worked_continuously),
    bind(bonusLevel, special_bonus_level));

cout << seniority_level << position << " " << first_name << "
  " << last_name << " (" << years_worked_continuously << "yrs)"
    << ", " << employee_id << ", has salary (bonus level  " <<
    special_bonus_level << ") " << roundedSalary << endl;
```

Why is this approach interesting? Well, let's look at it from a software design perspective. We created small pure functions that each have a clear responsibility. Then, we bound them to specific values. Afterward, we passed them as arguments to another lambda that uses them to compute the result we need.

What would that mean in an **object-oriented programming (OOP)** style? Well, functions would be part of a class. Binding a function to a value is equivalent to calling the constructor of the class. Passing the object to another function is called DI.

Wait a minute! What we are actually doing is separating responsibilities and injecting dependencies, only by using pure functions instead of objects! Because we use pure functions, the dependencies are made evident by the compiler. Therefore, we have a method to refactor code that has a very small probability of error, because we use the compiler a lot. This is a very useful process for refactoring.

I have to admit that the result is not as nice as I'd like. Let's refactor our lambda.

Refactoring lambdas

I'm not happy with what the `computeSalary` lambda we've extracted looks like. It's quite complex due to receiving many parameters and multiple responsibilities. Let's take a closer look at it, and see how we can improve it:

```
auto computeSalary = [](auto baseSalaryForPosition, auto
    factorForSeniority, auto factorForContinuity, auto bonusLevel){
        int baseSalary = baseSalaryForPosition();
        double factor = factorForSeniority();
        double continuityFactor = factorForContinuity();
        int specialBonusLevel =  bonusLevel();

        double specialBonusFactor = specialBonusLevel * 0.03;

        double currentSalary = baseSalary * factor * continuityFactor;
        double salary = currentSalary + specialBonusFactor *
            currentSalary;

        int roundedSalary = ceil(salary);
         return roundedSalary;
};
```

All the signs seem to point to the fact that the function has multiple responsibilities. What if we extract more functions from it? Let's start with the `specialBonusFactor` computation:

```
auto specialBonusFactor = [](auto bonusLevel){
    return bonusLevel() * 0.03;
};
auto computeSalary = [](auto baseSalaryForPosition, auto
factorForSeniority, auto factorForContinuity, auto bonusLevel){
    int baseSalary = baseSalaryForPosition();
    double factor = factorForSeniority();
    double continuityFactor = factorForContinuity();

    double currentSalary = baseSalary * factor * continuityFactor;
    double salary = currentSalary + specialBonusFactor() *
```

```
        currentSalary;

    int roundedSalary = ceil(salary);
    return roundedSalary;
};
```

We can now inject `specialBonusFactor`. However, notice that `specialBonusFactor` is the only lambda that needs `bonusLevel`. This means that we can replace the `bonusLevel` lambda with the `specialBonusFactor` lambda partially applied to `bonusLevel`, as shown in the following example:

```
int main(){
            ...
    auto bonusFactor = bind(specialBonusFactor, [&](){ return
        bonusLevel(special_bonus_level); } );
    auto roundedSalary = computeSalary(
            bind(baseSalaryForPosition, position),
            bind(factorForSeniority, seniority_level),
            bind(factorForContinuity, years_worked_continuously),
            bonusFactor
        );
    ...
}

auto computeSalary = [](auto baseSalaryForPosition, auto
factorForSeniority, auto factorForContinuity, auto bonusFactor){
    int baseSalary = baseSalaryForPosition();
    double factor = factorForSeniority();
    double continuityFactor = factorForContinuity();

    double currentSalary = baseSalary * factor * continuityFactor;
    double salary = currentSalary + bonusFactor() * currentSalary;

    int roundedSalary = ceil(salary);
    return roundedSalary;
};
```

Our `computeSalary` lambda is now smaller. We can make it even smaller still, by inlining the temporary variables:

```
auto computeSalary = [](auto baseSalaryForPosition, auto
    factorForSeniority, auto factorForContinuity, auto bonusFactor){
        double currentSalary = baseSalaryForPosition() *
            factorForSeniority() * factorForContinuity();
    double salary = currentSalary + bonusFactor() * currentSalary;
    return ceil(salary);
};
```

That's pretty good! However, I'd like to get it closer to a mathematical formula. First, let's rewrite the line computing `salary` (highlighted in bold in the code):

```
auto computeSalary = [](auto baseSalaryForPosition, auto
    factorForSeniority, auto factorForContinuity, auto bonusFactor){
        double currentSalary = baseSalaryForPosition() *
            factorForSeniority() * factorForContinuity();
        double salary = (1 + bonusFactor()) * currentSalary;
    return ceil(salary);
};
```

Then, let's replace the variable with the functions. We are then left with the following code example:

```
auto computeSalary = [](auto baseSalaryForPosition, auto
    factorForSeniority, auto factorForContinuity, auto bonusFactor){
        return ceil (
            (1 + bonusFactor()) * baseSalaryForPosition() *
                factorForSeniority() * factorForContinuity()
    );
};
```

Therefore, we have a lambda that receives multiple lambdas and uses them to compute a value. We could still make improvements to the other functions, but we have reached an interesting point.

So where do we go from here? We've injected dependencies, the code is more modular, easier to change, and easier to test. We can inject lambdas from tests that return the values we want, which is actually a stub in unit testing. While we haven't improved the whole code, we have separated dependencies and responsibilities by extracting pure functions and using functional operations. We can leave the code like this if we want to. Or, we can take another step and regroup the functions into classes.

From lambdas to classes

We've already made the point a few times in this book, that a class is nothing more than a set of cohesive partially applied pure functions. With our technique until now, we've created a bunch of partially applied pure functions. Turning them into classes is a simple task now.

Let's see a simple example of the `baseSalaryForPosition` function:

```
auto baseSalaryForPosition = [](const string& position){
    int baseSalary;
    if(position == "Tester") baseSalary = 1500;
    if(position == "Analyst") baseSalary = 1600;
    if(position == "Developer") baseSalary = 2000;
    if(position == "Team Leader") baseSalary = 3000;
    if(position == "Manager") baseSalary = 4000;
    return baseSalary;
};
```

We use it in `main()` as in the following example:

```
auto roundedSalary = computeSalary(
        bind(baseSalaryForPosition, position),
        bind(factorForSeniority, seniority_level),
        bind(factorForContinuity, years_worked_continuously),
        bonusFactor
    );
```

To turn it into a class, we just need to create a constructor that will receive the `position` parameter and then change it to be a class method. Let's see it in the following example:

```
class BaseSalaryForPosition{
    private:
        const string& position;

    public:
        BaseSalaryForPosition(const string& position) :
            position(position){};

        int baseSalaryForPosition() const{
            int baseSalary;
            if(position == "Tester") baseSalary = 1500;
            if(position == "Analyst") baseSalary = 1600;
            if(position == "Developer") baseSalary = 2000;
            if(position == "Team Leader") baseSalary = 3000;
            if(position == "Manager") baseSalary = 4000;
            return baseSalary;
        }
};
```

Instead of passing the partially applied function into the `computeSalary` lambda, we can simply initialize it and pass the object, as shown in the following code:

```
auto bonusFactor = bind(specialBonusFactor, [&](){ return
    bonusLevel(special_bonus_level); } );
auto roundedSalary = computeSalary(
    theBaseSalaryForPosition,
    bind(factorForSeniority, seniority_level),
    bind(factorForContinuity, years_worked_continuously),
    bonusFactor
);
```

For this to work, we also need to change our `computeSalary` lambda as shown here:

```
auto computeSalary = [](const BaseSalaryForPosition&
    baseSalaryForPosition, auto factorForSeniority, auto
        factorForContinuity, auto bonusFactor){
        return ceil (
            (1 + bonusFactor()) *
                baseSalaryForPosition.baseSalaryForPosition() *
                    factorForSeniority() * factorForContinuity()
        );
};
```

Now, to allow the injection of different implementations, we actually need to extract an interface from the `BaseSalaryForPosition` class and inject it as an interface, instead of a class. This is especially useful for injecting doubles from tests, such as stubs or mocks.

From now on, nothing stops you regrouping the functions into classes as you see fit. I will leave this as an exercise for the reader because I believe we have shown how to use pure functions to refactor code, even when we want to obtain the object-oriented code at the end.

Recapping the refactoring method

What have we learned so far? Well, we went through a structured process of refactoring that can be used at any level in the code, reduces the probability of errors, and enables changeability and testing. The process is based on two fundamental ideas—any program can be written as a combination of immutable functions and I/O functions, or as a functional core within an imperative shell. In addition, we have shown that this property is fractal—we can apply it to any level of code, from a few lines up to a whole module.

Since immutable functions can be the core of our programs, we can extract them little by little. We write the new function name, copy and paste the body, and use the compiler to pass any dependencies as arguments. When the code is compiled, and if we're carefully and slowly changing it, we are fairly sure that the code still works properly. This extraction reveals the dependencies of our function, thus allowing us to make design decisions.

Going forward, we will extract more functions that receive other partially applied pure functions as parameters. This leads to a clear distinction between dependencies and actual breaking dependencies.

Finally, since the partially applied functions are equivalent to classes, we can easily encapsulate one or more of them, based on cohesion. This process works whether we start from classes or functions, and it's no matter if we want to end with functions or classes as well. However, it allows us to use functional constructs to break dependencies and to separate responsibilities in our code.

Since we are improving the design, it's time to see how design patterns apply in functional programming and how to refactor toward them. We'll visit a few of the Gang of Four patterns, as well as DI, which we've already used in our code.

Design patterns

Many of the good things in software development come from people who notice how programmers work and extract certain lessons from it; in other words, looking at the practical approaches and extracting common and useful lessons rather than speculating a solution.

The so-called Gang of Four (Erich Gamma, Richard Helm, Ralph Johnson, and John Vlissides) took this exact approach when they documented, in a precise language, a list of design patterns. After noticing how more programmers were solving the same problems in similar ways, they decided to write these patterns down and introduced the world of programming to the idea of reusable solutions to specific problems within a clear context.

Since the design paradigm of the day was OOP, the *Design Patterns* book they published shows these solutions using object-oriented approaches. As an aside, it's quite interesting to notice that they documented at least two types of solutions wherever possible—one based on careful inheritance and the other on object composition. I've spent many hours studying the design patterns book, and I can tell you that it's a very interesting lesson in software design.

We'll be exploring a few design patterns and how to implement them using functions in the next section.

The strategy pattern, functional style

The strategy pattern can be described briefly as a way to structure your code, which allows the selection of an algorithm at runtime. The OOP implementation uses DI, and you're probably familiar with both the object-oriented and functional design from STL.

Let's take a look at the STL `sort` function. Its most complex form requires a functor object as shown in the following example:

```
class Comparator{
    public:
        bool operator() (int first, int second) { return (first < second);}
};

TEST_CASE("Strategy"){
    Comparator comparator;
    vector<int> values {23, 1, 42, 83, 52, 5, 72, 11};
    vector<int> expected {1, 5, 11, 23, 42, 52, 72, 83};

    sort(values.begin(), values.end(), comparator);

    CHECK_EQ(values, expected);
}
```

The `sort` function uses the `comparator` object to compare elements from the vector and sort it in place. It's a strategy pattern because we can exchange `comparator` with anything that has the same interface; in fact, it just requires the `operator()` function to be implemented. We could imagine, for example, a UI in which a human user selects the comparison function and sorts a list of values using it; we would only need to create the right instance of `comparator` at runtime and send it to the `sort` function.

You can already see the seeds of the functional solution. In fact, the `sort` function allows a much simpler version, as shown in the following example:

```
auto compare = [](auto first, auto second) { return first < second;};

TEST_CASE("Strategy"){
    vector<int> values {23, 1, 42, 83, 52, 5, 72, 11};
    vector<int> expected {1, 5, 11, 23, 42, 52, 72, 83};

    sort(values.begin(), values.end(), compare);
```

```
        CHECK_EQ(values, expected);
    }
```

This time, we drop the ceremony and jump straight into implementing what we need—a comparison function that we plug into `sort`. No more classes, no more operators—a strategy is just a function.

Let's see how this works in a more complex context. We will use the problem from the Wikipedia page on the *Strategy pattern*, `https://en.wikipedia.org/wiki/Strategy_pattern`, and write it using a functional approach.

Here's the problem: we need to write a billing system for a pub that can apply a discount for the happy hour. The problem lends itself to the usage of the strategy pattern since we have two strategies for computing the final price of the bill—one that returns the full price, while the second returns a happy hour discount on the full bill (we'll use 50% in our case). Once again, the solution is to simply use two functions for the two strategies—the `normalBilling` function that just returns the full price it receives and the `happyHourBilling` function that returns half the value it receives. Let's see this in action in the following code (resulting from my **test-driven development (TDD)** approach):

```cpp
map<string, double> drinkPrices = {
    {"Westmalle Tripel", 15.50},
    {"Lagavulin 18y", 25.20},
};

auto happyHourBilling = [](auto price){
    return price / 2;
};

auto normalBilling = [](auto price){
    return price;
};

auto computeBill = [](auto drinks, auto billingStrategy){
    auto prices = transformAll<vector<double>>(drinks, [](auto drink){
    return drinkPrices[drink]; });
    auto sum = accumulateAll(prices, 0.0, std::plus<double>());
    return billingStrategy(sum);
};

TEST_CASE("Compute total bill from list of drinks, normal billing"){
    vector<string> drinks;
    double expectedBill;

    SUBCASE("no drinks"){
        drinks = {};
```

```
            expectedBill = 0;
        };

        SUBCASE("one drink no discount"){
            drinks = {"Westmalle Tripel"};
            expectedBill = 15.50;
        };

        SUBCASE("one another drink no discount"){
            drinks = {"Lagavulin 18y"};
            expectedBill = 25.20;
        };

      double actualBill = computeBill(drinks, normalBilling);

      CHECK_EQ(expectedBill, actualBill);
    }

    TEST_CASE("Compute total bill from list of drinks, happy hour"){
        vector<string> drinks;
        double expectedBill;

        SUBCASE("no drinks"){
            drinks = {};
            expectedBill = 0;
        };

        SUBCASE("one drink happy hour"){
            drinks = {"Lagavulin 18y"};
            expectedBill = 12.60;
        };

        double actualBill = computeBill(drinks, happyHourBilling);

        CHECK_EQ(expectedBill, actualBill);
    }
```

I think this shows that the simplest implementation for a strategy is a function. I personally enjoy the simplicity this model brings to the strategy pattern; it's liberating to write minimal useful code that makes things work.

The command pattern, functional style

The command pattern is one that I've used extensively in my work. It fits perfectly with MVC web frameworks, allowing the separation of the controller into multiple pieces of functionality, and at the same time allows separation from the storage format. Its intent is to separate a request from the action—that's what makes it so versatile, since any call can be seen as a request.

A simple example of usage for the command pattern is in games that support multiple controllers and changing the keyboard shortcuts. These games can't afford to link the *W* key press event directly to the code that moves your character up; instead, you bind the *W* key to a `MoveUpCommand`, thus neatly decoupling the two. We can easily change the controller event associated with the command or the code for moving up, without interference between the two.

When we look at how commands are implemented in object-oriented code, the functional solution becomes equally obvious. A `MoveUpCommand` class would look like the following example:

```
class MoveUpCommand{
    public:
        MoveUpCommand(/*parameters*/){}
        void execute(){ /* implementation of the command */}
}
```

I said it was obvious! What we're actually trying to accomplish is easily done with a named function, as shown in the following example:

```
auto moveUpCommand = [](/*parameters*/{
/* implementation */
};
```

The simplest command pattern is a function. Who would have thought it?

Dependency injection with functions

We can't talk about widely spread design patterns without touching on DI. While not defined in the Gang of Four book, the pattern has become so common in modern code that many programmers know it as being part of a framework or library rather than as the design pattern.

The intent of the DI pattern is to separate the creation of dependencies for a class or function from their behavior. To understand the problem it solves, let's look at this code:

```
auto readFromFileAndAddTwoNumbers = [](){
    int first;
    int second;
    ifstream numbersFile("numbers.txt");
    numbersFile >> first;
    numbersFile >> second;
    numbersFile.close();
    return first + second;
};

TEST_CASE("Reads from file"){
    CHECK_EQ(30, readFromFileAndAddTwoNumbers());
}
```

This is pretty fair code to write if all you need to do is add together two numbers read from a file. Unfortunately, in the real world, our clients will most likely require more sources for reading the numbers, such as, a console, as shown in the following:

```
auto readFromConsoleAndAddTwoNumbers = [](){
    int first;
    int second;
    cout << "Input first number: ";
    cin >> first;
    cout << "Input second number: ";
    cin >> second;
    return first + second;
};

TEST_CASE("Reads from console"){
    CHECK_EQ(30, readFromConsoleAndAddTwoNumbers());
}
```

Before moving on, please note that the test for this function will pass only if you introduce from the console 2 numbers whose sum is 30. Because they require input at every run, the test case is commented in our code sample; please feel free to enable it and play around with it.

The two functions look very similar. To solve such similarities, DI can help as shown in the following example:

```cpp
auto readAndAddTwoNumbers = [](auto firstNumberReader, auto
    secondNumberReader){
        int first = firstNumberReader();
        int second = secondNumberReader();
        return first + second;
};
```

Now we can implement readers that use files:

```cpp
auto readFirstFromFile = [](){
    int number;
    ifstream numbersFile("numbers.txt");
    numbersFile >> number;
    numbersFile.close();
    return number;
};

auto readSecondFromFile = [](){
    int number;
    ifstream numbersFile("numbers.txt");
    numbersFile >> number;
    numbersFile >> number;
    numbersFile.close();
    return number;
};
```

We can also implement readers who use the console:

```cpp
auto readFirstFromConsole = [](){
    int number;
    cout << "Input first number: ";
    cin >> number;
    return number;
};

auto readSecondFromConsole = [](){
    int number;
    cout << "Input second number: ";
    cin >> number;
    return number;
};
```

As usual, we can test that they work correctly in various combinations, as shown in the following:

```
TEST_CASE("Reads using dependency injection and adds two numbers"){
    CHECK_EQ(30, readAndAddTwoNumbers(readFirstFromFile,
        readSecondFromFile));
    CHECK_EQ(30, readAndAddTwoNumbers(readFirstFromConsole,
        readSecondFromConsole));
    CHECK_EQ(30, readAndAddTwoNumbers(readFirstFromFile,
        readSecondFromConsole));
}
```

We are injecting the code that reads the numbers through a lambda. Please note in the test code that using this method allows us to mix and match the dependencies as we see fit—the last check reads the first number from a file, while the second is read from the console.

Of course, the way we usually implement DI in object-oriented languages uses interfaces and classes. However, as we can see, the simplest way to implement DI is with a function.

Purely functional design patterns

So far, we've seen how some of the classic object-oriented design patterns can be turned into a functional variant. But can we imagine design patterns that stem from functional programming?

Well, we've actually already used some of them. map/reduce (or transform/accumulate in STL) is one example. Most of the higher-order functions (such as filter, all_of, and any_of, among others) are also examples of patterns. However, we can go even further and explore a common, but opaque, design pattern that comes from functional programming.

The best way to understand it is by starting from specific problems. First, we'll see how we can maintain state in an immutable context. Then, we'll learn about the design pattern. Finally, we'll see it in action in another context.

Maintaining state

How can we maintain state in functional programming? This may seem like a strange question, given that one of the ideas behind functional programming is immutability, which, in turn, seems to prevent state change.

However, this limitation is an illusion. To understand it, let's think for a moment about how time passes. If I put on a hat, I change my state from hat off to hat on. If I could look back in time second by second from the moment I reached for the hat until I had it on, I would be able to see how my movement advanced each second toward this goal. But I can't change anything from any past second. The past is immutable, whether we like it or not (after all, maybe I look silly with the hat, but I can't revert it). So nature makes time work in such a way that the past is immutable, yet we can change state.

How can we model this conceptually? Well, think about it this way—first, we have an initial state, Alex with hat off, and a definition of a movement with the intent to reach the hat and put it on. In programming terms, we model the movement with a function. The function receives the position of the hand and the function itself, and returns the new position of the hand plus the function. Therefore, by copying nature, we end up with the sequence of states in the following example:

```
Alex wants to put the hat on
Initial state: [InitialHandPosition, MovementFunction (HandPosition -> next
HandPosition)]
State₁ = [MovementFunction(InitialHandPosition), MovementFunction]
State₂ = [MovementFunction(HandPosition at State₁),MovementFunction]...
Stateₙ = [MovementFunction(HandPosition at Stateₙ₋₁), MovementFunction]
until Alex has hat on
```

By applying `MovementFunction` repeatedly, we end up with a sequence of states. *Each of the states is immutable, yet we can store the state.*

Now let's see a simple example in C++. The simplest example we can use is an autoincrement index. The index needs to remember the last value used and use an `increment` function to return the next value from the index. Normally, we would be in trouble when trying to implement this using immutable code, but can we do it with the method described previously?

Let's find out. First, we need to initialize the auto-increment index with the first value—let's say it's 1. As usual, I'd like to check that the value is initialized to what I expect, as shown in the following:

```
TEST_CASE ("Id") {
    const auto autoIncrementIndex = initAutoIncrement(1);
    CHECK_EQ(1, value(autoIncrementIndex));
}
```

Note that, since the `autoIncrementIndex` does not change, we can make it `const`.

How do we implement `initAutoIncrement`? As we said, we need to initialize a structure that holds both the current value (1 in this case) and the increment function. I will start with a pair like this:

```
auto initAutoIncrement = [](const int initialId){
    function<int(const int)> nextId = [](const int lastId){
        return lastId + 1;
    };

    return make_pair(initialId, nextId);
};
```

As for the previous `value` function, it just returns the value from the pair; it is the first element from the pair, as shown in the following snippet:

```
auto value = [](const auto previous){
    return previous.first;
};
```

Let's compute now the next element from our autoincrement index. We initialize it, then compute the next value, and check that the next value is 2:

```
TEST_CASE("Compute next auto increment index"){
    const auto autoIncrementIndex = initAutoIncrement(1);

    const auto nextAutoIncrementIndex =
        computeNextAutoIncrement(autoIncrementIndex);

    CHECK_EQ(2, value(nextAutoIncrementIndex));
}
```

Once again, please note that both `autoIncrementIndex` variables are `const` because they never mutate. We have the value function already, but what does the `computeNextAutoIncrement` function look like? Well, it has to take the current value and the function from the pair, apply the function to the current value, and return a pair between the new value and the function:

```
auto computeNextAutoIncrement = [](pair<const int, function<int(const
    int)>> current){
        const auto currentValue = value(current);
        const auto functionToApply = lambda(current);
        const int newValue = functionToApply(currentValue);
        return make_pair(newValue, functionToApply);
};
```

We're using a utility function, `lambda`, that returns the lambda from the pair:

```
auto lambda = [](const auto previous){
    return previous.second;
};
```

Does this really work? Let's test the next value:

```
TEST_CASE("Compute next auto increment index"){
    const auto autoIncrementIndex = initAutoIncrement(1);
    const auto nextAutoIncrementIndex =
        computeNextAutoIncrement(autoIncrementIndex);
    CHECK_EQ(2, value(nextAutoIncrementIndex));

    const auto newAutoIncrementIndex =
        computeNextAutoIncrement(nextAutoIncrementIndex);
    CHECK_EQ(3, value(newAutoIncrementIndex));
}
```

All the tests pass, showing that we have just stored the state in an immutable way!

Since this solution seems very simple, the next question is—can we generalize it? Let's try.

First, let's replace `pair` with `struct`. The struct needs to have a value and function that will compute the next value as data members. This will remove the need for our `value()` and `lambda()` functions:

```
struct State{
    const int value;
    const function<int(const int)> computeNext;
};
```

The `int` type repeats itself, but why should it? A state can be more complex than just `int`, so let's turn our `struct` into a template:

```
template<typename ValueType>
struct State{
    const ValueType value;
    const function<ValueType(const ValueType)> computeNext;
};
```

With this, we can initialize an autoincrement index and check the initial value:

```
auto increment = [](const int current){
    return current + 1;
};

TEST_CASE("Initialize auto increment"){
```

```
        const auto autoIncrementIndex = State<int>{1, increment};

        CHECK_EQ(1, autoIncrementIndex.value);
    }
```

Lastly, we need a function that computes the next State. The function needs to return a State<ValueType>, so it's best to encapsulate it into the State struct. Also, it can use the current value, so there is no need to pass a value into it:

```
    template<typename ValueType>
    struct State{
        const ValueType value;
        const function<ValueType(const ValueType)> computeNext;

        State<ValueType> nextState() const{
            return State<ValueType>{computeNext(value), computeNext};
        };
    };
```

With this implementation, we can now check the next two values of our autoincrement index:

```
    TEST_CASE("Compute next auto increment index"){
        const auto autoIncrementIndex = State<int>{1, increment};

        const auto nextAutoIncrementIndex = autoIncrementIndex.nextState();

        CHECK_EQ(2, nextAutoIncrementIndex.value);

        const auto newAutoIncrementIndex =
            nextAutoIncrementIndex.nextState();
        CHECK_EQ(3, newAutoIncrementIndex.value);
    }
```

The tests pass, so the code works! Now let's play with it some more.

Let's imagine we are implementing a simple Tic-Tac-Toe game. We'd like to use the same pattern to compute the next state of the board after a move.

First, we need a structure that can hold a TicTacToe board. For simplicity, I will use vector<vector<Token>>, where Token is an enum that can hold the Blank, X, or O values:

```
    enum Token {Blank, X, O};
    typedef vector<vector<Token>> TicTacToeBoard;
```

Then, we need a `Move` structure. The `Move` structure needs to contain the board coordinates of the move and the token used to make the move:

```
struct Move{
    const Token token;
    const int xCoord;
    const int yCoord;
};
```

We also need a function that can take a `TicTacToeBoard`, apply a move, and return the new board. For simplicity, I will implement it with local mutation, as follows:

```
auto makeMove = [](const TicTacToeBoard board, const Move move) ->
    TicTacToeBoard {
        TicTacToeBoard nextBoard(board);
        nextBoard[move.xCoord][move.yCoord] = move.token;
         return nextBoard;
};
```

We also need an empty board to initialize our `State`. Let's just fill it with `Token::Blank` by hand:

```
const TicTacToeBoard EmptyBoard{
    {Token::Blank,Token::Blank, Token::Blank},
    {Token::Blank,Token::Blank, Token::Blank},
    {Token::Blank,Token::Blank, Token::Blank}
};
```

We'd like to make the first move. However, our `makeMove` function doesn't have the signature allowed by the `State` structure; it takes an additional parameter, `Move`. For a first test, we can just bind the `Move` parameter to a hardcoded value. Let's say that `X` moves to the upper left corner, coordinates *(0,0)*:

```
TEST_CASE("TicTacToe compute next board after a move"){
    Move firstMove{Token::X, 0, 0};
    const function<TicTacToeBoard(const TicTacToeBoard)> makeFirstMove
        = bind(makeMove, _1, firstMove);
    const auto emptyBoardState = State<TicTacToeBoard>{EmptyBoard,
        makeFirstMove };
    CHECK_EQ(Token::Blank, emptyBoardState.value[0][0]);

    const auto boardStateAfterFirstMove = emptyBoardState.nextState();
    CHECK_EQ(Token::X, boardStateAfterFirstMove.value[0][0]);
}
```

As you can see, our `State` structure works fine in this case. However, it has a limitation: it will only allow one move. The problem is that the function that computes the next stage cannot change. But what if we passed it as a parameter to the `nextState()` function instead? We end up with a new structure; let's call it `StateEvolved`. It holds a value and a `nextState()` function that takes the function that computes the next state, applies it, and returns the next `StateEvolved`:

```
template<typename ValueType>
struct StateEvolved{
    const ValueType value;
    StateEvolved<ValueType> nextState(function<ValueType(ValueType)>
        computeNext) const{
            return StateEvolved<ValueType>{computeNext(value)};
    };
};
```

We can now make a move by passing into `nextState` the `makeMove` function with the `Move` parameter bound to the actual move:

```
TEST_CASE("TicTacToe compute next board after a move with
    StateEvolved"){
    const auto emptyBoardState = StateEvolved<TicTacToeBoard>
        {EmptyBoard};
    CHECK_EQ(Token::Blank, emptyBoardState.value[0][0]);
    auto xMove = bind(makeMove, _1, Move{Token::X, 0, 0});
    const auto boardStateAfterFirstMove =
        emptyBoardState.nextState(xMove);
    CHECK_EQ(Token::X, boardStateAfterFirstMove.value[0][0]);
}
```

We can now make a second move. Let's say O moves in the center to coordinates *(1, 1)*. Let's check the before-and-after state:

```
    auto oMove = bind(makeMove, _1, Move{Token::O, 1, 1});
    const auto boardStateAfterSecondMove =
        boardStateAfterFirstMove.nextState(oMove);
    CHECK_EQ(Token::Blank, boardStateAfterFirstMove.value[1][1]);
    CHECK_EQ(Token::O, boardStateAfterSecondMove.value[1][1]);
```

As you can see, using this pattern we can store any state in an immutable way.

The reveal

The design pattern we discussed previously seems very useful for functional programming, but you may have realized that I've avoided naming it.

In fact, the pattern we have discussed so far is one example of a monad, specifically a `State` monad. I've avoided telling you its name until now because monads are a particularly opaque topic in software development. For this book, I have watched hours of videos on monads; I have also read blog posts and articles, and for some reason none of them was understandable. Since a monad is a mathematical object from category theory, some of the resources I mentioned take the mathematical approach and explain them using definitions and operators. Other resources try to explain by example, but they are written in programming languages with native support for the monad pattern. None of them fit our goals for this book—a practical approach to complex concepts.

To understand monads better, we need to look at more examples. The easiest one is probably the `Maybe` monad.

Maybe

Consider trying to compute an expression such as the following in C++:

```
2  + (3/0) * 5
```

What is likely to happen? Usually, an exception will be thrown since we are attempting to divide by `0`. But, there are situations in which we'd like to see a value such as `None` or `NaN`, or some kind of message. We've seen that we can use `optional<int>` to store data that may be an integer or a value; we could, therefore, implement a divide function that returns an `optional<int>`, as shown in the following:

```
function<optional<int>(const int, const int)> divideEvenWith0 = []
    (const int first, const int second) -> optional<int>{
        return (second == 0) ? nullopt : make_optional(first / second);
};
```

However, when we try to use the `divideEvenWith0` in an expression, we realize that we also need to change all the other operators. For example, we could implement a `plusOptional` function that returns `nullopt` when either parameter is `nullopt`, or the value if not, as shown in the following example:

```
auto plusOptional = [](optional<int> first, optional<int> second) -
    > optional<int>{
        return (first == nullopt || second == nullopt) ?
            nullopt :
        make_optional(first.value() + second.value());
};
```

While it works, this requires writing more functions and a lot of duplication. But hey, could we write a function that takes a `function<int(int, int)>` and turns it into a `function<optional<int>(optional<int>, optional<int>)>`? Sure, let's write the function as follows:

```
auto makeOptional = [](const function<int(int, int)> operation){
    return [operation](const optional<int> first, const
        optional<int> second) -> optional<int>{
        if(first == nullopt || second == nullopt) return nullopt;
        return make_optional(operation(first.value(),
            second.value()));
    };
};
```

This works fine, as shown in the following passing tests:

```
auto plusOptional = makeOptional(plus<int>());
auto divideOptional = makeOptional(divides<int>());

CHECK_EQ(optional{3}, plusOptional(optional{1}, optional{2}));
CHECK_EQ(nullopt, plusOptional(nullopt, optional{2}));

CHECK_EQ(optional{2}, divideOptional(optional{2}, optional{1}));
CHECK_EQ(nullopt, divideOptional(nullopt, optional{1}));
```

However, this doesn't solve one problem—we still need to return `nullopt` when dividing by 0. So, the following test will fail as follows:

```
//    CHECK_EQ(nullopt, divideOptional(optional{2}, optional{0}));
//    cout << "Result of 2 / 0 = " << to_string(divideOptional
        (optional{2}, optional{0})) << endl;
```

We can solve this problem by using our own `divideEvenBy0` method instead of the standard divide:

```
function<optional<int>(const int, const int)> divideEvenWith0 = []
    (const int first, const int second) -> optional<int>{
    return (second == 0) ? nullopt : make_optional(first / second);
};
```

This time, the test passes, as shown here:

```
auto divideOptional = makeOptional(divideEvenWith0);

CHECK_EQ(nullopt, divideOptional(optional{2}, optional{0}));
cout << "Result of 2 / 0 = " << to_string(divideOptional
    (optional{2}, optional{0})) << endl;
```

Moreover, the display after running the tests looks like this:

```
Result of 2 / 0 = None
```

I have to say, there's something weirdly satisfying about escaping the tyranny of dividing by 0 and getting a result instead. Maybe that's just me.

Anyway, this leads us to the definition of the `Maybe` monad. It stores a value and a function called `apply`. The `apply` function takes an operation (`plus<int>()`, `minus<int>()`, `divideEvenWith0`, or `multiplies<int>()`), and a second value to which we apply the operation, and returns the result:

```
template<typename ValueType>
struct Maybe{
    typedef function<optional<ValueType>(const ValueType, const
        ValueType)> OperationType;
    const optional<ValueType> value;
    optional<ValueType> apply(const OperationType operation, const
        optional<ValueType> second){
            if(value == nullopt || second == nullopt) return nullopt;
            return operation(value.value(), second.value());
    }
};
```

We can use the `Maybe` monad to make computations as follows:

```
TEST_CASE("Compute with Maybe monad"){
    function<optional<int>(const int, const int)> divideEvenWith0 = []
      (const int first, const int second) -> optional<int>{
        return (second == 0) ? nullopt : make_optional(first / second);
    };

    CHECK_EQ(3, Maybe<int>{1}.apply(plus<int>(), 2));
    CHECK_EQ(nullopt, Maybe<int>{nullopt}.apply(plus<int>(), 2));
    CHECK_EQ(nullopt, Maybe<int>{1}.apply(plus<int>(), nullopt));

    CHECK_EQ(2, Maybe<int>{2}.apply(divideEvenWith0, 1));
    CHECK_EQ(nullopt, Maybe<int>{nullopt}.apply(divideEvenWith0, 1));
    CHECK_EQ(nullopt, Maybe<int>{2}.apply(divideEvenWith0, nullopt));
    CHECK_EQ(nullopt, Maybe<int>{2}.apply(divideEvenWith0, 0));
    cout << "Result of 2 / 0 = " << to_string(Maybe<int>
        {2}.apply(divideEvenWith0, 0)) << endl;
}
```

Once again, we can compute expressions, even with `nullopt`.

So what is a monad?

A **monad** is a functional design pattern that models computations. It comes from mathematics; more precisely, from the domain called **category theory**.

What is computation? A basic computation is a function; however, we are interested in adding more behaviors to the functions. We've seen two examples of maintaining state and allowing operations with an optional type, but monads are quite widespread in software design.

A monad basically has a value and a higher-order function. To understand what they do, let's compare the `State` monad shown in the following code:

```
template<typename ValueType>
struct StateEvolved{
    const ValueType value;

    StateEvolved<ValueType> nextState(function<ValueType(ValueType)>
        computeNext) const{
            return StateEvolved<ValueType>{computeNext(value)};
    };
};
```

With the `Maybe` monad shown here:

```
template<typename ValueType>
struct Maybe{
    typedef function<optional<ValueType>(const ValueType, const
        ValueType)> OperationType;
    const optional<ValueType> value;
    optional<ValueType> apply(const OperationType operation, const
        optional<ValueType> second) const {
            if(value == nullopt || second == nullopt) return nullopt;
            return operation(value.value(), second.value());
    }
};
```

They both hold a value. The value is encapsulated in the monad structure. They both hold a function that makes computation on that value. The `apply/nextState` (called `bind` in the literature) functions receive a function themselves that encapsulates the computation; however, the monad does something in addition to the computation.

There's more to the monads than just these simple examples. However, they show how to encapsulate certain computations and how to remove certain types of duplication.

It's worth noting that the `optional<>` type from C++ is actually inspired from the `Maybe` monad, as well as the promises, so you're probably already using monads in your code that are waiting to be discovered.

Summary

We've learned a lot of things in this chapter, all around improving design. We learned that refactoring means restructuring the code without changing the external behavior of a program. We saw that to ensure the preservation of behavior, we need to make very small steps and tests. We learned that legacy code is code that we're afraid to change, and in order to write tests for it, we need to change the code first, which leads to a dilemma. We've also learned that, fortunately, we can make some small changes in the code that are guaranteed to preserve behavior, but that break dependencies and thus allow us to plug into the code with tests. We saw then that we can use pure functions to identify and break the dependencies, leading to lambdas that we can regroup into classes based on cohesiveness.

Finally, we learned that we can use design patterns with functional programming, and we saw a few examples. Even if you don't use anything else from functional programming, using functions such as strategy, command, or injected dependencies will make your code easier to change with minimal fuss. We touched on a strikingly abstract design pattern, the monad, and we saw how to use the `Maybe` monad and the `State` monad. Both can help a lot in our quest to write less code with richer functionality.

We've discussed quite a lot about software design. But does functional programming apply to architecture? That's what we'll visit in the next chapter—event sourcing.

13
Immutability and Architecture - Event Sourcing

Event sourcing is an architectural pattern that takes advantage of immutability for storage. The fundamental idea of event sourcing is the following—instead of storing the current state of data, how about we store the events that modify the data? This idea may seem radical, but it's not new; in fact, you're already using tools based on this principle—source-control systems such as Git follow this architecture. We will explore this idea in more detail, including a discussion about its advantages and disadvantages.

The following topics will be covered in this chapter:

- How the concept of immutability can be applied to data storage
- What event sourcing architecture looks like
- What to take into account when deciding whether to use event sourcing

Technical requirements

You will need a compiler that supports C++ 17. I used GCC 7.4.0.

The code can be found on GitHub at `https://github.com/PacktPublishing/Hands-On-Functional-Programming-with-Cpp` in the `Chapter13` folder. It includes and uses `doctest`, which is a single-header open source unit testing library. You can find it on its GitHub repository at `https://github.com/onqtam/doctest`.

Immutability and architecture – event sourcing

Until around 2010, the choice of data storage was quite limited. Whether your preferred choice was Oracle, MySQL, or PostgreSQL, you were pretty much bound to using a relational model for your data.

Then, suddenly, a plethora of new database engines popped up out of nowhere, with partial-to-no support for relational data. They were so different that they defied positive categorization, so the world ended up naming them based on what they didn't do—NoSQL databases. Indeed, their only commonality was that the support for SQL was little-to-none. The list of engines is long and changing, but at the time of writing, a few are prevalent—Redis, MongoDB, DynamoDb, Cassandra, and Couchbase, among others. Each of these engines has its own strengths and weaknesses, and the reason for their appearance is optimizing for various scenarios, usually in the context of cloud computing. For example, Cassandra is highly distributed, while MongoDB allows the easy storage of many types of data.

Around the same time I heard about NoSQL, I started hearing about a new architectural pattern called event sourcing. Event sourcing takes a radically different approach to data storage compared to the usual UI-server-RDBMS pattern. Instead of storing the current state of the system, the event sourcing pattern says—why don't we store the incremental changes to the system encoded as *domain events*?

The astute reader will notice two things about this idea:

- It sounds like something that would come out of the **domain-driven design (DDD)** movement, and indeed it has. Domain events can be just another pattern that we use as part of our DDD approach to architecture and as part of the evolution of our domain models.
- The idea of storing incremental changes in a data store, although radical for business applications, is not new in software architecture. In fact, I have been using a tool that is based on this pattern throughout the writing of this book. You probably also used it to get the code samples. While using a more complex model for history than what we'll discuss for event sourcing, Git stores incremental changes alongside the current state of the code.

Git is not the only tool using this pattern. We have been using such tools in operations for data backup for years. Since a full backup can take a very long time, a good strategy mixes frequent incremental backups with infrequent full backups. However, the trick is that, when recovery is needed, we can apply the incremental backups one after another, leading to the same state as a full backup. It's a good trade-off between the time and storage used for backups on one side and the time needed to restore a backup on the other.

By this point, you may wonder what event sourcing has to do with NoSQL databases, other than being related to storage? While I can't prove it, I believe the two ideas came from the same current of thought surrounding programming in the 2010s—optimize development speed by removing technical obstacles and optimize systems for various web and cloud-based architectures.

Let's think for a moment about Twitter. In terms of data flow, Twitter has two main features—posting a message and seeing the messages other people have posted. If you don't immediately see the message that another user has posted, you won't even know about it, so high latency is allowed. However, we don't want to lose data so we need the user message to be stored as quickly as possible.

The standard way to implement something like this has been to save the message directly into a database upon request and return the updated feed on response. This allows us to see the message immediately, but it has a few disadvantages. First, it makes the database a bottleneck, because every posted message executes both an `INSERT` and a `SELECT` statement. Second, it requires more resources on the server, thus increasing costs for cloud-based servers.

What if we think differently? When you post a message, we just save an event into a fast event store and return it immediately. Upon a future request to update the feed, the event is taken into account and the updated feed is returned. The data store is not a bottleneck anymore and we've reduced the server load. However, we have added a new element in the system, the event store, which may cost a bit more, but it turns out that, at high scale, this can be less expensive and more responsive than the alternative. This is an example of event sourcing.

Another option is to solve this at the data engine level and separate the writes and reads as previously stated; however, we use a data store that is optimized for writing. The downside is that the data will be available for reading with a higher latency than before, but that's OK. At some point in the future, it becomes available and the message feed is updated. This is an example of using a NoSQL database instead of an RDBMS.

The 2010s were very interesting indeed, giving rise to a number of new ideas in software architecture and design while introducing functional programming into mainstream programming languages. Incidentally, they were also interesting for the release of the interconnected series of superhero movies from **Marvel Cinematic Universe** (**MCU**). There's no connection between the two, I just like the MCU! However, I have to stop fanboying (about the history of software design and MCU) and move on to another weird idea—taking immutability into data storage.

Taking immutability to architecture

We've seen that immutability has a profound effect on code structure, and, therefore, on software design. We've also discussed, on multiple occasions, that I/O is fundamentally mutable. We're about to show that data storage is not necessarily mutable and that immutable data storage also has a profound effect on architecture.

How can data storage be immutable? After all, the whole reason for many software applications is to do CRUD—create, retrieve, update, and delete. The only operation that doesn't change data is retrieve, although, in some cases, retrieving data can have additional side effects such as analytics or logging.

However, remember that we face the same problem with data structures. A mutable data structure will change its structure when adding to an element or deleting from it. Yet, pure functional languages support immutable data structures.

An immutable data structure has the following property—adding or deleting items does not change the data structure. Instead, it returns a copy of the initial data structure plus the changes. To optimize memory, purely functional programming languages don't actually clone the data, they just make smart use of pointers to reuse the existing memory. However, for the programmer, it is as if the data structure has been completely cloned.

Consider applying the same idea to storage. Instead of changing the existing data, every write or delete creates a new version of the data with the applied changes, while leaving the previous version intact. Imagine the possibilities; we get the whole history of data changes and we can always recover them because we have a very recent version of the data.

That's not so easy though. Stored data tends to be large and duplicating it on every change will eat up huge storage space and become extremely slow in the process. The same optimization technique as for in-memory data doesn't work so well since stored data tends to be more complex and pointers aren't (yet?) as easy to manage for filesystems.

Fortunately, there's an alternative—store a version of data to begin with and just store a number of changes to the data. We could implement this in a relational database (the changes are just entities after all), but fortunately, we don't have to. To support this storage model, storage engines collectively called **event stores** have been implemented. They allow us to store events and get the latest version of data when we need it.

How would such a system work? Well, we need to model the domain and domain events. Let's do this for Twitter as an example:

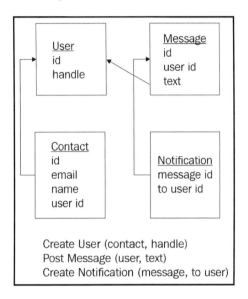

If we were using traditional data storage, we would just save the entities somehow, but we want to store events, so what we'll have is a long list of incremental changes, conceptually looking like this:

```
CreateUser name:alexboly -> userid 1
CreateUser name: johndoe -> userid 2
PostMessage userid: 1, message: 'Hello, world!' -> messageid 1
PostMessage userid: 2, message: 'Hi @alexboly' -> messageid 2
CreateNotification userid: 1, notification: "Message from johndoe"
PostMessage userid: 1, message: 'Hi @johndoe' -> messageid 3
CreateNotification userid: 2, notification: "Message from alexboly"
LikeMessage userid: 2, messageid: 3
...
```

Before we move on to see an example of implementation, we need to remember we're discussing software architecture, and no solution is perfect. Therefore, we have to stop and consider for a moment the trade-offs we're making when using event sourcing.

Advantages of event sourcing

We wouldn't be talking about event sourcing if it didn't have advantages.

On a conceptual level, the domain model and domain events can be easily extracted from domain experts in very fast, lightweight sessions. Event storming is a facilitated session that allows us to design a complex system in hours, through collaboration between tech and domain experts. The knowledge created in this event is not to be underestimated; such common understanding is a strong basis for any collaboration across areas in a complex endeavor in knowledge work.

On a software design level, event sourcing reveals intent better than other code structures. Domain operations tend to hide inside entities; with event sourcing, the changes to the domain model are front and center to the architecture. We can actually search for all the changes that data can go through, and obtain a list—something that's difficult for other code structures.

On a coding level, event sourcing simplifies programming. While thinking in events may be difficult at first, it can quickly become second nature. This model allows us to write code that reflects the most important business features, thus leading to an easier understanding between programmers and product owners or clients. It also neatly encapsulates each type of change, thus simplifying our testing and code.

On a data-storage level, event sourcing allows us to see a list of changes made to the data, an extreme feat for other data-storage models. Incremental backups fit better in this model since it's fundamentally incremental. Recovery is built into the data storage, allowing us to start from any past materialized storage and apply all the events.

Moreover, event sourcing allows us to go back in time. If every event has an opposite event, which is usually quite easy to do, we can play the opposite events from the end to a certain timestamp, leading us to the exact data we had at that time.

On a performance level, event sourcing optimizes writing data, making it very useful for most applications that require fast writes but can deal with latency on reads (also known as **most web-based systems**).

But nothing comes for free, so what can go wrong?

Disadvantages and caveats of event sourcing

With all its advantages, event sourcing could become a prevalent way of architecting complex applications, but it has a few important drawbacks that you need to consider before jumping on the wagon.

Changing an event schema

The first issue comes from the core model of event sourcing—what if we need to change the structure of an event after we already have a bunch of data? For example, what if we need to add a timestamp to each of our events? Or what if we need to change our `PostMessage` event to include a field for visibility, which could be only receiver, only followers, or everyone?

This problem has solutions, but each comes with its own problems. One solution is to version the event schema and have multiple schemas side by side, which works but complicates the materialization. Another solution would be to use data migration scripts to change past events, but it breaks the concept of immutability and has to be done right. Another option is to never change an event schema, just add a new event type, but this can lead to confusion due to multiple deprecated event types.

Delete past data

The second issue is with privacy. The **General Data Protection Regulation (GDPR)** adopted recently in the **European Union** (**EU**), affecting many software systems around the world, gives a user the right to ask for the complete deletion of private data from a system. When using a normal database, this is relatively easy—just delete the records related to the user ID—but how do we do this in an event store?

We can start by deleting all of the events related to a user. But can we do that? We may hit a problem if the events have a temporal relationship. Imagine, for example, the following scenario for collaboratively editing a document:

```
CreateAuthor alexboly => authorid 1
CreateAuthor johndoe => authorid 2
...
AddText index: 2400, authorid:1, text: "something interesting here."
AddText index: 2427, authorid:2, text: "yes, that's interesting" =>
    "something interesting here. yes that's interesting"
DeleteText index: 2400, length: 10, authorid: 1 =>"interesting here.
    yes that's interesting"
...
```

Let's mark the events we need to delete if the user `alexboly` asks us to:

```
CreateAuthor alexboly => authorid 1
CreateAuthor johndoe => authorid 2
. . .
AddText index: 2400, authorid:1, text: "something interesting here."
AddText index: 2427, authorid:2, text: "yes, that's interesting" =>
    "something interesting here. yes that's interesting"
DeleteText index: 2400, length: 10, authorid: 1 =>"interesting here.
    yes that's interesting"
. . .
```

Do you see the problem? Not only do we lose data from the document if we delete the highlighted events, but the indexes don't match anymore either! Applying the events in order to a blank document will, therefore, lead to errors or corrupted data.

There are a few things we could do:

- One solution is to delete the user's identity but preserve the data. While this could work in particular contexts, this solution depends on the outreach of the delete request. There's a special case where a user has added personal data (for example, an address, email address, or an ID number) into a document. If we delete the user's identity, but also need to delete the personal data, we will need to scan all events for the personal data and remove or replace it with the same number of blank characters.
- Another solution is to materialize the database, to delete the data, and to start from the new checkpoint with future events. This breaks one of the core ideas of event sourcing—the ability to reconstruct the data from an empty store—and it can prove difficult for systems that have many events or many deletions. It is possible though, with proper planning and structure.
- A third solution is to take advantage of the architecture and use a special event for `DeletePrivateData`. However, this event is different because it will have to change the event store rather than the data. While it fits with the architecture, it is risky and will require extensive testing, since it can break everything.
- A fourth solution is to design the events so that they are not temporally coupled. In theory, this sounds good, but we have to admit it may not always be possible in practice. In the previous example, we needed some kind of position for the text, and I challenge you to find a way of specifying the position that is independent of existing text. Also consider that we would carry out this design effort in a rare situation, potentially making all events less comprehensible. If it's possible with minimal changes, great; but if not, you'll need to make a decision yourself.

An example of implementation

We will look next at a simple example of implementation using event sourcing. We'll start with our Twitter example, and start writing some tests.

First, let's create a user and check the event store for the right events, in pseudocode:

```
TEST_CASE("Create User"){
    EventStore eventStore;
    ...
    auto alexId = createUser("alexboly", eventStore);
    ...
    CHECK_EQ(lastEvent, expectedEvent);
}
```

We need a few things to compile this test. First, an event store that can store events, but how do we express an event that can be stored? We need some kind of data structure that can hold property names and values. The simplest one is a map<string, string> structure that will map the names of properties to their values. To see it in action, let's create the event structure for CreateUser:

```
auto makeCreateUserEvent = [](const string& handle, const int id){
    return map<string, string>{
            {"type", "CreateUser"},
            {"handle", handle},
            {"id", to_string(id)}
    };
};
```

The CreateUser event has a type, CreateUser, and needs a handle, for example, alexboly, and an id for the user. Let's make it nicer and more explicit with typedef:

```
typedef map<string, string> Event;
auto makeCreateUserEvent = [](const string& handle, const int id){
    return Event{
            {"type", "CreateUser"},
            {"handle", handle},
            {"id", to_string(id)}
    };
};
```

We can now create our EventStore. Since it's basically a list of events, let's just use it:

```
class EventStore : public list<Event>{
    public:
```

```
        EventStore() : list<Event>(){
        };
};
```

So, now our test can use the `EventStore` and the `makeCreateUserEvent` function to check that, after calling `createUser`, the right event will be in event store:

```
TEST_CASE("Create User"){
    auto handle = "alexboly";
    EventStore eventStore;

    auto alexId = createUser(handle, eventStore);

    auto expectedEvent = makeCreateUserEvent(handle, alexId);
    auto event = eventStore.back();
    CHECK_EQ(event, expectedEvent);
}
```

We only have to implement `createUser` now for this test to work. It is simple enough; call `makeCreateUserEvent` and add the result to `EventStore`. We need an `id`, but since we only have one element, for now, let's use a hardcoded value of 1:

```
int id = 1;
auto createUser = [](string handle, EventStore& eventStore){
    eventStore.push_back(makeCreateUserEvent(handle, id));
    return id;
};
```

The test passes; now we can execute events and they'll go to the event store.

Let's see now how the new user can post a message. We will need a second event type, `PostMessage`, and a similar code infrastructure. Let's write the test. First, we need to create a user. Second, we need to create a message that is linked to the user through the `userId`. Here's the test:

```
TEST_CASE("Post Message"){
    auto handle = "alexboly";
    auto message = "Hello, world!";
    EventStore eventStore;

    auto alexId = createUser(handle, eventStore);
    auto messageId = postMessage(alexId, message, eventStore);
    auto expectedEvent = makePostMessageEvent(alexId, message,
        messageId);
    auto event = eventStore.back();
    CHECK_EQ(event, expectedEvent);
}
```

The `makePostMessageEvent` function will just create an `Event` structure with all the required information. It also needs a type and `messageId`:

```
auto makePostMessageEvent = [](const int userId, const string& message, int
id){
    return Event{
            {"type", "PostMessage"},
            {"userId", to_string(userId)},
            {"message", message},
            {"id", to_string(id)}
    };
};
```

Finally, `postMessage` just adds the result of `makePostMessageEvent` into the `EventStore`. We need an ID once again, but we only have one message, so we can use the same ID, `1`:

```
auto postMessage = [](const int userId, const string& message,
    EventStore& eventStore){
        eventStore.push_back(makePostMessageEvent(userId, message, id));
        return id;
};
```

So, now we have a user that can post a message, all through events. That's quite neat, and not as difficult as it may have seemed in the beginning.

This implementation raises a few interesting questions though.

How do you retrieve data?

Firstly, what if I want to search for a user by their handle or their `id`? That's a real use scenario on Twitter. If I mention another user in a message with `@alexboly`, a notification should be posted to the user with the handle `alexboly`. Also, I'd like to display all messages relevant to the user `@alexboly` on the timeline.

I have two options for this. The first option is to store just the events and run all of them whenever reading data. The second option is to maintain a domain store with the current values and query it like any other database. It's important to note that each or both of these stores may be in-memory for very fast access.

Regardless of whether the current values are cached or computed, we need a way to execute the events and obtain them. How do we do that?

Let's write a test to describe what we need. After running one or more events, we need to execute the events and get the current values, allowing us to retrieve them as needed:

```
TEST_CASE("Run events and get the user store"){
    auto handle = "alexboly";
    EventStore eventStore;

    auto alexId = createUser(handle, eventStore);
    auto dataStore = eventStore.play();

    CHECK_EQ(dataStore.users.back(), User(alexId, handle));
}
```

To make the test pass, we need a few things. First, a `User` domain object, which we'll keep very simple:

```
class User{
    public:
        int id;
        string handle;
        User(int id, string handle): id(id), handle(handle){};
};
```

Second, a data store that has a list of `users`:

```
class DataStore{
    public:
        list<User> users;
};
```

Finally, the `play` mechanism. Let's just use an ugly implementation for now:

```
class EventStore : public list<Event>{
    public:
        DataStore play(){
            DataStore dataStore;
            for(Event event :  *this){
                if(event["type"] == "CreateUser"){
                    dataStore.users.push_back(User(stoi(event["id"]),
                        event["handle"]));
                }
            };
            return dataStore;
        };
}
```

Knowing higher-order functions, we can, of course, see that our `for` statement in the preceding snippet can be turned into a functional approach. In fact, we can filter all the events by the `CreateUser` type and then transform each event into an entity through a call to `transform`. First, let's extract some smaller functions. We need one function that turns a `CreateUser` event into a user:

```
auto createUserEventToUser = [](Event event){
    return User(stoi(event["id"]), event["handle"]);
};
```

And we need another one that filters a list of events by type:

```
auto createUserEventToUser = [](Event event){
    return User(stoi(event["id"]), event["handle"]);
};
```

We can now extract a `playEvents` function, which takes a list of events, filters it by type, and runs the transformation, obtaining a list of entities:

```
template<typename Entity>
auto playEvents = [](const auto& events, const auto& eventType,
    auto playEvent){
        list<Event> allEventsOfType;
        auto filterEventByThisEventType = bind(filterEventByEventType,
            _1, eventType);
        copy_if(events.begin(),events.end(),back_insert_iterator
            (allEventsOfType), filterEventByThisEventType);
        list<Entity> entities(allEventsOfType.size());
        transform(allEventsOfType.begin(), allEventsOfType.end(),
            entities.begin(), playEvent);
        return entities;
};
```

We can now use this function in our `EventStore` to both replace the treatment of `CreateUser` and generalize it to other events:

```
class EventStore : public list<Event>{
    public:
        EventStore() : list<Event>(){
        };
        DataStore play(){
            DataStore dataStore;
            dataStore.users = playEvents<User>(*this, "CreateUser",
                createUserEventToUser);
            return dataStore;
        };
};
```

We now have a way to retrieve data from our store based on events. Time to look at the next question.

What about referential integrity?

So far, we've seen that relationships between entities when using events are based on IDs, but what if we call an event using the wrong `id`? Look at the example in the following snippet:

```
CreateUser handle:alexboly -> id 1
DeleteUser id: 1
PostMessage userId: 1, text: "Hello, world!" -> user with id 1 doesn't
                                                 exist anymore
```

I see a few solutions to this problem:

- The first solution is to run the event anyway. This will work if it doesn't create additional issues on display. On Twitter, if I see a message, I can navigate to the user who posted the message. In this case, the navigation would lead to an inexistent page. Is this a problem? I would argue that for something like Twitter, it's not such a big problem, as long as it doesn't happen very often, but you'll have to judge it in the context of your own product.
- The second solution is to run the event without any checks, but run a repeated job that checks for referential issues and cleans them up (through events, of course). This method allows you to eventually clean up the data using event sourcing, without slowing down updates with integrity checks. Once again, you'll need to figure out whether this works in your context.
- The third solution is to run integrity checks on each event run. While this ensures referential integrity, it will also slow everything down.

The checks can run in two ways—either by checking the data store or checking the event store. For example, you could check that `DeleteUser` for ID 1 never occurred, or that it didn't occur after `CreateUser` (but you'll need the user handle for that).

Keep this in mind when choosing event sourcing for your application!

Summary

Event sourcing is a method of immutable data storage, starting from a simple idea—instead of storing the current state of the world, what if we stored all the events that lead to the current state? The advantages of this approach are many and interesting—the ability to move forward and backward in time, built-in incremental backup, and thinking in a timeline rather than in a state. It also comes with a few caveats—deleting past data is very difficult, the event schema is difficult to change, and referential integrity tends to become looser. You also need to pay attention to possible errors and define policies for treating them in a structured and repeatable manner.

We've also seen how a simple event sourcing architecture can be implemented with the help of lambdas as events. We could also look at event sourcing for storing lambdas, since a stored event is basically a command pattern, and the simplest implementation of a command pattern is a lambda. The curious reader can try to serialize/deserialize the events into lambdas and see how it changes the design.

Like any architectural pattern, my advice is to carefully consider the trade-offs and to have answers to the most important challenges raised by the implementation. If you choose to try event sourcing, I also advise you to try a production-ready event store rather than building your own. The one we wrote in this chapter is useful for showcasing the core principles and challenges of event sourcing, but it's far from being ready to be used in production.

It's now time to move on to the future of functional programming in C++. In the next chapter, we will walk through the existing functional programming features in C++ 17, and look at the news about C++ 20.

Section 4: The Present and Future of Functional Programming in C++

We have visited a lot of techniques that we can use in functional programming, from the basic building blocks, through the way we can design in a function-centric style, to how we can take advantage of functional programming for various goals. It's time to look at the present and future of functional programming in Standard C++ 17 and 20.

We will first play with the amazing ranges library, available as an external implementation for C++ 17 and as part of the C++ 20 standard. We will see how a simple idea, wrapping existing containers in a lightweight manner, combined with a composition operator and with a new take on the higher-order functions that we've extensively used, allows us to write code that is simpler, faster, and much lighter than the alternatives from Standard C++ 17.

We'll then visit STL support and see what's coming next. Finally, we'll take a look at the main building blocks of functional programming and how they are, and will be, supported in C++.

The following chapters will be covered in this section:

- Chapter 14, *Lazy Evaluation Using the Ranges Library*
- Chapter 15, *STL Support and Proposals*
- Chapter 16, *Standard Language Support and Proposals*

14
Lazy Evaluation Using the Ranges Library

We discussed at length in this book how to think in terms of functions, and how function chaining and composition helps to create designs that are modular and composable. Yet, we hit a problem—with our current approach, a lot of data needs to be copied from one collection to another.

Fortunately, Eric Niebler took it upon himself to work on a library that enables a solution available in purely functional programming languages—lazy evaluation. The library, called **ranges**, was then officially accepted into the C++ 20 standard. In this chapter, we will see how to take advantage of it.

The following topics will be covered in this chapter:

- Why and when lazy evaluation is useful
- Introduction to the ranges library
- How to use lazy evaluation using the ranges library

Technical requirements

You will need a compiler that supports C++ 17. I used GCC 7.4.0.

The code can be found on GitHub at `https://github.com/PacktPublishing/Hands-On-Functional-Programming-with-Cpp` in the `Chapter14` folder. It includes and uses `doctest`, which is a single header open source unit testing library. You can find it on its GitHub repository at `https://github.com/onqtam/doctest`.

An overview of the ranges library

The ranges library offers a variety of helpful new tools for the C++ programmer. All of them are useful, but many are particularly so for our functional programming needs.

But first, let's see how to set it up. To use the ranges library with C++ 17, you need to use the instructions from `https://ericniebler.github.io/range-v3/`. Then, you just need to include the `all.hpp` header file:

```
#include <range/v3/all.hpp>
```

As for C++ 20, you just need to include the `<ranges>` header since the library was included in the standard:

```
#include <ranges>
```

However, if you get a compilation error when trying out the previous line of code, don't be surprised. At the time of writing, the latest version of g++ is 9.1, but the ranges library hasn't yet been included in the standard. Due to its size, the implementations are expected to be quite late. Until then, if you want to try it out, you can still use Eric Niebler's version.

So, what does the ranges library offer? Well, it all starts from the concept of range. A range is formed by a begin and an end iterator. This allows us, for starters, to add a range on top of an existing collection. Then, we can pass a range to an algorithm that requires a begin and end iterator (such as `transform`, `sort`, or `accumulate`), hence removing the inconvenient calls to `begin()` and `end()`.

With ranges, we can build views. Views specify that we are interested in a partial or full collection through the two iterators, but also to allow lazy evaluation and composability. Since views are just lightweight wrappers on top of a collection, we can declare a chain of operations without actually executing them until the result is needed. We will see in detail how this works in the next section, but here's a simple example composing two operations that will filter all numbers from a collection that are multiples of six by filtering first *all of the even numbers*, followed by filtering the numbers that are *multiples of 3*:

```
numbers | ranges::view::filter(isEven) |
ranges::view::filter(isMultipleOf3)
```

Mutations are also possible on ranges, with the help of actions. Actions are similar to views, except that they mutate the underlying container in-place rather than creating a copy. As we've discussed many times previously, we prefer not to mutate data in functional programming; however, there are cases when we can optimize performance with this solution, so it's worth mentioning. Here's an example of an action in...well, in action:

```
numbers |= action::sort | action::take(5);
```

The | operator is very interesting for functional programmers, since it's a kind of functional composition operator. It's also natural to use for Unix/Linux users, who are very used to composing operations. As we've seen in Chapter 4, *The Idea of Functional Composition*, such an operator would be very useful. Unfortunately, it doesn't yet support the composition of any two functions—just views and actions.

Finally, the ranges library supports custom views. This opens up possibilities such as data generation, which is useful for many things, but Chapter 11, *Property-Based Testing*, in particular.

Let's visit the features of the range library in more detail and with examples.

Lazy evaluation

We have seen, in past chapters, how to structure code in a functional way, by taking advantage of small transformations on data structures. Let's take a simple example—compute the sum of all even numbers from a list. The structured programming approach would be to write a loop that goes over the whole structure and adds all elements that are even:

```
int sumOfEvenNumbersStructured(const list<int>& numbers){
    int sum = 0;
    for(auto number : numbers){
        if(number % 2 == 0) sum += number;
    }
    return sum;
};
```

The test for this function runs correctly on a simple example:

```
TEST_CASE("Run events and get the user store"){
    list<int> numbers{1, 2, 5, 6, 10, 12, 17, 25};

    CHECK_EQ(30, sumOfEvenNumbersStructured(numbers));
}
```

Of course, this method mutates data and we have seen that it's not always a good idea. It also does too many things at once. We'd rather compose more functions. The first function needed decides whether a number is even:

```
auto isEven = [](const auto number){
    return number % 2 == 0;
};
```

The second picks the numbers from a collection that satisfy a predicate:

```
auto pickNumbers  = [](const auto& numbers, auto predicate){
    list<int> pickedNumbers;
    copy_if(numbers.begin(), numbers.end(),
        back_inserter(pickedNumbers), predicate);
    return pickedNumbers;
};
```

The third computes the sum of all elements from a collection:

```
auto sum = [](const auto& numbers){
    return accumulate(numbers.begin(), numbers.end(), 0);
};
```

This leads us to the final implementation, which composes all of these functions:

```
auto sumOfEvenNumbersFunctional = [](const auto& numbers){
    return sum(pickNumbers(numbers, isEven));
};
```

And then it passes the test, like the structured solution:

```
TEST_CASE("Run events and get the user store"){
    list<int> numbers{1, 2, 5, 6, 10, 12, 17, 25};

    CHECK_EQ(30, sumOfEvenNumbersStructured(numbers));
    CHECK_EQ(30, sumOfEvenNumbersFunctional(numbers));
}
```

The functional solution has distinct advantages—it's simple, composed of small functions that can be recombined, and it's immutable, which also means it can run in parallel. However, it does have a disadvantage—it copies data.

We've seen in Chapter 10, *Performance Optimization*, how to deal with this issue, but the truth is that the simplest solution is lazy evaluation. Imagine what it would mean if we could chain the function calls, but the code wouldn't actually execute until the moment we need its result. This solution opens the possibility of writing the code we need to write, and how we need it, with the compiler optimizing, to the maximum, the chain of functions.

That's what the ranges library is doing and other things on top.

Lazy evaluation using the ranges library

The ranges library offers a facility called **views**. Views allow the construction of immutable and cheap data ranges from iterators. They don't copy the data—they just refer to it. We can use view to filter all of the even numbers from our collection:

```
ranges::view::filter(numbers, isEven)
```

Views can be composed without any copying and by using the composition operator, |. For example, we can obtain the list of numbers divisible by 6 by composing two filters: the first one on even numbers, and the second on numbers divisible by 3. Given a new predicate that checks whether a number is multiple of 3, we use the following:

```
auto isMultipleOf3 = [](const auto number){
    return number % 3 == 0;
};
```

We obtain the list of numbers divisible by 6 through the following composition:

```
numbers | ranges::view::filter(isEven) |
ranges::view::filter(isMultipleOf3)
```

It's important to notice that nothing was actually computed when writing this code. The views were initialized and are waiting for a command. So, let's compute the sum of the elements from the views:

```
auto sumOfEvenNumbersLazy = [](const auto& numbers){
    return ranges::accumulate(ranges::view::
        filter(numbers, isEven), 0);
};
TEST_CASE("Run events and get the user store"){
    list<int> numbers{1, 2, 5, 6, 10, 12, 17, 25};

    CHECK_EQ(30, sumOfEvenNumbersLazy(numbers));
}
```

The `ranges::accumulate` function is a special implementation of accumulate that knows how to work with the views. Only when calling `accumulate` is the view acting; moreover, no data is actually copied—instead, the ranges use smart iterators to compute the result.

Let's also see the result of composing the views. As expected, the sum of all numbers from the vector that are divisible by 6 is 18:

```
auto sumOfMultiplesOf6 = [](const auto& numbers){
    return ranges::accumulate(
            numbers | ranges::view::filter(isEven) |
                ranges::view::filter(isMultipleOf3), 0);
};
TEST_CASE("Run events and get the user store"){
    list<int> numbers{1, 2, 5, 6, 10, 12, 17, 25};

    CHECK_EQ(18, sumOfMultiplesOf6(numbers));
}
```

What a nice way of writing code! It is much easier than both previous options, while having a low memory footprint.

But that's not all ranges can do.

Mutable changes with actions

In addition to views, the ranges library offers actions. Actions allow eager, mutable operations. For example, to sort the values in the same vector, we can use the following syntax:

```
TEST_CASE("Sort numbers"){
    vector<int> numbers{1, 12, 5, 20, 2, 10, 17, 25, 4};
    vector<int> expected{1, 2, 4, 5, 10, 12, 17, 20, 25};

    numbers |= ranges::action::sort;

    CHECK_EQ(expected, numbers);
}
```

The |= operator is similar to the `ranges::action::sort(numbers)` call, sorting the vector in place. Actions are also composable, either through a direct method call or with the | operator. This allows allows us to write code that sorts and keeps the unique items from a container through composition of the `sort` and `unique` actions with the | operator:

```
TEST_CASE("Sort numbers and pick unique"){
    vector<int> numbers{1, 1, 12, 5, 20, 2, 10, 17, 25, 4};
    vector<int> expected{1, 2, 4, 5, 10, 12, 17, 20, 25};

    numbers |= ranges::action::sort | ranges::action::unique;

    CHECK_EQ(expected, numbers);
}
```

Still, that's not everything ranges can do.

Infinite series and data generation

Since views are lazy evaluated, they allow us to create infinite series. For example, to generate a series of integers, we can use the `view::ints` function. Then, we need to limit the series so we can use `view::take` to keep the first five elements from the series:

```
TEST_CASE("Infinite series"){
    vector<int> values = ranges::view::ints(1) | ranges::view::take(5);
    vector<int> expected{1, 2, 3, 4, 5};

    CHECK_EQ(expected, values);
}
```

Additional data generation can be done using `view::iota` for any type that allows increments, for example, for `chars`:

```
TEST_CASE("Infinite series"){
    vector<char> values = ranges::view::iota('a') |
        ranges::view::take(5);
    vector<char> expected{'a', 'b', 'c', 'd', 'e'};

    CHECK_EQ(expected, values);
}
```

In addition, you can generate linearly distributed values with the `linear_distribute` view. Given a value interval and a number of items to include in the linear distribution, the view includes both interval boundaries, plus enough values from inside the interval. For example, taking five linearly distributed values from the $[1, 10]$ interval leads to the values $\{1, 3, 5, 7, 10\}$:

```
TEST_CASE("Linear distributed"){
    vector<int> values = ranges::view::linear_distribute(1, 10, 5);
    vector<int> expected{1, 3, 5, 7, 10};

    CHECK_EQ(expected, values);
}
```

What if we need more complex data generators? Fortunately, we can create custom ranges. Let's say that we want to create a list of each tenth power of 2 starting from 1 (that is, 2^1, 2^{11}, 2^{21}, and so on). We could do that with a transform call; however, we can also do this using the `yield_if` function in combination with the `for_each` view. The line in bold from the following code shows you exactly how to use these two together:

```
TEST_CASE("Custom generation"){
    using namespace ranges;
    vector<long> expected{ 2, 2048, 2097152, 2147483648 };

    auto everyTenthPowerOfTwo = view::ints(1) | view::for_each([](int
        i){ return yield_if(i % 10 == 1, pow(2, i)); });
    vector<long> values = everyTenthPowerOfTwo | view::take(4);

    CHECK_EQ(expected, values);
}
```

We first generate an infinite series of integers starting from 1. Then, for each of them, we check whether the value divided by 10 has the remainder 1. If it does, we return 2 to that power. To obtain a finite vector, we pipe the previous infinite series into the `take` view, which keeps only the first four elements.

Of course, this type of generation is not optimal. For every useful number, we need to visit 10, and it would be better to start from a range that goes 1, 11, 21, and so on.

It's worth mentioning here that an alternative to writing this code is to use the stride view. The `stride` view takes every n[th] element from a series, exactly as we need it to. In combination with the `transform` view, we can achieve exactly the same result:

```
TEST_CASE("Custom generation"){
    using namespace ranges;
    vector<long> expected{ 2, 2048, 2097152, 2147483648 };
```

```
auto everyTenthPowerOfTwo = view::ints(1) | view::stride(10) |
    view::transform([](int i){ return pow(2, i); });
vector<long> values = everyTenthPowerOfTwo | view::take(4);

CHECK_EQ(expected, values);
}
```

By now, you've probably realized that data generation is very interesting for testing, in particular, property-based testing (as we discussed in Chapter 11, *Property-Based Testing*). For testing, however we often need to generate strings. Let's see how.

Generating strings

To generate strings, first, we need to generate characters. For ASCII characters, we can start from a range of integers from 32 to 126, that is, the ASCII code for the interesting, printable characters. We take a random sample and transform the code into characters. How do we take a random sample? Well, there's a view for that called view::sample, which, given a number of items, takes a random sample from the range. Finally, we just need to turn it into a string. This is how we get a random string of the length 10 formed out of ASCII characters:

```
TEST_CASE("Generate chars"){
    using namespace ranges;

    vector<char> chars = view::ints(32, 126) | view::sample(10) |
        view::transform([](int asciiCode){ return char(asciiCode); });
    string aString(chars.begin(), chars.end());

    cout << aString << endl;

    CHECK_EQ(10, aString.size());
}
```

Here are a few samples resulted from running this code:

```
%.0FL[cqrt
#0bfgiluwy
4PY]^_ahlr
;DJLQ^bipy
```

As you can see, these are interesting strings to use in our tests. Moreover, we can vary the size of the strings by changing the argument of view::sample.

This example is limited to ASCII characters. However, with support for UTF-8 now being part of the C++ standard, it should be easy to expand to support special characters.

Summary

Eric Niebler's ranges library is a rare feat in software engineering. It manages to simplify the use of existing STL high-order functions, while adding lazy evaluation, with a topping of data generation. Not only is it part of the C++ 20 standard, but it is also useful for older versions of C++.

Even if you don't use a functional style of structuring your code, and whether you prefer mutable or immutable code, the ranges library allows you to make it elegant and composable. Therefore, I advise you to play with it and try for yourself how it changes your code. It's definitely worth it, and it's an enjoyable exercise.

We're closing in on the end of this book. It's now time to have a look at STL and the language standard support functional programming, and what we can expect from C++ 20, and this will be the topic of the next chapter.

15
STL Support and Proposals

The **Standard Template Library** (**STL**) has been a useful companion to C++ programmers since the 90s. Starting from concepts such as generic programming and value semantics, it has grown to support many useful scenarios. In this chapter, we will look at how STL supports functional programming in C++ 17 and see what some of the new features that have been introduced in C++ 20 are.

The following topics will be covered in this chapter:

- Using functional features from the `<functional>` header
- Using functional features from the `<numeric>` header
- Using functional features from the `<algorithm>` header
- `std::optional` and `std::variant`
- C++20 and the ranges library

Technical requirements

You will need a compiler that supports C++ 17. I used GCC 7.4.0c.

The code is on GitHub at `https://github.com/PacktPublishing/Hands-On-Functional-Programming-with-Cpp` in the `Chapter15` folder. It includes and uses `doctest`, which is a single-header open source unit testing library. You can find it on its GitHub repository here: `https://github.com/onqtam/doctest`.

The <functional> header

We need to start somewhere in our exploration of functional programming support in STL, and the header aptly named <functional> seems like a good start. This header defines the fundamental function<> type, which we can use for functions and have used a few times in this book for lambdas:

```
TEST_CASE("Identity function"){
    function<int(int)> identity = [](int value) { return value;};

    CHECK_EQ(1, identity(1));
}
```

We can use the function<> type to store any type of function, be it a free function, a member function, or a lambda. Let's look at an example of a free function:

```
TEST_CASE("Free function"){
    function<int()> f = freeFunctionReturns2;

    CHECK_EQ(2, f());
}
```

Here's an example of a member function:

```
class JustAClass{
    public:
        int functionReturns2() const { return 2; };
};

TEST_CASE("Class method"){
    function<int(const JustAClass&)> f = &JustAClass::functionReturns2;
    JustAClass justAClass;

    CHECK_EQ(2, f(justAClass));
}
```

As you can see, in order to call a member function through the function<> type, a valid reference to an object needs to be passed in. Think of it as the *this instance.

In addition to this fundamental type, the <functional> header offers a few already-defined function objects that come in handy when using functional transformations on collections. Let's look at a simple example of using the sort algorithm in combination with the defined greater function in order to sort a vector in descending order:

```
TEST_CASE("Sort with predefined function"){
    vector<int> values{3, 1, 2, 20, 7, 5, 14};
```

```
    vector<int> expectedDescendingOrder{20, 14, 7, 5, 3,  2, 1};

    sort(values.begin(), values.end(), greater<int>());

    CHECK_EQ(expectedDescendingOrder, values);
}
```

The `<functional>` header defines the following useful function objects:

- **Arithmetic operations**: `plus`, `minus`, `multiplies`, `divides`, `modulus`, and `negate`
- **Comparisons**: `equal_to`, `not_equal_to`, `greater`, `less`, `greater_equal`, and `less_equal`
- **Logical operations**: `logical_and`, `logical_or`, and `logical_not`
- **Bit-wise operations**: `bit_and`, `bit_or`, and `bit_xor`

These function objects spare us the trouble of encapsulating common operations in functions when we need to use them with higher-order functions. While it's a great collection, I would dare to suggest that an identity function would be equally useful, as weird as that may sound. Fortunately, it's easy to implement one.

However, that's not all the `<functional>` header has to offer. The `bind` function implements partial functional application. We've seen it in action multiple times in this book, and you can see its usage in detail in Chapter 5, *Partial Application and Currying*. Its basic function is to take a function, bind one or more parameters to values, and obtain a new function:

```
TEST_CASE("Partial application using bind"){
    auto add = [](int first, int second){
        return first + second;
    };

    auto increment = bind(add, _1, 1);

    CHECK_EQ(3, add(1, 2));
    CHECK_EQ(3, increment(2));
}
```

With the `function<>` type allowing us to write lambdas, the predefined function objects reducing duplication, and `bind` allowing partial application, we have the bases for structuring our code in a functional way. But we couldn't do so effectively without higher-order functions.

The <algorithm> header

The <algorithm> header file contains algorithms, with some of them implemented as higher-order functions. In this book, we have seen examples of use for many of them. Here's a list of useful algorithms:

- all_of, any_of, and none_of
- find_if and find_if_not
- count_if
- copy_if
- generate_n
- sort

We have seen how focusing on data and combining these higher-order functions to transform input data into the desired output is one of the ways in which you can think in small, composable, pure functions. We have also seen the drawbacks of this approach—the need to copy data, or make multiple passes through the same data—and we have seen how the new ranges library solves these issues in an elegant manner.

While all of these functions are extremely useful, there is one function from the <algorithm> namespace that deserves a special mention—the implementation of the functional map operation, transform. The transform function takes an input collection and applies a lambda to each element of the collection, returning a new collection with the same number of elements but with the transformed values stored in it. This opens infinite possibilities of adapting data structures to our needs. Let's look at a few examples.

Projecting one property of each object from a collection

We often need to get the value of a property from each element from a collection. In the following example, we use transform to get the list of all the names of people from a vector:

```
TEST_CASE("Project names from a vector of people"){
    vector<Person> people = {
        Person("Alex", 42),
        Person("John", 21),
        Person("Jane", 14)
    };
```

```
    vector<string> expectedNames{"Alex", "John", "Jane"};
    vector<string> names = transformAll<vector<string>>(
            people,
            [](Person person) { return person.name; }
    );

    CHECK_EQ(expectedNames, names);
}
```

Once again, we use a wrapper over `transform` and `transformAll` in order to avoid writing the boilerplate code:

```
template<typename DestinationType>
auto transformAll = [](auto source, auto lambda){
    DestinationType result;
    transform(source.begin(), source.end(), back_inserter(result),
        lambda);
    return result;
};
```

Computing conditionals

Sometimes, we need to compute whether a condition applies or not for a collection of elements. In the following example, we will compute whether people are minors or not by comparing their age with 18:

```
TEST_CASE("Minor or major"){
    vector<Person> people = {
        Person("Alex", 42),
        Person("John", 21),
        Person("Jane", 14)
    };

    vector<bool> expectedIsMinor{false, false, true};
    vector<bool> isMinor = transformAll<vector<bool>>(
            people,
            [](Person person) { return person.age < 18; }
    );

    CHECK_EQ(expectedIsMinor, isMinor);
}
```

Converting everything into a displayable or serializable format

We often need to save or display a list. To do so, we need to convert each element of the list into a displayable or serializable format. In the following example, we are computing the JSON representation of the `Person` objects from the list:

```
TEST_CASE("String representation"){
    vector<Person> people = {
        Person("Alex", 42),
        Person("John", 21),
        Person("Jane", 14)
    };

    vector<string> expectedJSON{
        "{'person': {'name': 'Alex', 'age': '42'}}",
        "{'person': {'name': 'John', 'age': '21'}}",
        "{'person': {'name': 'Jane', 'age': '14'}}"
    };
    vector<string> peopleAsJson = transformAll<vector<string>>(
            people,
            [](Person person) {
            return
            "{'person': {'name': '" + person.name + "', 'age':
                '" + to_string(person.age) + "'}}"; }
    );

    CHECK_EQ(expectedJSON, peopleAsJson);
}
```

Even with the infinite possibilities that are opened by the `transform` function, it becomes even more powerful in combination with the `reduce` (`accumulate` in C++) higher-order function.

The <numeric> header – accumulate

It's interesting to see that the two higher-order functions that form the `map`/`reduce` pattern, one of the most commonly known patterns in functional programming, ended up in two different header files in C++. The `transform`/`accumulate` combination, requiring both the `<algorithm>` and the `<numeric>` header files, allow us to solve many problems that have the following pattern:

- A collection is provided.

- The collection needs to be transformed into something else.
- An aggregated result needs to be computed.

Let's look at a few examples.

Computing the total price with tax for a shopping cart

Let's say we have a `Product` structure, as follows:

```
struct Product{
    string name;
    string category;
    double price;
    Product(string name, string category, double price): name(name),
        category(category), price(price){}
};
```

Let's also assume that we have different tax levels based on product categories:

```
map<string, int> taxLevelByCategory = {
    {"book", 5},
    {"cosmetics", 20},
    {"food", 10},
    {"alcohol", 40}
};
```

Say we were given a list of products, such as the following:

```
vector<Product> products = {
    Product("Lord of the Rings", "book", 22.50),
    Product("Nivea", "cosmetics", 15.40),
    Product("apple", "food", 0.30),
    Product("Lagavulin", "alcohol", 75.35)
};
```

Let's compute the total price, with and without tax. We also have a helper wrapper, `accumulateAll`, at our disposal:

```
auto accumulateAll = [](auto collection, auto initialValue,  auto
    lambda){
        return accumulate(collection.begin(), collection.end(),
            initialValue, lambda);
};
```

To compute the price without tax, we just need to get all the product prices and add them up. It's a typical map/reduce scenario:

```cpp
auto totalWithoutTax = accumulateAll(transformAll<vector<double>>
    (products, [](Product product) { return product.price; }), 0.0,
        plus<double>());
CHECK_EQ(113.55, doctest::Approx(totalWithoutTax));
```

First, we map (transform) the list of Products into a list of prices, and then reduce (or accumulate) them into a single value—its total.

A similar, albeit more complex, process applies when we need the total price with tax:

```cpp
auto pricesWithTax = transformAll<vector<double>>(products,
        [](Product product){
            int taxPercentage =
                taxLevelByCategory[product.category];
            return product.price + product.price *
                taxPercentage/100;
        });
auto totalWithTax = accumulateAll(pricesWithTax, 0.0,
    plus<double> ());
CHECK_EQ(147.925, doctest::Approx(totalWithTax));
```

First, we map (transform) the list of Products with the list of prices with tax, then reduce (or accumulate) all the values into the total with tax.

In case you're wondering, the doctest::Approx function allows for a comparison between floating point numbers with a small rounding error.

Converting a list into JSON

In the previous section, we saw how to convert each item from a list into JSON through a transform call. It's easy to turn it into a full JSON list with the help of accumulate:

```cpp
string expectedJSONList = "{people: {'person': {'name': 'Alex',
    'age': '42'}}, {'person': {'name': 'John', 'age': '21'}},
        {'person': {'name': 'Jane', 'age': '14'}}}";
string peopleAsJSONList = "{people: " + accumulateAll(peopleAsJson,
    string(),
        [](string first, string second){
            return (first.empty()) ? second : (first + ", " +
                second);
        }) + "}";
CHECK_EQ(expectedJSONList, peopleAsJSONList);
```

We use `transform` to turn the list of people into a list of JSON representations for each object, and then we use `accumulate` to join them and use a few additional operations to add the front and back of the list representation in JSON.

As you can see, the `transform`/accumulate (or `map`/reduce) combination serves a lot of different uses, depending on the functions we pass into it.

Back to <algorithm> – find_if and copy_if

We can accomplish a lot of things with `transform`, `accumulate`, and `any_of`/all_of/none_of. Sometimes, however, we need to filter out some of the data from collections.

The usual style of doing this is with `find_if`. However, `find_if` is cumbersome if what we need is to find all the items from a collection that fit a specific condition. Therefore, the best option to solve this problem in a functional way using the C++ 17 standard is `copy_if`. The following example uses `copy_if` to find all the minors in a list of people:

```
TEST_CASE("Find all minors"){
    vector<Person> people = {
        Person("Alex", 42),
        Person("John", 21),
        Person("Jane", 14),
        Person("Diana", 9)
    };

    vector<Person> expectedMinors{Person("Jane", 14),
                                  Person("Diana", 9)};
    vector<Person> minors;
    copy_if(people.begin(), people.end(), back_inserter(minors), []
        (Person& person){ return person.age < 18; });

    CHECK_EQ(minors, expectedMinors);
}
```

<optional> and <variant>

We have discussed happy path cases a lot, which are when the data is valid for our data transformations. What do we do for edge cases and errors? Sure, in exceptional cases, we can throw exceptions or return error cases, but what about situations when we need to return an error message?

The functional way is to return data structures in these cases. After all, we need to return an output value even when the input isn't valid. But we hit a challenge—the type we need to return in the case of an error is an error type, while the type we need to return in the case of valid data is some more valid data.

Fortunately, we have two structures that support us in these cases—`std::optional` and `std::variant`. Let's take an example of a list of people, some of whom are valid and some of whom are invalid:

```
vector<Person> people = {
    Person("Alex", 42),
    Person("John", 21),
    Person("Jane", 14),
    Person("Diana", 0)
};
```

The last person has an invalid age. Let's try to write, in a functional way, the code that will display the following string:

```
Alex, major
John, major
Jane, minor
Invalid person
```

To have a chain of transformations, we need to use the `optional` type, as follows:

```
struct MajorOrMinorPerson{
    Person person;
    optional<string> majorOrMinor;

    MajorOrMinorPerson(Person person, string majorOrMinor) :
        person(person), majorOrMinor(optional<string>(majorOrMinor)){};

    MajorOrMinorPerson(Person person) : person(person),
        majorOrMinor(nullopt){};
};
    auto majorMinorPersons = transformAll<vector<MajorOrMinorPerson>>
        (people, [](Person& person){
            if(person.age <= 0) return MajorOrMinorPerson(person);
            if(person.age > 0 && person.age < 18) return
                MajorOrMinorPerson(person, "minor");
            return MajorOrMinorPerson(person, "major");
            });
```

With this call, we obtain a list of pairs between the person and a value that is either `nullopt`, `minor`, or `major`. We can use this in the following `transform` call in order to obtain the list of strings according to the validity condition:

```
auto majorMinorPersonsAsString = transformAll<vector<string>>
    (majorMinorPersons, [](MajorOrMinorPerson majorOrMinorPerson){
        return majorOrMinorPerson.majorOrMinor ?
        majorOrMinorPerson.person.name + ", " +
            majorOrMinorPerson.majorOrMinor.value() :
                "Invalid person";
    });
```

Finally, the call to accumulate creates the expected output string:

```
auto completeString = accumulateAll(majorMinorPersonsAsString,
    string(), [](string first, string second){
        return first.empty() ? second : (first + "\n" + second);
    });
```

We can check this out with a test:

```
string expectedString("Alex, major\nJohn, major\nJane,
                            minor\nInvalid person");

CHECK_EQ(expectedString, completeString);
```

An alternative method is possible with the use of `variant`, if we need to, for example, return an error code combined with the person.

C++ 20 and the ranges library

We discussed the ranges library at length in Chapter 14, *Lazy Evaluation Using the Ranges Library*. If you can use it, either because you use C++ 20 or because you can use it as a third-party library, the previous function becomes extremely simple and much faster:

```
TEST_CASE("Ranges"){
    vector<Person> people = {
        Person("Alex", 42),
        Person("John", 21),
        Person("Jane", 14),
        Person("Diana", 0)
    };
    using namespace ranges;
```

```
        string completeString = ranges::accumulate(
            people |
            view::transform(personToMajorMinor) |
            view::transform(majorMinor),
            string(),
            combineWithNewline
            );
        string expectedString("Alex, major\nJohn, major\nJane,
                                    minor\nInvalid person");

        CHECK_EQ(expectedString, completeString);
    }
```

Similarly, finding the list of minors from a list of people is very easy with the ranges' `view::filter`:

```
    TEST_CASE("Find all minors with ranges"){
        using namespace ranges;

        vector<Person> people = {
            Person("Alex", 42),
            Person("John", 21),
            Person("Jane", 14),
            Person("Diana", 9)
        };
        vector<Person> expectedMinors{Person("Jane", 14),
                                        Person("Diana", 9)};

        vector<Person> minors = people | view::filter(isMinor);

        CHECK_EQ(minors, expectedMinors);
    }
```

Once we have the `isMinor` predicate, we can pass it to `view::filter` to find the minors from the list of people.

Summary

In this chapter, we went on a tour of the functional programming features that are available in the STL of C++ 17, and of the new features in C++ 20. With functions, algorithms, the help provided by `variant` and `optional` in error or edge cases, and the simplified and optimized code that can be achieved using the ranges library, we have pretty good support for functional programming features.

Now, it's time to move on to the next chapter and look at the C++ 17 language support for functional programming, and at the interesting things that are coming for functional programming in C++20.

16
Standard Language Support and Proposals

We've gone through a lot of topics in this book, so now it's time to group them all in a handy chapter that you can use to help remember how to use the functional programming techniques we covered. We will take this opportunity to look at the C++ 20 standard as well, mentioning how we can use these new features in our code.

The following topics will be covered in this chapter:

- Supported ways of writing pure functions in C++, and future proposals
- Supported ways of writing lambdas in C++, and future proposals
- Supported ways for currying in C++, and future proposals
- Supported ways for functional composition in C++, and future proposals

Technical requirements

You will need a compiler that supports C++ 17; I used GCC 7.4.0c.

The code is on GitHub at `https://github.com/PacktPublishing/Hands-On-Functional-Programming-with-Cpp` in the `Chapter16` folder. It includes and uses `doctest`, which is a single-header open source unit testing library. You can find it in the GitHub repository at `https://github.com/onqtam/doctest`.

Standard language support and proposals

So far, we've explored several ways of writing code in a functional style in C++. Now, we'll take a look at some additional options that are allowed by the C++ 17 standard, and at a few options that are enabled by C++ 20. So, let's start by writing pure functions.

Pure functions

Pure functions are functions that return the same outputs when receiving the same inputs. Their predictability makes them useful for understanding how the written code correlates with its runtime performance.

We discovered in `Chapter 2`, *Understanding Pure Functions*, that writing pure functions in C++ requires a combination of `const` and `static`, depending on whether the function is part of a class or is a free function, and on how we pass the parameters to the function. For your ease, I will reproduce the conclusions we reached on the syntax for pure functions here:

- Class functions, pass by value:
    - `static int increment(const int value)`
    - `int increment(const int value) const`
- Class functions, pass by reference:
    - `static int increment(const int& value)`
    - `int increment(const int&value) const`
- Class functions, pass pointer by value:
    - `static const int* increment(const int* value)`
    - `const int* increment(const int* value) const`
- Class functions, pass pointer by reference:
    - `static const int* increment(const int* const& value)`
    - `const int* increment(const int* const& value) const`
- Standalone function, pass by value `int increment(const int value)`
- Standalone function, pass by reference `int increment(const int& value)`
- Standalone function, pass pointer by value `const int* increment(const int* value)`
- Standalone function, pass pointer by reference `const int* increment(const int* const& value)`

We've also discovered that while the compiler is helpful for reducing side effects, it doesn't always tell us when a function is pure or not. We always need to remember to use these three criteria when writing a pure function, and be careful to apply them:

- It always returns the same output values for the same input values.
- It has no side effects.
- It does not change its parameter values.

Lambdas

Lambdas are a fundamental part of functional programming, allowing us to make operations with functions. C++ has had lambdas since C++11, but there were some recent additions to the syntax. Additionally, we will explore some lambda features that we haven't used until now in this book, but which can come in handy for your own code.

Let's begin with a simple lambda—increment has one input and returns the incremented value:

```
TEST_CASE("Increment"){
    auto increment =  [](auto value) { return value + 1;};

    CHECK_EQ(2, increment(1));
}
```

The square brackets ([]) specify the list of captured values, as we'll see in the following code. We can specify the type of the parameter in the same way we do for any function:

```
TEST_CASE("Increment"){
    auto increment =  [](int value) { return value + 1;};

    CHECK_EQ(2, increment(1));
}
```

We can also specify the return value immediately after the list of parameters and a -> sign:

```
TEST_CASE("Increment"){
    auto increment =  [](int value) -> int { return value + 1;};

    CHECK_EQ(2, increment(1));
}
```

If there's no input value, the list of parameters and the round parentheses, `()`, can be ignored:

```
TEST_CASE("One") {
    auto one =  []{ return 1;};

    CHECK_EQ(1, one());
}
```

We can capture a value by specifying its name, in which case it's captured by copy:

```
TEST_CASE("Capture value") {
    int value = 5;
    auto addToValue =  [value](int toAdd) { return value + toAdd;};

    CHECK_EQ(6, addToValue(1));
}
```

Alternatively, we can capture a value by reference, using the `&` operator in the capture specification:

```
TEST_CASE("Capture value by reference") {
    int value = 5;
    auto addToValue =  [&value](int toAdd) { return value + toAdd;};

    CHECK_EQ(6, addToValue(1));
}
```

If we capture multiple values, we can either enumerate them or just capture all of them. For capture by value, we use the `=` specifier:

```
TEST_CASE("Capture all values by value") {
    int first = 5;
    int second = 10;
    auto addToValues = [=](int toAdd) { return first + second +
        toAdd;};
    CHECK_EQ(16, addToValues(1));
}
```

To capture all values by reference, we use the `&` specifier without any variable name:

```
TEST_CASE("Capture all values by reference") {
    int first = 5;
    int second = 10;
    auto addToValues = [&](int toAdd) { return first + second +
        toAdd;};
    CHECK_EQ(16, addToValues(1));
}
```

While not recommended, we can make the lambda call mutable with the `mutable` specifier after the argument list:

```
TEST_CASE("Increment mutable - NOT RECOMMENDED"){
    auto increment =  [](int& value) mutable { return ++value;};

    int value = 1;
    CHECK_EQ(2, increment(value));
    CHECK_EQ(2, value);
}
```

Additionally, starting in C++ 20, we can specify that the function call is `consteval` instead of the default `constexpr`:

```
TEST_CASE("Increment"){
    auto one = []() consteval { return 1;};

    CHECK_EQ(1, one());
}
```

Unfortunately, this use case is not yet supported in g++8.

Exceptions specifiers are also possible; that is, if the lambda throws no exception, then `noexcept` may come in handy:

```
TEST_CASE("Increment"){
    auto increment =  [](int value) noexcept { return value + 1;};

    CHECK_EQ(2, increment(1));
}
```

If the lambda throws an exception, it can be specified as either general or specific:

```
TEST_CASE("Increment"){
    auto increment =  [](int value) throw() { return value + 1;};

    CHECK_EQ(2, increment(1));
}
```

But what if you want to use generic types? Well, in C++ 11, you can use the `function<>` type for this. Starting with C++ 20, all the goodness of type constraints is available for your lambdas in a neat syntax:

```
TEST_CASE("Increment"){
    auto increment =  [] <typename T>(T value) -> requires
        NumericType<T> { return value + 1;};

    CHECK_EQ(2, increment(1));
}
```

Unfortunately, this is not yet supported in g++8 either.

Partial application and currying

Partial application means obtaining a new function by applying a function with N arguments on 1 (or more, but fewer than N) arguments.

We can implement partial application manually by implementing a function or a lambda that passes the arguments along. Here's an example of partial application that uses the `std::plus` function to obtain an `increment` function by setting one of its parameters to 1:

```
TEST_CASE("Increment"){
    auto increment =  [](const int value) { return plus<int>()(value,
        1); };

    CHECK_EQ(2, increment(1));
}
```

In this book, we've mainly focused on how to use lambdas in these situations; it's worth mentioning, however, that we can use pure functions for the same goal. For example, the same increment function can be written as a normal C++ function:

```
namespace Increment{
    int increment(const int value){
        return plus<int>()(value, 1);
    };
}

TEST_CASE("Increment"){
    CHECK_EQ(2, Increment::increment(1));
}
```

Partial application can be done in C++ with the help of the `bind()` function. The `bind()` function allows us to bind parameters to values for a function, allowing us to derive the `increment` function from `plus`, as follows:

```
TEST_CASE("Increment"){
    auto increment = bind(plus<int>(), _1, 1);

    CHECK_EQ(2, increment(1));
}
```

`bind` takes the following parameters:

- The function that we want to bind.
- The arguments to bind to; these can either be a value or a placeholder (such as `_1`, `_2`, and so on). Placeholders allow arguments to be forwarded to the final function.

In pure functional programming languages, partial application is linked with currying. **Currying** is the decomposition of a function that takes N arguments into N functions that take one argument. There is no standard way to curry a function in C++, but we can do it through the use of lambdas. Let's take a look at an example that curries the `pow` function:

```
auto curriedPower = [](const int base) {
    return [base](const int exponent) {
        return pow(base, exponent);
    };
};

TEST_CASE("Power and curried power"){
    CHECK_EQ(16, pow(2, 4));
    CHECK_EQ(16, curriedPower(2)(4));
}
```

As you can see, with the help of currying, we can naturally do a partial application by simply calling the curried function with just one parameter instead of two:

```
auto powerOf2 = curriedPower(2);
CHECK_EQ(16, powerOf2(4));
```

This mechanism is enabled by default in many pure functional programming languages. However, it is more difficult to do in C++. There is no standard support for currying, but we can create our own `curry` function that takes an existing function and returns its curried form. Here's an example of a generalized `curry` function for functions with two parameters:

```
template<typename F>
auto curry2(F f){
    return [=](auto first){
        return [=](auto second){
            return f(first, second);
        };
    };
}
```

Additionally, here's how we can use it to curry and do partial application:

```
TEST_CASE("Power and curried power"){
    auto power = [](const int base, const int exponent){
        return pow(base, exponent);
    };
    auto curriedPower = curry2(power);
    auto powerOf2 = curriedPower(2);
    CHECK_EQ(16, powerOf2(4));
}
```

Let's now look at ways to implement functional composition.

Functional composition

Functional composition means taking two functions, *f* and *g*, and obtaining a new function, *h*; for any value, *h(x) = f(g(x))*. We can implement functional composition manually, either in a lambda or in a normal function. For example, given two functions, `powerOf2`, which computes powers of 2, and `increment`, which increments a value, we will see the following:

```
auto powerOf2 = [](const int exponent){
    return pow(2, exponent);
};

auto increment = [](const int value){
    return value + 1;
};
```

We can compose them by simply encapsulating the call into a lambda called
`incrementPowerOf2`:

```
TEST_CASE("Composition"){
    auto incrementPowerOf2 = [](const int exponent){
        return increment(powerOf2(exponent));
    };

    CHECK_EQ(9, incrementPowerOf2(3));
}
```

Alternatively, we could just use a simple function, as follows:

```
namespace Functions{
    int incrementPowerOf2(const int exponent){
        return increment(powerOf2(exponent));
    };
}

TEST_CASE("Composition"){
    CHECK_EQ(9, Functions::incrementPowerOf2(3));
}
```

However, an operator that takes two functions and returns the composed function is
handy, and it's implemented in many programming languages. The closest thing available
in C++ to a functional composition operator is the | pipe operator from the ranges library,
which is currently in the C++ 20 standard. However, while it implements composition, it
does not work for general functions or lambdas. Fortunately, C++ is a powerful language
and we can write our own compose function, as we discovered in Chapter 4, *The Idea of
Functional Composition*:

```
template <class F, class G>
auto compose(F f, G g){
    return [=](auto value){return f(g(value));};
}

TEST_CASE("Composition"){
    auto incrementPowerOf2 = compose(increment, powerOf2);

    CHECK_EQ(9, incrementPowerOf2(3));
}
```

Going back to the ranges library and the pipe operator, we can use this form of functional composition within the context of ranges. We've explored this topic extensively in `Chapter 14`, *Lazy Evaluation Using the Ranges Library,* and here's an example of using the pipe operator to compute the sum of all numbers that are multiples of both 2 and 3 from a collection:

```cpp
auto isEven = [](const auto number){
    return number % 2 == 0;
};

auto isMultipleOf3 = [](const auto number){
    return number % 3 == 0;
};

auto sumOfMultiplesOf6 = [](const auto& numbers){
    return ranges::accumulate(
            numbers | ranges::view::filter(isEven) |
                ranges::view::filter(isMultipleOf3), 0);
};

TEST_CASE("Sum of even numbers and of multiples of 6"){
    list<int> numbers{1, 2, 5, 6, 10, 12, 17, 25};

    CHECK_EQ(18, sumOfMultiplesOf6(numbers));
}
```

As you can see, there are multiple options for functional programming in standard C++, and a few exciting developments coming in C++ 20.

Summary

This is it! We have gone through a quick overview of the most important operations in functional programming and how we can implement them using C++ 17 and C++ 20. I trust that you are now in possession of more tools in your toolkit—including pure functions, lambdas, partial application, currying, and functional composition, to name only a few.

From now on, it's your choice in terms of how to use them. Pick a few, or combine them, or slowly move your code based on mutable state to immutability; mastering these tools will enable more choice and flexibility in the way you write code.

Whatever you choose to do, I wish you good luck with your projects and your programming career. Happy coding!

Assessments

Chapter 1

1. **What is an immutable function?**

   An immutable function is a function that doesn't change its argument values or the state of the program.

2. **How do you write an immutable function?**

   If you want the compiler to help you, make the arguments `const`.

3. **How do immutable functions support code simplicity?**

   Since they don't change their arguments, they remove any potential complexity from the code, thus allowing programmers to understand it better.

4. **How do immutable functions support a simple design?**

   Immutable functions are boring because they only do computation. Therefore, they facilitate maintenance over long periods of time.

5. **What is a high-level function?**

   A high-level function is a function that receives another function as a parameter.

6. **What examples of high-level functions can you give from STL?**

   There are many examples of high-level functions in STL, particularly in the algorithms. `sort` is the example that we used in this chapter; however, if you look in the `<algorithm>` header, you will find many others, including `find`, `find_if`, `count`, `search`, and more.

7. **What are the advantages of functional loops over structured loops? What are their potential disadvantages?**

   Functional loops avoid off-by-one errors and express the intent of the code more clearly. They are also composable, thus allowing complex operations by chaining multiple loops. However, when composed, they require multiple passes through the collection, which could otherwise be avoided by using simple loops.

8. **What is OOP from the perspective of Alan Kay? How does it relate to functional programming?**

   Alan Kay saw OOP as a way to structure code on the principles of cellular organisms. Cells are separate entities that communicate through chemical signals. Therefore, communication between small objects is the most important part of OOP.

   This means that we can use functional algorithms on data structures that are represented as objects without any conflict.

Chapter 2

1. **What is a pure function?**

   A pure function is a function that has two constraints, as follows:

   - It always returns the same output values for the same argument values.
   - It doesn't have side effects.

2. **How is immutability related to pure functions?**

   Pure functions are immutable because they don't change anything in the program state.

3. **How can you tell the compiler to prevent changes to a variable that's passed by value?**

   Simply define the parameter as `const`, as follows:

   ```
   int square(const int value)
   ```

4. **How can you tell the compiler to prevent changes to a variable that's passed by reference?**

   Simply define the parameter as `const&`, as follows:

   ```
   int square(const int& value)
   ```

5. **How can you tell the compiler to prevent changes to a pointer address that's passed by reference?**

   If the pointer is passed by value, nothing is needed since all the changes will be local to the function:

   ```
   int square(int* value)
   ```

   If the pointer is passed by reference, we need to tell the compiler that the address cannot change:

   ```
   int square(int*& const value)
   ```

6. **How can you tell the compiler to prevent changes to the value that's pointed by a pointer?**

   If the pointer is passed by value, we apply the same rule as for simple values that are passed by value:

   ```
   int square(const int* value)
   ```

   To prevent changes to both the value and the address when passing the pointer by reference, more use of the `const` keyword is required:

   ```
   int square(const int&* const value)
   ```

Chapter 3

1. **What is the simplest lambda you can write?**

   The simplest lambda receives no parameters and returns a constant; it can be something like the following:

   ```
   auto zero = [](){return 0;};
   ```

2. **How can you write a lambda that concatenates two string values passed as parameters?**

   There are a few variations to this answer, depending on your preferred way of concatenating strings. The simplest way using STL is as follows:

   ```
   auto concatenate = [](string first, string second){return first
   + second;};
   ```

3. **What if one of the values is a variable that's captured by value?**

   The answer is similar to the preceding solution, but using the value from context:

   ```
   auto concatenate = [first](string second){return first +
   second;};
   ```

   Of course, we can also use the default capture by value notation, as follows:

   ```
   auto concatenate = [=](string second){return first + second;};
   ```

4. **What if one of the values is a variable that's captured by reference?**

   There's very little change from the previous solution, as shown in the following code, except if you want to protect against value changes:

   ```
   auto concatenate = [&first](string second){return first +
   second;};
   ```

   If you want to protect against a value change, we need to cast to `const`:

   ```
   auto concatenate = [&firstValue = as_const(first)](string
   second){return firstValue + second;};
   ```

5. **What if one of the values is a pointer that's captured by value?**

   We could ignore the immutability, as follows:

   ```
   auto concatenate = [=](string second){return *pFirst +
   second;};
   ```

   Alternatively, we could use a pointer to a `const` type:

   ```
   const string* pFirst = new string("Alex");
   auto concatenate = [=](string second){return *pFirst +
   second;};
   ```

Or, we could just use the value, as follows:

```
string* pFirst = new string("Alex");
first = *pFirst;
auto concatenate = [=](string second){return first + second;}
```

6. **What if one of the values is a pointer that's captured by reference?**

   This allows us to change both the value pointed to and the pointer address inside the lambda.

   The simplest way is to ignore immutability, as follows:

   ```
   auto concatenate = [&](string second){return *pFirst +
   second;};
   ```

   If we want to constrain immutability, we could use the cast to const:

   ```
   auto concatenate = [&first = as_const(pFirst)](string
   second){return *first + second;};
   ```

   However, it's usually best to simply use the value instead, as follows:

   ```
   string first = *pFirst;
   auto concatenate = [=](string second){return first + second;};
   ```

7. **What if both values are captured by value using the default capture specifier?**

   This solution requires no arguments, just two values captured from the context:

   ```
   auto concatenate = [=](){return first + second;};
   ```

8. **What if both values are captured by reference using the default capture specifier?**

   If we don't care about mutating the values, we can do the following:

   ```
   auto concatenate = [&](){return first + second;};
   ```

   To preserve immutability, we need to do the cast to const:

   ```
   auto concatenate = [&firstValue = as_const(first), &secondValue
   = as_const(second)](){return firstValue + secondValue;}
   ```

   There's no way to ensure immutability using just the default capture by reference specifier. Use capture by value instead.

9. **How can you write the same lambda as a data member in a class that has the two string values as data members?**

   In a class, we need to specify the type of the lambda variable and whether we capture either the two data members or this.

   The following code shows how to capture values by copy with the `[=]` syntax:

   ```
   function<string()> concatenate = [=](){return first + second;};
   ```

   The following code shows how to capture `this` instead:

   ```
   function<string()> concatenate = [this](){return first + second;};
   ```

10. **How can you write the same lambda as a static variable in the same class?**

    We need to receive the data members as parameters, as follows:

    ```
    static function<string()> concatenate;
    ...
    function<string()> AClass::concatenate = [](string first, string second){return first + second;};
    ```

    We've seen that this is better than passing as parameter a whole instance of `AClass` because it reduces the coupling area between the function and the class.

Chapter 4

1. **What is functional composition?**

   Functional composition is an operation on functions. It takes two functions, f and g, and creates a third function, C, with the following property for any argument: x, $C(x) = f(g(x))$.

2. **Functional composition has a property that is usually associated with mathematical operations. What is it?**

   Functional composition is not commutative. For example, squaring the increment of a number is not the same as incrementing the square of a number.

3. **How can you turn an add function with two parameters into two functions with one parameter?**

Consider the following function:

```
auto add = [](const int first, const int second){ return first
+ second; };
```

We can turn the preceding function into the following:

```
auto add = [](const int first){
    return [first](const int second){
        return first + second;
    };
};
```

4. **How can you write a C++ function that comprises two single parameter functions?**

In the chapter, we saw that it's very easy to do so with the help of templates and the magic of `auto` types:

```
template <class F, class G>
auto compose(F f, G g){
   return [=](auto value){return f(g(value));};
}
```

5. **What are the advantages of functional composition?**

Functional composition allows us to create complex behaviors by composing very simple functions. Additionally, it allows us to remove certain types of duplication. It also raises the probability of reuse by allowing small functions to be recomposed in infinite ways.

6. **What are the potential disadvantages of implementing operations on functions?**

The operations on functions can have very complex implementations and can become very difficult to understand. Abstractions come with a cost, and the programmer must always balance the benefits of composability and small code with the costs of using abstract operations.

Chapter 5

1. **What is partial function application?**

    Partial function application is the operation of obtaining a new function that takes *N-1* parameters from a function, which in turn takes *N* parameters by binding one of the parameters to a value.

2. **What is currying?**

    Currying is the operation of splitting a function that takes *N* parameters into *N* function, with each taking one parameter.

3. **How does currying help to implement partial application?**

    Given the curried function *f(x)(y)*, the partial application of *f* on *x = value* can be obtained by simply calling *f* with the value like this: *g = f(value)*.

4. **How can we implement partial application in C++?**

    Partial application can be implemented manually in C++, but it's easier to implement it using the `bind` function from the `functional` header.

Other Books You May Enjoy

If you enjoyed this book, you may be interested in these other books by Packt:

The Modern C++ Challenge
Marius Bancila

ISBN: 978-1-78899-386-9

- Serialize and deserialize JSON and XML data
- Perform encryption and signing to facilitate secure communication between parties
- Embed and use SQLite databases in your applications
- Use threads and asynchronous functions to implement generic purpose parallel algorithms
- Compress and decompress files to/from a ZIP archive
- Implement data structures such as circular buffer and priority queue
- Implement general purpose algorithms as well as algorithms that solve specific problems
- Create client-server applications that communicate over TCP/IP
- Use design patterns to solve real-world problems

Hands-On Design Patterns with C++
Fedor G. Pikus

ISBN: 978-1-78883-256-4

- Recognize the most common design patterns used in C++
- Understand how to use C++ generic programming to solve common design problems
- Explore the most powerful C++ idioms, their strengths, and drawbacks
- Rediscover how to use popular C++ idioms with generic programming
- Understand the impact of design patterns on the program's performance

Leave a review - let other readers know what you think

Please share your thoughts on this book with others by leaving a review on the site that you bought it from. If you purchased the book from Amazon, please leave us an honest review on this book's Amazon page. This is vital so that other potential readers can see and use your unbiased opinion to make purchasing decisions, we can understand what our customers think about our products, and our authors can see your feedback on the title that they have worked with Packt to create. It will only take a few minutes of your time, but is valuable to other potential customers, our authors, and Packt. Thank you!

Index